WOMEN AND SEXUALITY
IN THE NOVELS OF THOMAS HARDY

ABBREVIATIONS

Throughout this study I have used the fourteen-volume New Wessex edition of Hardy's novels, published by Macmillan in 1974–6. The exceptions to this are the following:

Far From the Madding Crowd (Macmillan, London, 1949)
The Return of the Native (Macmillan, London, 1943)
Jude the Obscure (Macmillan, London, 1971)

References to these editions are given in parentheses in the text and are abbreviated as follows:

Desperate Remedies DR
Under The Greenwood Tree UGT
A Pair of Blue Eyes PBE
Far From the Madding Crowd FFMC
The Return of the Native RN
Two on a Tower TT
The Mayor of Casterbridge MC
The Woodlanders W
Tess of the d'Urbervilles TD
Jude the Obscure JO

Florence Emily Hardy's *The Life of Thomas Hardy 1840–1928* (Macmillan, London, 1975) is abbreviated to *Life* and references to this text are also given in parentheses.

Acknowledgments

My book has been helped by so many generous individuals that I almost hesitate to begin a list in case I cannot make it complete. Nonetheless, I must express my deep gratitude first and foremost to those members of St Andrews University who, in my thesis-writing days, helped to bring the project into being. My warmest thanks go to my doctoral supervisor, Phillip Mallett, who guided, invigorated, inspired and consoled me, put up with my stubborness and contrariness, and became my valued friend. I owe him a debt of special importance which can never be repaid. I would also like to express my deepest thanks to Professor Peter Bayley, whose unfailing support and encouragement sustained me through many hard times, and to Dr Neil Rhodes, whose scholarly criticisms of my text were as enlightening as the dinner conversations I enjoyed in his home. And of all the generous individuals who shared their lives with me at St Andrews, I owe a special debt of affection to Peter Coxon, whose infectious enthusiasm for all things Hardyan enlivened my days immeasurably. Among those who have helped with the final stages of the book, I would like to thank Professor J. Hillis Miller for his patient readings of my text, Tolin Duda for her special skills in structural organisation, Rona Davies for her sensitive and insightful comments on the final draft, and Luis Ortiz who went well out of his way to guide me through the hazards of computer typesetting. Finally, my deepest appreciation goes to my editor, Andrew Wheatcroft, whose availability above and beyond the call of duty, whose sense of organisation when I had none, and whose infinite care in working with me on final revisions completed the incomplete and brought the book through.

CONTENTS

v

to Adam, Ruthie, Mimi and Alice,
with love

First published in 1988 by
Routledge
11 New Fetter Lane, London EC4P 4EE

Published in the USA by
Routledge
in association with
Routledge, Chapman and Hall, Inc.
29 West 35th Street, New York, NY 10001

Set in 11/13pt Baskerville
and printed in Great Britain
by Butler & Tanner Ltd
Frome and London

Library of Congress Cataloging in Publication Data
Morgan, Rosemarie.
Women and sexuality in the novels of Thomas Hardy.
Revision of thesis (Ph.D.)—St. Andrews University.
Bibliography: p.
Includes index
1. Hardy, Thomas, 1840–1928—Characters—Women.
2. Women in literature. 3. Sex in literature.
4. Sex role in literature. I. Title.
PR4757.W6M67 1988 823'.8 87–28623

British Library CIP Data also available

ISBN 0–415–00268–0

Women and Sexuality
in the Novels of
Thomas Hardy

Rosemarie Morgan

ROUTLEDGE
London and New York

INTRODUCTION

For Hardy, the physical world holds within its form and structure as many meanings as the imagination of the observer has powers to encompass. The physical expression of things – the way the world looks and is looked upon – yields due significance to the acute observer but immeasurable significance to the imaginative poet whose endeavour, as Hardy saw it, should be to draw out the essential existence of things unseen and render them visible. This is also the part real, part imaginary world of the Wessex novels, a world shaped by an imaginative seeing into nature, human and pastoral, but a world bound no less by hard material fact, life as it is lived.

Life as it is lived by the characters in Hardy's novels, takes material, physical shape, colour, dimension, and form, from sense impressions, sense experience, the life of the senses, and even, on occasion, the sixth senses. Hardy speaks of Tess's existence as a structure of sensations; and indeed sensory experience, for Tess, not only intensifies the physical expression of things so that trees have inquisitive eyes – seeing into her innermost self as Angel cannot – but it also intensifies her mental powers: by fixing her attention on a distant star she moves mind out of body and transcends the material world altogether. Like the poet-Hardy, she moves within and beyond the physical world to discover inner powers, hidden essences and, again like Hardy, she shapes form into feeling, into imaginative vision, into dreams of the new and strange.

Visible essences – Tess's trees with eyes, or her own peony mouth (in form, tone, texture and mobility, the manifest expression of her sexuality) – are, by nature and definition, physical. But it is not so much the visibility as the palpability of female sensations that, with Hardy's women, gives expression to their physicality. Even the so-called 'ethereal' Sue Bridehead has a palpable flesh-and-blood presence: her spirit, Hardy says, could be seen 'trembling through her limbs'. This brings her (descriptively) close to certain other, rather more voluptuous flesh-and-blood presences whom no one except Hardy would think to align (imaginatively) with the superficially sexless Sue: those earthy, hot-blooded milkmaids at Talbothays 'under whose bodices the life throbbed quick and warm'.

I lay stress upon the physicality of Hardy's women for two reasons. The first has to do with the Victorian critics' discomfiture with Hardy's women, which none perceived as an embarrassment with, or fear of, the female body, and which most couched in terms of moral censure. The second has to do with Hardy's less-than-typical Victorian view of female sexuality: his complete lack of puritanical censure, his complete faith in the healthy, life-giving force of free, unrepressed sexual activity, his complete commitment to active, assertive, self-determined women of the kind satirised in the pages of *Punch* as 'masculine', hag-like or gross.[1] In Hardy, the active, assertive woman appears in none of these guises. On the contrary, whether she appears as farmer (Bathsheba), or field-labourer (Tess), or text-illuminator (Sue), or as a highly competent head of household (Paula Power and Ethelberta), she is personable, desirable and by no means mannish or grotesque.

Victorian women were rarely offered fresh active fictions bearing imaginative possibilities of challenge, renewal and change. The tales of discovery, of travel, of work, of exploration, were men's stories where they were not the stories of fallen women – Little Em'ly, Hetty Sorrel. In Hardy's Wessex world the sphere is broadened yet kept well within the range of plausibility and possibility. Women work outside the home in both conventional and unconventional occupations, from teaching to negotiating the price of corn, from serving as barmaids to inaugurating telegraphic systems, from working as milkmaids to organising public readings. Women travel unaccompanied beyond the neighbourhood, embark upon enterprises of their own volition, initiate relationships. In other words, they struggle to shape their own lives with a vigour and energy and resilience that is, to the reader, the more remarkable for the fact that theirs is a struggle against all odds, a struggle in a world that, as Hardy says in *The Return of the Native*, is *not* friendly to women.

In the first instance, I shall argue in this book that Hardy sets at odds those social and literary conventions which mutually reinforced the culturally based induction, in Victorian England, of a sexual 'amnesia' in women. From infancy women were kept in ignorance of their own bodies to experience puberty, defloration and sexual intercourse as *mystery*. Necessarily, the fullness of woman's physical and sexual experience is bound, in Hardy, by his own observations and empathy and, of course, by the censor – dubbed by Hardy, the 'Grundyist'[2] – but demystification there is, no less. His women toil and labour, for example, and bear the marks of their physical activity; if they weep, their skin blotches, their eyelids puff, redden and ache; if restless and hot in sleep, they sweat; if ill-tempered or depressed, their features slacken; and the physical reality of exhaustion leaves woman as it leaves man – visibly 'jaded' and 'fagged' (*TD*, pp.382, 383). The important point here is that neither the marks of toil nor, indeed, any visible signs of the body's functioning, of physical exertion, of stress or fatigue, renders any of Hardy's women less than worthy, less than noble, less than womanly for their imperfections, or their soiling in the world of work. Hardy begins where the majority of Victorian novelists left off, with 'real', flesh-and-blood women; and he begins with radical verve: the soiled and soiling world of work was not, or so many Victorians argued, a suitable place for noble womankind.

In the same radical spirit, Hardy not only acknowledges, or gives due recognition to female volatile emotions, female sensations, but he also treats them with the same devotion to physical detail as he gives to the male. Hence the potential for the physically active life (as opposed to passive), the active struggle, the active experience, is not reserved exclusively for the hero; and the life of the senses, *women's* senses, does not elude the reader's powers of visualisation and is not, therefore, rendered invisible, or beyond the bounds of common experience.

Hardy's women experience their bodies in ways that drew shudders from his critics, which one of the more outspoken among them, Mrs Oliphant, did not try to hide. Her feelings ran high about *Jude* in particular, whose 'grossness, indecency, and horror' lay, she felt, at the door of the women: the 'revolting ... disgusting' Arabella, more 'brutal in depravity than anything which the darkest slums could bring forth', and the 'indecent' 'other woman', who 'completes the circle of the unclean' by 'keeping the physical facts' of life 'in constant prominence by denying . . . them'.[3]

This brings me back to the second of my reasons for stressing the physicality of Hardy's women. Whereas critics reviled their voluptuousness, Hardy kept firmly to his practice of celebrating the life of the senses and, most important, of presenting the voluptuous woman, the sexy woman, as neither dumb nor loose in morals. To bring moral seriousness and sexiness together in the single female form was not only to fly in the face of current convention, code and belief, it was also subversive. The Victorian conceptual bifurcation of woman (madonna and whore) may seem to the modern mind to be primarily iconographical, but it carried sufficient influence within society to generate its likeness in form: notably, the concept of two types of women, one fit for sex and the other for wife. The social usefulness of this bifurcation in a male-dominated society is that it consolidates division, not only between the sexes – for there is no equivalent among men of the madonna/whore polarisation – but also between women themselves, in that they are divided against their own kind. In every sense of the word they are divided against their own sex. Hardy, then, in presenting Victorians with female models who did not conform to the stereotypes, not only offended against proprieties but also threatened the status quo, hitting at the very structure and foundation of society itself.

It is not simply that moral seriousness and sexiness come together, subversively, in Hardy's more noteworthy heroines, where current belief upheld the view that the latter undoubtedly negated the former, where the prevailing conviction was that the voluptuous woman was by definition morally degenerate. More substantially, as I shall demonstrate in the following chapters, the fusion of these qualities in the single female form brings forth, in Hardy's novels, a set of fit and healthy, brave and dauntless, remarkably *strong* women. The sexual vitality which infuses their animate life generates vigour of both body and mind; from thence springs intelligence, strength, courage and emotional generosity, and that capacity so many Hardy heroines possess for self-exposure expressing both daring and intimacy – the ultimate intimacy which demands facing the fear of ego-loss in those moments which call for abandon.

In terms of presenting a revisionary reading of Hardy's texts, or, within the specific context of female sexuality, of treading in his narrative footsteps, one has to begin, I think, with the reaction of Victorian critics and their disciples speaking today in literary publications and academies. Aside from possible fears of, or embarrassments by, confrontations with the physical, flesh-and-blood reality of women's lives, it seems to me that even while shuddering at the voluptuousness of Hardy's women Victorian critics shielded their eyes or, at any rate, did not fully expose the picture they had before them. For example, Hardy's most sexually passionate heroines, Bathsheba and Tess, conveyed nothing whatsoever, to contemporary readers, of their erotic ecstasy and orgasmic rapture – as, for instance, in those scenes where first the one sinks blissfully in the throes of ecstasy, her 'blood beating ... stinging as if aflame to the very hollows of her feet', 'enlarged', 'swamped', liquidly streaming, stung to tears (Ferns episode), and where the other ecstatically undulates on her orgasmic plateau, beyond 'consciousness of time and space', in 'exaltation', with 'tears in her eyes' (Garden episode). Certainly reviewers vilified the voluptuousness of both these women but, significantly, critical hostility was not activated by these passages but by Hardy's *literal* presentation of the heroine's physical contact with the male body, notably Bathsheba's first ensnarement by Troy in the plantation scene, and Tess's trip across the flooded lane in Angel's arms. This critical perspective, in so far as indecorum is measured solely in relation to male/ female body contact, speaks of far more than delicacy of mind or a distaste for things physical. It speaks of total obliviousness to, or ignorance of, female sexuality: outside or beyond the physical presence of the male, beyond his compass, a woman's erotic life did not exist.

In an age that placed a high value on reticence, self-restraint, and certain 'feminine' qualities such as delicacy of health, a retiring disposition, a physical and intellectual timidity, and so forth, Hardy's women, with their admixture of qualities – transcending the stereotypes of madonna and whore – must have confused many readers caught with mixed feelings of admiration and alarm. Indeed, for removing the paragon from her pedestal and for raising the fallen woman from the gutter, for presenting humanly imperfect but lovable heroines, Hardy was, to his hurt and indignation, charged with misrepresenting womankind. The charge was unanswerable for, in a sense, his critics were right: the representative model, as personified by Coventry Patmore's Angel in the House, or Ruskin's Stainless Sceptre of Womanhood, was, in the amalgam, and in Victorian eyes, the most desirable, the most perfect of all representations.

Models of perfection are, however, in their very unattainability, tyrannical. And since women like men must fall short of perfection, their 'fall' and ensuing experience of guilt, shame and self-hatred inevitably ensured the continuance of their suffering and subordination and, ultimately, the perpetuation of sexual inequality and female bondage. It may well be for these reasons alone that Hardy abhorred what he called the 'perfect woman in fiction'. Indeed, one of the most important aspects of his conceptual framework is that he presents no perfect women in his fiction. On the contrary, his heroines' best faculties are presented in the context of their less-than-perfect natures in a less-than-perfect world not yet ready to take them at face value. But that the worthy and desirable must acquire angelic proportions if they are to remain worthy and desirable, that the world is unable to dispense with the sexual double-standard, that female sexuality still presents a threat to the dominant culture which refuses to grant women the opportunities granted to men, becomes, for Hardy, a tortuous theme of increasing importance to his work. The 'prosaic reality' in *Far From the Madding Crowd*, where two aspiring farmers rise to prosperity but only the female contender is denied legal rights and privileges, constitutes a primary motif modulating into a dominant theme in the darker work of *Jude the Obscure*. This motif finds its true parallel in the iniquitous Victorian marriage and divorce laws, in *Jude*, which are seen to be more intransigently ratified by secular law.[4]

Hardy relished the company of women and expressed no reservations about their powers, moral, intellectual, sexual, emotional, psychic; but he was not drawn to the liberal feminism of his day. While many liberal feminists agitated for equal rights with men, with which Hardy was in full sympathy, and while many others were divided, as was Hardy, over the question of enfranchisement and the problem of the under-educated voter, the majority of liberal feminists joined with the prominent emancipationist, Millicent Garrett Fawcett, in upholding the view that woman's true destiny lay in fulfilling the role of wife and mother. Indeed, liberal feminists regarded marriage as woman's highest vocation, as in a calling to the religious life with complete abdication of the self to the institution.

Hardy was moving in a completely different direction. Early on in his career he had studied, taken notes and made diagrams of, Charles Fourier's[5] work. The French socialist and philosopher held, amongst other things, strong anti-marriage views, but while the extent of his influence on Hardy has yet to be fully documented, one thing is clear: Hardy was deeply opposed to the liberal feminist's idealisation of marriage. Tending, instead, towards socialistic views and the abolition of marriage in its current institutionalised form, he was more readily drawn to the radical feminist fringe as, for example, in his support of the singular activist and anti-marriage campaigner, Mona Caird.[6]

Yet, while the lone anti-marriage campaigner, as embodied in Sue Bridehead, arrives late on the scene in Hardy's novels, she is nascent in earlier incarnations of his more dissident, rebellious women. Bathsheba's views on marriage, for example, while more tentative than Sue's, spring from a shared ideology and a shared feminine consciousness which hotly denounces the notion that marriage should be the expressed goal of a woman's sexuality.

The lone campaigner inevitably drew Hardy's immediate interest for he was one himself. Indeed, his intense feelings of isolation, his deep sense of alienation from the Victorian middle-class world he had entered as a popular, if controversial, novelist, must have urged him to a close understanding of the condition of women, in so far as he and they felt, sorely, the impact of the society's institutionalised values; in so far as each had to struggle to be heard, to gain recognition; in so far as oppression by either class or sexual division was the experience of both. Not only did Hardy identify with the oppressed classes, seeing himself (to use his word) a 'misfit' in the society, and not only did he have to bowdlerise his own texts to tailor them to the Victorian drawing-room where public readings were encouraged in polite company, but he was also constantly, painfully, at loggerheads with critics. Such perpetual censure, such unremitting condescension on the part of critics, such a sense of suffocation, frustration and humiliation must surely have intensified what is in my opinion his acute sensitivity towards, and sympathetic insight into, the plight of women curbed and bound to 'fit' the world of men.

Yet critical opinion does not favour Hardy as a champion of those women, who, as critics would have it, 'disrupt' the community, the social order, the status quo. These disruptive women evidently unsettle more worlds than their own, and Hardy stands, I would argue, firmly behind them. From El-fride's embattled sexual confrontations with Knight to Sue's outrage at the notion that a married woman should be regarded as man's property, Hardy's platform remains consistent and forthright: the world that denies autonomy, identity, purpose and power to women, is to be, on his terms, the loser.

Opinion can be, even while one disagrees with it, opinion-shaping. At the same time, while discovering in Victorian criticism on Hardy an underlying troubled spirit, an under-standable resentment at his iconoclasm, a rancour, even, at his intimate knowledge of women in an age that left intimate knowledge of women to women, so it seems to me that twentieth-century criticism in so far as it reflects and perpetuates the doubts and fears of Victorians on matters of female sexuality, has long outlived its usefulness as an opinion-shaping force.

My aim, in this book, is to present a revisionary study of Hardy's treatment of female sexuality, a new vision of his work, reshaping our impression of him through the refracting lens of his view of women. There was a consistency in his thinking on the condition of women, although he was forced, at first, to hide or disguise his views. The disguise is not, however, im-penetrable, provided we follow Hardy closely, perceptively, and adjust our outlook to his phenomenalist view of the world, to look keenly into and beyond the physical expression of things – reading both their ostensible and their hidden meanings. In other words, we need to read Hardy's prose as we read his poetry, that is with an acute sensitivity, not simply to imagery, structure and language, but also to perspective and voice.

The re-reading here is a question of emphasis which turns

upon Hardy's own emphases: his skill in intercepting his own text with contrapuntal narrative voices, his poetic complex of metaphorical structures, his elaborate configuration of points of view. Closely interpreted, these poetic devices permit the reader access to an authorial perspective which can, and should, be differentiated from that of the principles.

The all-knowing, omniscient narrator has a range of approaches from which to choose. The principle ones are dramatic – recording actions, speech and gestures – and expository, revealing the characters' inner thoughts and feelings and commenting on the story as it progresses. Narrative point of view does, of course, all too often, fall between the two – between the dramatic and the expository. And with Hardy, given the subtlety and complexity of his narrative shifts, it becomes particularly important to differentiate between the perspectives of the primary and alternative narrators, whose points of view frequently diverge, and just as frequently conflict. I use the term primary narrator to mean the voice and perspective that, when distinguished from all others, proves to be recognisably coherent, consistent and stable, from the first chapter to the last.

For the sake of simplicity I shall speak of the primary narrator, throughout this book, as Hardy. For despite the constant re-alignment of perspectives and vantage points in his texts, a clearly defined, increasingly dominant Hardyan point of view does emerge. I say increasingly dominant because with time, experience, and a heightened reputation, he rapidly learned to exploit certain literary devices that allowed him to circumnavigate Mrs Grundy, thus gaining confidence in asserting his own voice – the iconoclastic voice we hear resounding loud and clear in *Tess* and *Jude*.

It is important, then, to an accurate reading of his texts, to trace perspectival shifts just as one traces patterns of images and tracks the rhythmic foot. Through this approach, of clarifying points of view and differentiating narrative discourses, of letting Hardy and his characters speak in their own voices, of separating surface text from underlying meanings and getting back to and beyond the physical expression of things, we will uncover hidden essences and new significations beneath the most darkly veiled utterance.

I

THE HERESY OF PASSION:
A Pair of Blue Eyes

In the post-Freudian age sexuality inheres in the psyche, or soul, whose guardians are the analyst and sexologist. In terms of professional focus the shift from Victorian physic to twentieth-century psychoanalytic is little more than a minor shift in emphasis from body to mind. A greater shift is evident in the sphere of professional influence. The monopolism exercised by the Victorian medical profession over scientific, biological, moral, ethical and empirical concerns scarcely finds its parallel today in what has become a profession of high specialisation and fundamentally scientific interest. We do not expect, these days, to have moral issues raised by our general practitioner, and emotional or sexual problems seem to belong, not so much to the surgery as to the guidance counsellor's office.

Mid- to late-Victorian medical theorists held that all serious discussion of female sexuality should properly be confined to the medical journals where, under the heading of pathological disorder, it would be addressed in terms of malfunction. In so far as all aspects of the subject – physical, moral, psychological – were confined to professional investigations into physical and mental abnormalities, a close association inevitably grew up, in the cultural imagination, between the two areas: the mal-functioning organism and female sexuality.[1] And as *The Saturday Review* (1896) inadvertently reveals in a review of *Jude*, this close association had become, by the late century, fully assim-ilated into critical thought. In common with other critics, the *Saturday*'s 'Unsigned Reviewer' looks favourably upon Jude's sexuality but brings in the word 'malignant', more than once, in speaking of Sue's. The writer goes on to say that,

> The respectable public has now got to rejecting books wholly and solely for their recognition of sexuality, however incidental that recognition may be ... No novelist, however respectable, can deem himself altogether safe today from a charge of morbidity and unhealthiness.[2]

It is, of course, 'morbidity and unhealthiness' together with 'malignant', that reveal this author's attitudes while, no doubt, reinforcing those of the general reader.

Even as late as 1906, with the publication of Havelock Ellis's *Studies in the Psychology of Sex*, which shifted dialogues away from a clinical context, or from scientific discourses, into the oral histories of everyday men and women, members of the reading public were shocked at finding themselves exposed to 'unhealthy' issues now expressed in lay terms hitherto obscured by medicalese.

Some decades earlier, in the 1870s, Hardy, too, had felt the impact of this proscription as critics, reflecting the views of the medical theorists, accused him of misrepresenting women by making his heroines too voluptuous. In a mood of bitter reflection upon censorship and prudery he later observed that even the imagination had become the slave of stolid circumstance. It was conditioned, he said, by its surroundings like a river-stream. He was hitting back at his critics whose fidelity to social expedients, as he saw it, prevailed over what he called an honest portrayal of the relations between the sexes. And vitally important to that portrayal, to Hardy's mind, was the very real fact of female desire, sexual understanding, erotic love, none of which had any connection, as far as he was concerned, with physical or moral infirmity, with mental or moral derangement.

Hardy was not only struck by the manner in which critical fidelity to social expedients enslaved the creative imagination, he was also concerned about the social expediency of enslaving women by denying them a sexual reality. He was clearly on dangerous ground here, and, in every practical sense, had no choice but to disguise his oppositional views while patiently negotiating the proprieties – avoiding 'unhealthy' topics as best he may. I do not doubt that he must have found a certain satisfaction in covertly defying Mrs Grundy, in the earlier novels, by endowing his more unconventional heroines with a sexual reality which, in the main, defied and eluded the censor at one and the same time. For 'patiently negotiating the proprieties' does not have a very convincing Hardyan ring about it, despite the fact that it would be twenty years or so before he could openly declare himself, in *Tess*, an opponent of the league of medical theorists, an opponent of the prevailing sexual ethic, and an opponent of the sexual double-standard – his vindication of the voluptuous fallen woman challenging those very Victorian literary conventions that, in absenting or rarefying or mystifying sexuality, reinforced the notion of its unmentionability, its topical ineligibility.

Certain other literary conventions also found Hardy an avid opponent. Codes prescribing sexuality topically ineligible in works of fiction, were matched by equally well-observed conventions governing plot. For example, the marriage-and-happy-ending plot. This may have gained popularity partly because of its intrinsic reformist ethic. Marriage saves all, ensures happiness ever after, but before receiving her prize of husband and marriage, convention dictated that the heroine should be brought to acknowledge her deficiencies, should then become penitent, should then reform. Love and courtship were thus co-terminous with moral reformation, and getting-married-and-living-happily-ever-after provided the most desirable consummation for both character and plot.

Behind this convention lay the principle that moral growth was synonymous with becoming socialised according to prevailing sexual codes and prescribed roles. This was not an equation Hardy, himself, would have made. Both the convention and its underlying principle came under attack in his later novels, and the equivocation that supervenes at certain critical points in his early texts points in the same direction. Where, for example, convention demanded reformation of a headstrong, wilful young woman, the kind of reformation Gabriel Oak, in *Far From the Madding Crowd*, reserves for Bathsheba whom he would fashion 'meek and comely', Hardy confounds the issue by adopting an openly ambivalent stance, or, alternatively, by openly reserving his judgement – clearly very ill-at-ease with such conventions and all that they represented.

I do not mean to suggest that the more dominant Victorian literary conventions inscribed passionless configurations over the outlines of love and romance. For, indeed, sexual mystique did generate a conventional language of love and courtship in the mid- to late-century novel that was not exclusively of the sexually antiseptic lilies-and-lace category. Heroines might flush and glow, for example, or pant and palpitate, and heroes might stalk, or strut, or transfix or thrust, displaying erectile signals of stiffened bearing and stalwart posture (accented imagistically by the ubiquitous cane or uplifting wing-collar). But, typically, these postures and gestures, despite their resemblance to sexual signals and responses, do not lead to sexual encounters. Instead they flow as perceptible indicators towards the inevitable happy ending; not towards erotic sublimation for its own sake but towards marriage for propriety's sake. What then appears to be sexual passion, embedded in figurative narrative patterns, becomes a means to an end and not an end in itself. It becomes, in effect, a function of plot, to nudge the narrative to its due end, not a function of characterisation revealing depth of emotion, sexual responsiveness and desire.

In a similar way, channelling the erotic life to an end short of actual sexual fulfilment, the maiden possessing sexual knowledge is labelled fallen and denied, thereafter, sexual existence. Again, sexuality becomes a means to an end, not an end in itself. Sexual experience brings no new self-awareness, no enhancement of life, no self-renewal, no epiphanies. In classic Edenic tradition, woman's fall alone is the meaning. Having fallen, she is effectively cast out, excluded from love relationships. Either she adopts the celibate, penitential or vocational life, as in Gaskell's *Ruth*, or, lacking adventurous, self-renewing powers (in clear contrast to her predecessor, Moll Flanders), she limps forlornly into exile – the obvious example, George Eliot's Hetty Sorrel.

In *Candour in English Fiction* (1890), Hardy, arguing against Victorian literary conventions, complained that there were only two courses open to him. Either he produced in his characters, 'the spurious effect of their being in harmony with social forms and ordinances' or, 'by leaving them alone to act as they will, he must bring down the thunders of respectability upon his head'. By the 1890s his reputation, and to a lesser extent his nerves, could withstand the thunders; in the early 1870s, neither could. Yet, from the outset he deplored:

the false colouring best expressed by the regulation finish that 'they married and were happy ever after' ... a denouement ... indescribably unreal and meretricious, but dear to the Grundyist and subscriber.... In representations of the world, the passions ought to be proportioned as in the world itself, life being a physiological fact.[3]

There was a third course open to him which he does not mention but which he did adopt. Coventry Patmore was one of the first to distinguish Hardy's prose as the work of a poet, and indeed, it was by employing the epistemology of the poet that he succeeded in circumnavigating restrictive conventions and the Grundyist, even as early as *A Pair of Blue Eyes*. This, his third published novel, was well received, and while critical acclaim surpassed all his expectations (*Life*, p.95), 'a kind of defiance of conventionality' in the book did not escape the eagle eye of *The Saturday Review*. However, and this is the important point, the reviewer was unable to pinpoint the source or manner of the 'defiance'. And Hardy, in this instance, escaped the thunders.[4]

His first heroine, Cytherea Graye, in *Desperate Remedies* is not drawn into any form of 'defiance'. On the contrary, she is a thoroughly orthodox creation. Part Angel – self-effacing, noble, sexless, self-abnegating – and part Gothic personification of sensibility under pressure, she is, in her stereotypical ordinariness rare in the Hardy canon, betraying, I suspect, her author's sense of her feminine unreality, and hence unrealisableness in his imagination. But he does conceive of alternative possibilities of characterisation. This is suggested by one, very small, Hardyan impertinence tucked unobtrusively into the text where it is said of Cytherea's rival that,

She had been a girl of that kind which mothers praise as not forward, by way of contrast, when disparaging those warmer ones with whom loving is an end and not a means. (*DR*, p.148)

This covert approval of loving as an end in itself (the key word is of course 'warmer'), is too unrelated and understressed to signify in its immediate context as the narrative sweeps on apace; but it does signify in the wider context of Hardy's commitment to a sexual ethic, which, as his literary reputation improves, emerges with increasing force to re-state, in *Tess*, at far greater length, the very same principle – that loving should not be a means to an end but an end in itself. But the fact that it arises in *Desperate Remedies* at all signifies that, even given the most sexless of heroines, Hardy cannot be bound by the moral and literary conventions of the day, nor by the guise of respectability he had adopted in order to secure a market.

It is something of an irony that despite his efforts to conform, this, his first published novel, came in for censure not for small slips into forbidden ways of this kind, nor even for larger slips into closed areas of sensuality, but for falling into error on a simple matter of class distinction. The point of contention was not that his aristocratic Miss Aldclyffe develops a jealous, sensual attachment for the heroine, seeking her in her bed at night begging caresses and kisses. This the women could do with impunity since no male features in these embraces to give them sexual definition. Regarded as the emotional release of maternal or filial wells of feeling they were entirely innocuous; not a single reviewer discerned sensuality or erotic passion. Was Hardy gratified that in this respect at least his presentation of a deeply sensual feminine experience had passed muster? We do not know. But we do know of his shock at being attacked for 'daring to suppose it possible that an unmarried lady owning an estate could have an illegitimate child' (*Life*, p.84). That this should be the most perfidious of indiscretions was stupefying indeed!

To Hardy and his editor, Leslie Stephen, the Grundyists were both unpredictable and baffling: as late as *Far From the Madding Crowd*, Hardy's fourth published novel, he was still having trouble keeping one step ahead of them. Aware that the fallen maid of his draft version needed considerable refashioning if her entry into the Victorian drawing-room was not to offend, Hardy transformed the gay-young-woman-about-town (after the manner of 'Melia in 'The Ruined Maid', 1866) into something approaching the sexually-enfeebled fallen-woman stereotype. But despite Leslie Stephen's half-apologetic advice – he was abashed, he said, by his 'excessive prudery' – to treat the seduction of Fanny Robin in a 'gingerly fashion', (*Life*, pp.98–9), and despite Hardy's own attempts at re-fashioning, Fanny

Robin failed to conform to type. Part of her nonconformity lies, I think, in her initial rebounding after her 'fall', where convention dictated otherwise; and part in her lack of penitence and hot pursuit of the object of her desires; and, no doubt part of it also lies in her getting to the wrong church on time – distinctly a male privilege.

Hardy plays down this particular instance of Grundyist pressure, in the *Life*, as an amusing example of serial-writing politics. But the reality was harsher. Censorship, he later admitted, 'paralysed' him. This may well explain his excessive textual convolutions in *A Pair of Blue Eyes*, a narrative abounding in conflicting perspectives, contradictory voices and heavily veiled utterances.[5]

Stylistic convolutions also disfigure the text of *Desperate Remedies*, but they arise, I think, not from a struggle with non-conformist tendencies, but from a struggle with the genre. Following the rejection of his first book, *The Poor Man and the Lady*, Hardy was despatched by his publisher to try his hand at a Wilkie Collins-type novel. As his subsequent literary direction indicates he was not in the least predisposed to writing racy detective novels, so it seems perfectly understandable that *Desperate Remedies*, at its most stylistically awkward moments, tends to live up to the book's title.

Greatest difficulties arise here with the preliminaries; the result is an opening chapter embarrassingly pitted with falls. First Hardy enumerates a chronology. If the aim is to set a time-scale then it fails. The technique is far too tabular. Simultaneously, various settings are catalogued, presumably to establish location: Hocbridge, Christminster, Bloomsbury, Cambridge, London, Dukery St, and Russell Square – a proliferation of place-names all compressed into the introductory paragraphs on page one! Finally, a dramatis personae is shuffled out from the listings and data which is as ungainly as topography and chronology are lacklustre. Faceless, featureless, functionless, Cytherea Graye, Edward Springrove, Ambrose Graye, Huntway and Bradleigh are trundled out directory fashion – again, all on page one. They defy description, they defy even the imagination. And when the moment arrives for dialogue it is fairly evident that we are in the company of a very uncomfortable Hardy.

Fortunately this awkwardness in effecting an entry to the text does not disable the mechanics of plot once it gets under way, and by the time Hardy has completed *Under the Greenwood Tree* to embark upon *A Pair of Blue Eyes* he is no longer at odds with innovate technique. Instead he is at odds with propriety. Why? The answer lies in the arrival of the first in the line of his unconventional, voluptuous heroines, the first of his 'mis-representations' of womanhood.

Elfride Swancourt is no iconic Victorian maiden awaiting self-definition through male endowment: the marriage tie and its award of a man's name, identity, economic standing and status. Sexual development, exploration and understanding present themselves to Elfride, urged by an increasing awareness of her own psycho-sexual needs, to be of primary importance to her growth to maturity and fulfilment. If, then, we are drawn to her, identify and sympathise with her, this is not so much because she exemplifies oppressed, subordinated womanhood struggling to gain the love of a good man, but because in her daring she puts herself so much at risk, because in her candour she is so self-exposing, because she is strong and weak, brave and fearful, headstrong and vulnerable: she is utterly human and we care for her.

Problems arise for Hardy because he too cares for her. Yet can he be seen to ally himself with her without risking censure? For, according to prevailing views, her moral and intellectual seriousness should be undone by her sexiness; but Elfride is not so undone. Nor is her sexuality treated by Hardy as relative – that is to say merely activated by the male. Nor is it simply a means to an end: getting married and living happily ever after. Nor does it serve to aggrandise the male as the object of admiration, of respect, of adulation, of worship. Neither Stephen nor Knight enlarges in stature as the object of female desire. Rather, they diminish. Stephen, we are told, is not man enough for her, and Knight's fastidiousness opens up the question, in Elfride's mind, of his virility. She is not only sexually instigative, then, where the male is less so, she also sets the pace. This reversal of roles blatantly transgressed convention and openly subverted the ethical codes of the culture. Male control of the female depends in large measure upon his activating, and thereby regulating, her sexual responses, thus maintaining his supremacy. That she may not be beholden to him, dependent upon him, in this sense, undermines his power and considerably diminishes his authority – as is apparent in Knight's defensive reaction to Elfride's move towards activating *his* sexual responses:

'I almost wish you were of a grosser nature, Harry; in truth I do! Or rather, I wish I could have the advantages such a nature in you would afford me, and yet have you as you are.'

'What advantages would they be?'

'Less anxiety, and more security. Ordinary men are not so delicate in their tastes as you; and where the lover or husband is not fastidious, and refined, and of a deep nature things seem to go better, I fancy – as far as I have been able to observe the world.' (*PBE*, pp.324–5)

Not a little sexual knowledge informs these words, and Elfride is well aware of the transgression this implies even as she speaks. The tonal alteration in her language aptly reflecting what we imagine to be his coldly appraising stare, her candour gives way to camouflage. Criticism is veiled as flattering euphemism and sexual knowledge is presented as speculation. Initially hesitant ('I almost wish'), then eager, ('grosser nature', or sexually passionate in Victorian parlance), then less ardent ('not so delicate ... tastes'), her verbal thrust gradually loses impetus. By the time 'fastidious' and 'delicate' have been covered by 'refined' the *volte-face* from courage to fear is virtually concluded. 'Deep nature' compounds the retrenchment, the speculative 'I fancy' counteracts the knowledge revealed, and 'as far as I have been able to observe the world' mollifies. However, because Elfride's fear, as well as her courage, is based on the strength of her insight,[6] she arouses dread in her male listener. To eclipse the import of her words and no less her obvious power to disturb, Knight blandly cuts across her argument with cold reason:

Yes I suppose it is right. Shallowness has this advantage, that you can't be drowned there. (*PBE*, p.325)

That he so clings to the life-line with 'deep nature' that she hands him, turning the moment to personal advantage, belies his superficial air of calm.

Elfride's startlingly unconventional inclination, then, is to assess her lover's sexual adequacy not his wealth or social status.

The pitfalls, for Hardy, are obvious. Her heresy, together with her challenging alertness, sexual readiness and insurgent power to awaken in Knight an emotional latency as much to be feared as desired, presents her author with glaring problems of decorum. She is not only in danger of becoming alarmingly unwomanly in her awareness of sexual matters, in her assertion of her sexual desires, she is also (potentially) far too independent, far too lacking in submissiveness to be morally edifying. Hardy has no alternative. He must tailor his text to a more seemly fit.

Seemliness now appears in Grundyist guise – as a moralising, didactic narrator standing on the sidelines, so to speak. I shall refer to this speaker as the proprietary narrator, since its function here is to enter at intervals to provide moralistic asides with which to berate the wayward heroine, and, indeed, womanhood in general in so far as she might be identified (or identifying) with Elfride. The aside is a clumsy device. It is intrusive, platitudinous, self-righteous, and tonally discordant; although no doubt its edifying tone would have been reassuring to contemporary readers. Not so to Hardy, who, later in his career said as much:

The besetting sin of modern literature is its insincerity. Half its utterances are qualified, even contradicted, by an aside, and this particularly in morals and religion. (*Life*, p.215)

In fact, in making schematic use of the aside, Hardy exploits this contradictoriness to the full, in *A Pair of Blue Eyes*, incorporating it into a dialectic of opposing discourses and discordant voices of remarkable argumentative vigour.[7]

In Elfride's case, the aside has to be imbued with a guarded severity to ensure that an unconventional characterisation does not enter the Victorian middle-class drawing-room without bearing the marks of correction. Because the moralistic aside alludes to the world beyond the world of the novel it attracts notice yet shrugs off involvement in being noticed. At the same time, one cannot say it belongs solely to the reader's world since it fits rather too well into the world that Henry Knight inhabits and would have Elfride inhabit. However, for Hardy's purposes, it operates judiciously and effectively to oppose both the rebellious heroine and her dissident author wherever and whenever the nonconformity of either surfaces injudiciously within the text.

Let us take some examples. Following directly upon a candid confrontation with Stephen in which Elfride has owned to having had an earlier admirer, now in his grave – the very grave upon which Stephen is at this moment seated – and in which Stephen has admitted that he is not the blue-blood Elfride's father assumes him to be but a local stonemason's son, the troubled pair,

> Oppressed, in spite of themselves, by a foresight of impending complications ... returned down the hill hand in hand. At the door they paused wistfully, like children late at school. (*PBE*, p.110)

The proprietary narrator now intervenes with:

> Women accept their destiny more readily than men. Elfride had now resigned herself to the overwhelming idea of her lover's antecedents; Stephen had not forgotten the trifling grievance that Elfride had known earlier admiration than his own. (*PBE*, p.110)

From this we are meant to infer that Elfride's attitude partakes of a universal law of 'feminine' passive-acceptance. While Stephen still struggles with his grievance with a 'foresight of impending complications', Elfride makes no mental preparation for a confrontation with a class-conscious father far more likely to be swayed by reasoned argument than by resignation. If we are to trust the captious 'voice', we must either accept Elfride's unquestioning acceptance of her destiny or conclude that the author has lost sight of her altogether. For where *is* Hardy's ingenious, spirited young heroine customarily so quick in intelligence and daring? And surely her lack of class prejudice should be to her credit? That it should be made to appear to spring from an indiscriminative sense trivialises it beyond measure. The question to consider, then, is the veracity of the statement: 'Women accept their destiny more readily than men.' Elfride does not. She alters her course, with Stephen, not once, but twice (the broken elopement and the broken date to meet in the church), and finally rejects altogether the fate of becoming his wife. And she is patently not resigned to Knight's sexual fastidiousness, nor to his attempts at domination, nor to his repudiation of her, which spurs a hot pursuit to London where, on the brink of reconciliation, she is restrained by the interception of her father who snatches her back to Endelstow.

If any character readily accepts his destiny it is Stephen. His discovery of Elfride's engagement to Knight in his absence spurs no hot pursuit, no valiant attempts at reconciliation, but instead a passive, if not unemotional retreat from the locality. And where it is not Stephen, it is Knight – pathetic victim of his own sexual anxiety and, we infer, atrophied sexual potency, which have bred in him a predilection for what he calls 'untried' lips (metonymically, virgins). Perverse in his desire to brutalise the very thing he values, he fails to claim the one woman capable of altering his direction, the one woman sexually empowered to rekindle his potency as she also kindles in him a heightened emotional and perceptual sensitivity.

If the comment upon the nature of women in general and Elfride in particular is emptied of veracity and meaning, what is its function here? I would suggest that it is introduced at this point to 'play down' Elfride's active, sexually assertive role in her relationship with Stephen; that it acts as the foil Hardy requires to placate the Grundyists. It is a self-conscious move but a very self-knowing one. Hardy is touchily aware of where his allegiances lie, as he is also aware that the time is not yet ripe for revealing them. It is then, an essential prop in terms of both textual structure and publication stratagem. But that the proprietary commentator introduces a point of view that conflicts with the evidence as well as offering false, not to say prejudiced, information about Elfride, says more about Hardy than about his heroine: he may be paying lip-service to convention – the conventional practice of dictating in heavy moralistic tones to women – but he has no intention of winning the case.

It would be to misrepresent Hardy to suggest that each and every negative criticism directed at his heroine is painstakingly controverted by textual evidence. This would place him squarely, and uncomfortably, in the Ruskin camp advocating a model of perfection (Stainless Sceptre of Womanhood). His intention is not to present woman with so exalted a concept of perfection that she must inevitably fall short of the ideal, but rather to break with this stereotype, to characterise an individual who is human and flawed, whose lovability is not contingent upon her perfection. Morally sensible, sexually aware and mortally imperfect, Elfride is worthy in her own right and to be valued not for what she *ought* to be but for what she is. The only judgement Hardy controverts is that of the moraliser, the proprietary narrator, insinuating otherwise.

This stratagem of superimposing a Grundyist speaker to act the part of censor, as if to convey authorial disapproval of feminine nonconformity, functions throughout the entire novel. And the contradictoriness occasioned by the asides persists uniformly and with such frequency that I am persuaded of a purposeful conflict, an intentional conflict, thrust by Hardy into the text as he grapples, on the one hand with an unconventional heroine, and on the other with the Grundyists looking, as it were, over his shoulder. But let us take another example. Elfride, later caught up with Knight but not yet broken with Stephen, has it now said of her:

Woman's ruling passion to fascinate and influence those more powerful than she – though operant in Elfride, was decidedly purposeless. She had wanted her friend Knight's good opinion from the first: how much more than that elementary ingredient of friendship she now desired, her fears would hardly allow her to think. In originally wishing to please the highest class of man she had ever intimately known, there was no disloyalty to Stephen. She could not – and few women can – realize the possible vastness of an issue which has only an insignificant begetting. (*PBE*, pp.218–19)

Problems arise here as earlier. The prefatory glance aside at 'all women' is, with regard to Elfride, indefensible. There is no thematic evidence to support it. If her 'ruling passion (is) decidedly purposeless', why is Knight speeding back to Endelstow before the allotted time? The generalisation has no bearing upon (except to trivialise) Elfride's desire for 'much more than that elementary ingredient of friendship'. Delete the generalisation and there is no contradiction. Elfride desires; and this draws a response in Knight, who, as has been noted, is racing back to her prematurely. Reinstate the generalisation and there are immediate difficulties. The inference that Elfride (supposedly owning a 'ruling passion to fascinate and in-fluence') is vain and coquettish openly conflicts with what we know of her, quite apart from the fact that it is impugned by what follows: Hardy's evocation of her sincerity, her tremulous, fearful heart.

Similar problems arise over the speaker's final observation. Textual and thematic evidence shows that it is not Elfride who could not 'realize the possible vastness of an issue which has only an insignificant begetting', but Knight. It is he who lacks perspicacity, it is he who narrows Elfride's world as by means of 'instinctive acts so minute' he has forcibly narrowed his own.

Perhaps his lifelong constraint towards women, which he had attributed to accident, was not chance after all, but the natural result of instinctive acts so minute as to be indiscernible even by himself. (*PBE*, p.345)

Upon the insignificantly begotten issue of their first encounter as reviewer and reviewed, which becomes the less insignificant issue of their early intimacy, it is he, not she, who imposes limitations. Not broadness of vision but purblindness, exacerbated by his mincing sexuality, informs Knight's understanding of the world, human nature, himself, Elfride.

From the outset he engages obsessively in his relationship with her. Hardy dramatises this imaginatively by paralleling the 'earring' quest with the quest of the lover in pursuit of the beloved. It happens thus. Knight at first ridicules Elfride's perfectly natural liking for bodily adornment, then patronises it, then feverishly hunts down exactly the right pair of earrings and then races back to Endelstow to press them on her. When she spurns them, 'feeling less her master than heretofore' (*PBE*, p.221), he presses them on her again: 'let me dress you in them' (*PBE*, p.300). Finally, with his gifts accepted, he presses himself upon her: 'Elfride, when shall we be married?' (*PBE*, p.302). Knight's mode of courtship is neatly and suggestively paralleled by his obsession with the miniature artefacts which he laboriously seeks out and fastens in her lobes – those fated earrings which she admits to liking but, more tellingly, mislays.

His need to ridicule, patronise, dominate, 'dress', and at the last, to shame Elfride is illustrative: 'How can you be so fond of finery? I believe you are corrupting me into a taste for it' (*PBE*, p.303). The accusation appropriately mirrors his egomaniacal obsession with reducing her to the guilt-ridden, childlike dependency so necessary to his preservation of male supremacy. His obsession with the trifling and small, the miniature artefacts which afford him the opportunity of touching her person, is equally instructive. For as wooing gestures (the roaming caress, the tender stroking, the long lingering touch), his are cramped to fussy, fiddling activities accompanied by a contraction of his world to an area the size of a pinhead: the minute perforations in Elfride's lobes. This contracted focus sharpens Hardy's characterisation of Knight elsewhere in the novel.

Take, for example, his repudiation of Elfride: this provides an apt, if sad, logical, or rather psychological, conclusion to an affair which, on his part, has been conducted with unremitting condescension. Pointing to Knight's dismissive farewell, which takes into consideration none of the 'possible vastness' of the issue, Hardy reflects that:

It is a melancholy thought that men who at first will not allow the verdict of perfection they pronounce upon their sweethearts or wives to be disturbed by God's own testimony to the contrary, will, once suspecting their purity, morally hang them upon evidence they would be ashamed to admit in judging a dog. (*PBE*, p.358)

Sure enough Knight does dismiss Elfride as if she were a dog: 'Remain', 'You will not follow me', he orders (*PBE*, pp.359–60). Leaving the stricken girl racked with 'convulsive sobs [which] took all the nerve out of her utterance', Knight then

withdrew his eyes from the scene, swept his hand across them, as if to brush away the sight, breathed a low groan, and went on. (*PBE*, p.359)

As his dismissive words and blotting-out gestures indicate, and as Hardy's spatial allocations of bound and boundless areas emphasise – Elfride 'in the midst of it – up against the sky', Knight passing into interiors, 'going indoors' and thence to 'chambers' (*PBE*, pp.359–60) – there is no perspective on Knight's horizon that he does not constrict. The world, humanity, Elfride are reduced to specks by this man who comes close to perceiving this for himself as, to Stephen, he ponders:

All I know ... is a mass of generalities. I plod along, and occasionally lift my eyes and skim the weltering surface of mankind lying between me and the horizon as a crow might; no more. (*PBE*, p.162)

This is also the man, we recall, who has purposefully 'impregnated [her] with sentiments of her own smallness to an uncomfortable degree of distinctness' (*PBE*, p.206); and who was himself to be, in telling proximity to the heroic woman in the Cliff episode, 'with the small in his death' (*PBE*, p.240).

Elfride, by contrast, in her attempts to divert attention away from conflictful issues, does not so constrict her world. Her will to self-concealment itself testifies to an awareness of the possible vastness of begotten issues. When she declares herself to Knight, her words betray just how vast:

> I would gladly have told you; for I knew and know I had done wrong. But I dared not; I loved you too well! You have been everything in the world to me – and you are now. Will you not forgive me? (*PBE*, p.358)

These are not the words of a woman lacking perspicacity and foresight – as Hardy confirms: 'The reluctance to tell, arose from Elfride's simplicity in thinking herself so much more culpable than she really was' (*PBE*, p.358). In her newly reduced state of dependency upon Knight, Elfride's perception of her earlier independence and defiance looms disproportionately large. The issue of her indiscretion, which had earlier 'grieved her' (*PBE*, p.219), has now become an enormity fully realised in all its implications. Here again, the discrepancy between the worldly-wise commentator's observation and the characterisation and events which precede and follow it remains: that is, Elfride is quite justified in her self-concealment.

Invariably all attempts at sifting the evidence, of distinguishing between opposing voices and discourses, meet with the difficulty of identifying narrative shifts in perspective. This is the more problematical for Hardy's expertise in veiling such shifts, one might even say, his expertise in self-concealment. Take, for example, the following passage from the vault scene:

> Stephen's failure to make his hold on her heart a permanent one was his too timid habit of dispraising himself to her – a peculiarity which, exercised towards sensible men, stirs a kindly chord of attachment that a marked assertiveness would leave untouched, but inevitably leads the most sensible woman in the world to undervalue him who practises it. (*PBE*, p.279)

Because the narrative leads out towards 'the most sensible woman in the world' without unsettling its focus, the shift in perspective is almost imperceptible – although it does now sharpen instantly:

Directly domineering ceases in the man, snubbing begins in the woman; the trite but no less unfortunate fact being that the gentler creature rarely has the capacity to appreciate treatment from her natural complement. (*PBE*, p.279)

Fortunately there are verbal prompts here which should by now be registering their muffled cues. The 'creature' who 'rarely has the capacity' for this, that or the other, has that familiar enfeebled air about her which Hardy's choice of the word 'trite' assists us in recalling. Thus alerted, we suspect that he has lost sight of Elfride for she was never subject to Stephen's domination, and has not, to our knowledge, wittingly snubbed him – not even where he failed at the game of chess where she had shown above average skills.

And with the following reference to Elfride's snobbery we are assured that Hardy has, indeed, lost her, altogether:

To such girls poverty may not be, as to the more worldly masses of humanity, a sin in itself; but it is a sin because graceful and dainty manners seldom exist in such an atmosphere. Few women of old family can be thoroughly taught that a fine soul may wear a smock-frock, and an admittedly common man in one is but a worm in their eyes. (*PBE*, p.279)

'Such girls' are not Elfride – she whose rejoinder to Stephen's misery at his lowly origins had been:

'No; don't take trouble to say more ... It has become a normal thing that millionaires commence by going up to London with their tools at their back, and half-a-crown in their pockets. That sort of origin is getting so respected,' she continued cheerfully, 'that it is acquiring some of the odour of Norman ancestry'. (*PBE*, p.106)

Elfride cannot be accused of snobbery. Her opposition to her class-divisive father is clearly drawn, and even her impatient dismissal of Jethway as 'not good enough, even if I had loved him' (*PBE*, p.109) constitutes non-specific value judgement, not class-specific disparagement. In employing the same evaluative term later, but with reference to herself, her meaning is quite plain: 'If I had only known you had been coming' she tells Knight, 'what a nunnery I would have lived in to have been good enough for you!' (*PBE*, p.344). An appropriate match is surely the inference here. Aware that Jethway comes from a respectable, well-to-do background, Elfride is equally aware that her father (solely concerned with pedigree and not alto-gether satisfied with Knight's at that) would consider him decidedly ineligible. The issue of class in the Jethway colloquy is actually introduced not by Elfride but by Stephen, who, for understandable reasons, over-reacts to any suggestion of social difference.

To do justice to Hardy's close detailing in this context, Elfride's class attitudes might best be determined not only by her opposition to her father's views or those she expresses supportively to Stephen, but by her customary behaviour and actions. Her lack of concern for her own blue-blood or for appearances, as, for example, she rides hatless on horseback through the neighbourhood, stopping to chat at ease 'to old men and women' (*PBE*, p.136), and her natural affinity with sexton Cannister (*PBE*, p.110), more than adequately testify to her native lack of class prejudice. In addition, the nature of her relationship with parlour-maid Unity is more than egalitarian. It is sisterly (*PBE*, pp.88, 151). And Elfride certainly does not strike Unity as the kind of woman to whom the 'common man ... is but a worm'. To Knight's question, 'Was he [Luxellian] very fond of her?' Unity replies: 'Twas her nature to win people more when they knew her well' (*PBE*, p.402). Now while I take this to be a Hardyan backhander at Knight (in *not* having been won to Elfride as have her husband and 'people' generally, he is clearly not one who 'knew her well', hence defective in knowledge and understanding), it also vouches, in the words of one who does know her well, for Elfride's capacity to win people to her irrespective of their class.

Although this particular moralistic aside made by the pro-prietary narrator on Elfride's supposed snobbery is also con-troverted by what precedes and follows it, the confusion of 'voices' in the vault scene remains. However, this single difficult passage is hardly enough to disable what Hardy has already established: authorial non-alliance with the moralising pro-prietary narrator.[8]

Drawing out the sexual double-standard that shapes both Knight's philosophy and the proprietary narrator's com-mentary, Hardy now raises the question of Elfride's self-concealment; but first, tactically, from the point of view of the prejudiced narrator:

When women are secret they are secret indeed; and more often than not they only begin to be secret with the advent of a second lover. (*PBE*, p.281)

We do not have to look very far for the contrary evidence. Nor, at this point, should the inherent contradiction in this statement require much deciphering. First, there are enough precedents set in this novel to establish the withholding of information, or practice of secrecy, as normative and not, as the above observation implies, the practice of inconstant women generally or Elfride in particular. Parson Swancourt woos and weds Elfride's stepmother in secret. Stephen is secretive about his social origins, and secretive with Knight in London as to the nature of his relationship with Elfride. His failure to acknowledge her in the vault scene leads Knight falsely to assume that the couple are mere acquaintances. Stephen does not argue the point. Knight, too, is no exception. In fact, his deliberate attempt to deceive his trusted friend is perhaps the most treacherous of all deceptions. Having lulled Stephen into a sense of false security, Knight plots to reach Endelstow to claim Elfride (whom, of course, he has just been vociferously disclaiming) before Stephen has time to do the same (*PBE*, pp.382–7). That unknown to him, Stephen has changed his plans and is simultaneously making a dash for the ten o'clock train from Paddington is a rough justice that Hardy, with his predilection for chastening converging courses, cannot resist.

Second, Hardy provides alternative thematic evidence to show that Elfride is intentionally secretive, as is her father, right from the start: the minor concealment of the sermon writing, the less minor one of her elopement, and of course the major issue of her secret love. These concealments are in evidence long before Knight's arrival and are by no means contingent upon his 'advent'. Consequently, the imputation that 'women', and by inference Elfride, have an innate tendency to deceive lovers – stated as if it were a universal truth – comes, with all other such imputations, into the woman-in-the-wrong category of misinformation.

Yet again, Hardy's alternative evidence is convincing and none too esoteric. But in the sequence that follows matters become more complicated. We are invited to contemplate Elfride's 'vanity':

Perhaps to a woman it is almost as dreadful to think of losing her beauty as of losing her reputation. (*PBE*, p.299)

This commentary refers to Elfride's defensive reaction to Knight's baiting: 'a luxuriant head of hair', he claims, exhausts itself and 'gets thin as the years go on from eighteen to eight-and-twenty' (*PBE*, p.298). Slighted and alarmed, Elfride is further distressed as Knight insinuates that the thicker and more abundant the hair the greater the risk of balding as, he concludes mercilessly, statistical evidence would indicate. All our sympathies go to the cruelly baited girl, until, that is, the proprietary narrator intervenes to impute shameless vanity: 'to a woman it is almost as dreadful to think of losing her beauty as of losing her reputation'. Is Elfride's candid self-appraisal now to be read, then, as vanity? As earlier, the shift in the moral register in order to invoke censure manipulates characterisation against its natural direction. Hardy has long-since established his heroine's healthy, bounding awareness of her youth and beauty. But she has nothing of the coquette culturally conditioned to display allure and enticement while devoid of sexual feeling for her lover. And as the following spontaneous outburst suggests, and would openly attest but for the narrative contradiction, Hardy, himself, sees her as more ingenuous than vain: 'It is dreadful', she cries out,

to hear you talk so. For whatever dreadful name the weakness may deserve, I must candidly own that I am terrified to think my hair may ever get thin. (*PBE*, p.299)

In truth, there is more vanity in Knight's self-presentation, the upright, steely, masculine stance signalling power and potency where psycho-sexually he is a starveling, than there is in a single toss of the well-adorned Swancourt head. If, though, there is more sophistry than truth in the supposition that Elfride's protestations 'would be difficult for men to understand' (*PBE*, p.299) (the suggestion is that women are too unconscionably vain for any man's understanding), it would no doubt be true of Knight. Hardy has prepared for this contingency. Knight would indeed find her protestations difficult to understand because he himself is balding (*PBE*, p.203)! Her spontaneous outburst, revealing no sign of repressed anxiety, touches him to the quick. He would not dare to draw attention to himself in this way. Ironically, where he had set out to humiliate he now finds himself a possible target, for Elfride's aversion to thinning hair reflects rather poorly on him. Quick on the defensive – scorning her feelings which, in turn, permits him to misunderstand them – the scoffer turns an embarrassing moment to his advantage by shifting shame from himself to another, who now becomes the object of blame.

Whatever Elfride had felt before, she now feels the impact of ridicule while stoutly resisting 'whatever dreadful name' Knight might ascribe to her candid self-appraisal. He purposely misreads her self-evaluation and preoccupation with personal adornment, which is, simply, the outward expression of an innate grooming instinct. This perfectly natural instinct takes woman with her assistant, as it takes man with his barber, to the looking-glass in the expectation of enhancing self-presentation, which will in turn enhance display and signal sexual interest. Pointing to a double-standard in this context, Hardy draws attention to Knight's cultivation of:

a curly beard, and crisp moustache: the latter running into the beard on each side of the mouth, and ... hiding the real expression of that organ under a chronic aspect of impassivity. (*PBE*, p.159)

Knight's trimming and clipping springs solely from a desire to enhance display. Likewise his adoption of certain other grooming enhancers which Hardy takes pains to bring to the reader's attention. There is the urbane cosmopolitan, for example, who sports a 'stout walking-stick', a fashionable 'brown-holland sun-hat', not to mention a battered (well-travelled) leather case on his first foray out from the city to the Cornish wilds (*PBE*, p.183). Both Knight and Elfride are thus concerned with personal presentation in their different ways, although Knight would not, I think, invoke 'whatever dreadful name' to describe his own proud posture and cultivation of a hirsute persona.

If Elfride is at all representative of her time and clime (if not of her urban, bourgeois peers who were sporting hair-pieces during this period), she will display her fine head of hair to full advantage. Were she in reality merely vain, she would pose no threat. She would lack deep feeling for Knight and her gestures would be mannered rather than imbued with those subtle sex signals which he evidently finds too unsettling to handle. And if *he* is at all representative of his class and clime, her sensuous self-delight would be understood as voluptuousness threatening moral and mental disorder.

At one point, Knight does come quite close to discerning the true nature and function of what he calls, variously, 'vanity', 'womanly artifice' and 'showing off' (*PBE*, p.203). In his observations of Elfride's testing-out activities on Endelstow Tower, he notes:

An innocent vanity is of course the origin of these displays. 'Look at me,' say these youthful beginners in womanly artifice, without reflecting whether or not it may be to their advantage to show so very much of themselves. (*PBE*, p.203)

Coming close, but not quite close enough – unable, in the event, to suspend his deeply entrenched puritanical values – Knight rationalises Elfride's look-at-me sexual display as vain artifice, not female desire expressly testing male response. Moral judgement thus clouds the world which his sense-perceptions might at first register quite accurately, and female sexual receptivity, which urges testing behaviour, is marked down as mere vanity. Knight thus enacts the exemplary Victorian, and Elfride's sexuality remains unapproved, unproven and (for Knight's peace of mind) unconfronted.

Stylistic prolixities, authorial ambivalence and contradictory accounts notwithstanding, Hardy succeeds in breaking new ground in *A Pair of Blue Eyes* without jeopardising his reputation. Careful not to offend against propriety, he quietly but emphatically reverses Western literary chivalric tradition in his depiction of a heroine of some courage and nerve who plays knight gallant to the hero in a scene which also goes some way to discredit his intelligence about the world around him. Affined to these gathering heterodoxies, Elfride openly questions her lover on matters of sex and, when spurned, hotly pursues him, demonstrating to the last those galvanising qualities of nerve-steeled daring and fear in the face of danger that empowered her to heroic action on the Cliff. Defending herself to the last with a demand to be given full recognition as a person in her own right, she challenges Knight with the words:

'Am I such a – mere characterless toy – as to have no attract – tion
in me, apart from – freshness? Haven't I brains? You said – I was
clever and ingenious in my thoughts, and – isn't that anything? Have
I not some beauty? I think I have a little – and I know I have – yes
I do! You have praised my voice, and my manner, and my
accomplishments. Yet all these together are so much rubbish because
I – accidentally saw a man before you!' (*PBE*, p.344)

Knight is quick of course, to cut her across by his customary
method of re-stating the grounds of her argument.

'O come Elfride. "Accidentally saw a man" is very cool. You loved
him remember.' (*PBE*, p.344)

In order to undermine her he has to shift the focus away from
her point that her worth is not contingent, or should not be
contingent upon who may love her and whom she may love.
She has tactfully offered him an 'accidental'; he pushes beyond
it to make it symptomatic, not of her capacity to love more
than one man but of her inconstancy.

Hardy will not endorse this denial of her worth and self.
Returning the two heroes back to Endelstow at the last, each
intent upon claiming Elfride as his prize, he purposefully denies
her to them. Clearly there is no longer any question of inconstancy. On the contrary, it is belief in her constancy that impels
each hero to return and claim her – as Hardy illustrates well
in one of the last conversations between Stephen and Knight.
Conflated, their dialogue reads:

'Can it be that I have killed her?'/'You have killed her more than I?'

'I wish the most abject confession ... could ... make amends to my
darling'/'*Your* darling! ... Any man can say that, I suppose: any man
can. I know this, she was *my* darling before she was yours; and after
too. If anybody has a right to call her his own, it is I.' (*PBE*, p.396)

But neither is given the right to 'own' her and neither is given
the satisfaction of claiming her death as his trophy. Elfride dies
bearing another man's love and another man's life in her body.
There will be no victory and no vindication for either hero.

By drawing Elfride right out of Knight's sphere to die off-
stage, Hardy provides a fitting conclusion to a characterisation
which has demanded alternating shifts and displacements of
her person. Excluding her, finally, from Knight's bourgeois,

puritanical world is Hardy's way of vindicating her: she dies the woman she claimed the right in life to be. She is loved and lovable in her own right as Unity testifies. Her accomplishments, her clever and ingenious mind, her emotional generosity, are not only imprinted upon the hearts of those who know her deeply but are also no longer subject to effacement at the hands of man, time or change. Nothing and no one can render her personal qualities 'so much rubbish', nor can either reduce her to a 'mere characterless toy'.

The bitter irony of the denouement, Knight's journeying by train to the same destination as his dead beloved (lying in her coffin in the next carriage) yet moving in an altogether different direction, not towards burying but 'bedding' her, aesthetically provides the most perfect of finishes to the parallel voyages, in this novel, and their parallel significances. Not only does Hardy's narrative abound in restless authorial shifts but so, too, does the plot. Elfride's growth to womanhood is mapped out in a series of hazardous journeys each of which finds her accompanied by one or other of her lovers. One thing is plain: journeying alone she is safe! None of her solitary, wild, equestrian exploits endangers her. But every one of her voyages, ascents, or traversings with Knight, in particular, threatens or injures her, and on each there is a divergence of inner courses. Elfride mentally or emotionally voyages in one direction, towards an exploration and understanding of the world – he in quite the opposite. The Cliff scene is pivotal in this context, first and foremost at the subversive level of woman-as-heroic-rescuer, man-as-creature-in-distress, and second, at the level of divergent courses: Elfride sets out to watch for Stephen while Knight sets out to watch for her; she is sure of her course, he inadvertently sets her off it. She had been caught in a similar situation with Knight once before. Feeling for some days disturbed and slighted by his peremptory, superior manner, and, presumably, with an unconscious desire to disturb him in turn, she treads the crumbling parapet of the church tower, which in her youthful daring she had done many times before. Knight is certainly roused, but not to an animal alertness or to a fierce protectiveness, as Elfride might, instinctively, desire. Rather he raps out a schoolmasterly reprimand and, unnerved, Elfride trips and falls.

As the complexities of plot, or more precisely, the complexities of narrative stratagem, are unravelled, Knight's sexual exploitation, his parasitism, becomes increasingly apparent. As Elfride seeks routes of her own choosing either to settle her confusion, her sense of divided loyalties, or to arouse Knight to a recognition of her difficulties and of her need to test their relationship through a clash of feeling, thought and belief, so she loses vigour in his proximity while he thrives upon hers:

It was very odd to himself to look at his theories on the subject of love, and reading them now by the full light of experience, to see how much more his sentences meant than he had felt them to mean when they were written. People often discover the real force of a trite old maxim only when it is thrust upon them by a chance adventure; but Knight had never before known the case of a man who learnt the full compass of his own epigrams by such means. (*PBE*, p.216)

As Elfride passes through emotional conflict to deep humiliation and pain, so this is matched by the repression of her sexual energies. This 'rite of passage' (initiation into womanhood), finds its correlative journey in the sea-trip from London to the West Country which locates, yet again, the lovers travelling to the same destination but with hearts divergent within. As the 'staunch vessel' ploughs its way through 'floundering . . . rushing . . . dim and moaning' 'antagonistic currents', so Elfride, longing to throw off the burden of her secret past attempts another confrontation with her lover. But he will not, or cannot, respond. In the face of her tremulousness he is hearty, 'a certain happy pride in his tone', and as she falters so he is blithe; her unease is countered by his sanguinity, and as she is chilled by the minute both physically and emotionally – 'chilled . . . like a frost' – so he is 'warmed . . . all over' (*PBE*, pp.315–17).

If Elfride seeks closer sexual intimacy and understanding with Knight, he is determined to ground her. But she is intrepid. Like the staunch vessel bearing her, she rushes on: 'You are severe on women, are you not?' To this attempt to soften him Knight blandly responds with:

'No, I think not. I had a right to please my taste, and that was for untried lips. Other men than those of my sort acquire the taste as they get older – but don't find an Elfride.' (*PBE*, p.317)

Stricken by his assumptions, needing to curb his train of thought before presupposition hardens to conviction, she cries out with a revealing projection of her inner fears on to the outer world: 'What horrid sound is that we hear when we pitch forward?' Knight, impervious, 'pitches' on regardless: 'Only the screw – don't find an Elfride as I did. To think that I . . .' (*PBE*, p.317). Blandly overriding her feelings, he has just proved her right. He is severe indeed.

The congruent metaphors Hardy introduces in this sequence all too vividly conjure Elfride's staunch efforts to contain her passion in the face of Knight's sexual frigidity, which chills and drains her youthful, buoyant energies. Riveted by the 'horrid sound' of his steely words expressing distaste for all but untried lips, and with his words falling 'upon her like a weight', she drifts into a 'dim and moaning', restless sleep, later to awaken in terror at her own nightmares and his voice calmly assuring her that 'the clouds have completely cleared off whilst you have been sleeping' (*PBE*, pp.318–19). They have, however, amassed in Elfride's heart.

In lighthearted excursions across the cliffs with Stephen there had been a time for a playful testing of her immature sexuality, which later led to her greater need to develop nerve, the nerve which failed her in London. Her first, precipitate flight from the nest had brought her down to earth with a bump. Hardy elucidates this well by means of the 'journey' motif. He tells us, by way of a prefatory leader, that it had long since been Elfride's girlish practice to set out on small journeys from which she would return with little treasures she had found (*PBE*, p.142). But there are no treasures to be had on the journey to London with Stephen. Metaphorically shaping Elfride's journey on horseback to meet Stephen as a journey-without-direction, Hardy intimates that she is by no means ready to be launched into the adult world. Addressing himself to the most appropriate of symbolic actions, the young girl's manner of riding, he clusters all prose rhythms around the motion of her horse, the motion of turn and turn about. This aptly mirrors Elfride's strife-of-thought, her vacillation between emotional states of anxiety and expectation. Equally, the alternating pace of forward starts and sudden retreats bears a close rhythmic resemblance to the advance/retreat sexual behaviour of a young woman caught between desire and uncertainty. Unable to locate her true destination – onward or back – Elfride rides a distracted mental roundabout, patently unready for Stephen.

This premature journey, Elfride's first major attempt at finding direction, alone, unaided, and with only the ardent pressurisings of her lover to guide her, might plausibly be seen as the prologue to all other journeys that take place in her short career. By the time the day comes for embarking upon her sea-trip with Knight, expectation and anxiety have intensified to become, not closely related states propelling and retarding direction, but inseparable, unsegregated states. The rhythmic patterns and tensions of the earlier sequence, the gentle, rocking motion of the amenable pony, have become enlarged: the heaving, plunging motion of the sea-going vessel. Simultaneously, a contrapuntal effect introduced by the lovers' opposing moods highlights the tension: the complacent mind and the questing share no common ground. But the world, as Hardy presents the case, is not in accord with Knight. It is not with sanguine indifference that the staunch vessel's crew successfully navigates antagonistic currents, but with the applied energy, nerve and intuition that are Elfride's own attributes. She, however, has to manœuvre alone and unaided upon this voyage whose speed she cannot alter and whose direction she cannot control. There can be no voluntary turning back this time. To compound the journey metaphor Hardy reintroduces Mrs Jethway, who, as the personification of guilt and punishment (drawing herself inexorably into shadowy association with Knight), is fast closing in on Elfride. On the London trip she had appeared at the last terminus, now she appears mid-course, before disembarkation.

The implications are clear. Elfride's voyage to self-discovery, to sexual understanding, to forging new horizons cannot be accomplished in Knight's world. He is incapable of encompassing new directions despite his seniority and experience; he is unable to encourage her to be the kind of person she wants to be, feels herself to be; he is not warmed but alarmed by her emotional resilience, her assertiveness, her sexual responsiveness. He desires but cannot yield to a woman empowered by passions he feels he does not own or command.

Elfride's last journey brings no prizes for anyone, of course.

On the contrary, it brings forfeits for Stephen and Knight. This seems a harsh sentence upon the younger man, whose only failing has been to misplace his loyalties, to pledge too much trust, respect and confidence in Knight. As a 'Knight' in the making (his identification with the older man closely affiliated to the Grundyan world implies this) Stephen has, it seems, to pay a price. Yet so punishing a blow does sound a jarring note in what now appears to be a more coherently worked text than is customarily acknowledged. Alternatively displacing and reinstating his heroine as he grapples with propriety on the one hand and an unconventional characterisation on the other, Hardy ingeniously maps a course of increasingly fruitless voyages to mirror that unrewarding journey to womanhood which offers no prizes to the female challenger.

One of Hardy's most notable achievements in this novel is that he never permits himself to lose sight of his central character long enough to allow Knight the supremacy he demands for himself, and which propriety also demands of him. Neither hero nor superinduced proprietary consciousness so limits Hardy's imagination that he cannot find ways and means of steering between both and back to Elfride's struggle for recognition.

The struggle was also Hardy's own. I have laid considerable stress upon the contradictions and shifting perspectives in this early text to allay the misgivings of critics who put such elements down to faultiness of composition. Now that the internal organisation of the novel has been examined in close detail it is possible to regard them more in the light of a coherent, if complicated, literary stratagem. The more important part of this analysis, though, lies in the close attentive reading that is, to my mind, critical to an understanding of Hardy's radicalism, his defiance of convention, his rejection of prevailing sexual codes and practices, his commitment to the sexual reality of his women. If self-concealment was, in the early days of uncertain reader-response and uncertain reputation, as vital to his future as a novelist as to his deeply felt principles, it becomes all the more vital to our understanding of his work to examine, closely, the narrative guises and veiled utterances he adopts for this purpose. The radical Hardy, for whom female sexuality is neither to be degraded nor denied, for whom the sexually instigative Elfride is neither intellectually weak nor morally degenerate, shields, in each act of self-concealment, the icono-clastic spirit that must await fame and public recognition before coming out into the open.

Such a stratagem proved to be worthwhile. *A Pair of Blue Eyes* was well received, and the *Saturday Review* was the only observer to notice signs of unconventionality in Hardy's treat-ment of his subject. It is not surprising that he held a lifelong attachment to this early novel, given its experimental structure and final successful delivery. Yet his struggle for recognition, mirrored in the major Wessex novels in the intense struggle of his women, is by no means over – rather, it *begins* with the transgressive Elfride and his conflictful struggle to bring her into being.

2

SUBVERTING ORTHODOXY:
Far From the Madding Crowd

Reflecting on the first number of *Far From the Madding Crowd*, which came out, in serial form, in December 1873, Hardy responded with surprise to see his story placed at the beginning of the *Cornhill* magazine, with a 'striking illustration', for he 'had only expected, from the undistinguished rank of the characters in the tale, that it would be put at the end, and possibly without a picture' (*Life*, p.97).

The critical response which the book first generated in 1875 was by no means as quiet and unassuming; on the contrary, critical suppositions abounded. Reviewers were noticeably stirred by nostalgia, by dreams of a lost Albion, and by what they wistfully called Hardy's Wessex world of idylls and tranquil rural immobility. The great merit of the book, the French critic Leon Boucher claimed in his article entitled (typically) 'Le Roman Pastoral en Angleterre', lies in its rejuvenation of 'le genre antique et souvent ennuyeux de la pastoral'.[1] Resisting the novel's dissonant undertones, the *Guardian* called it 'in truth a purely pastoral idyll', *The Times* 'an idyll or a pastoral poem ... idyllic ... romantic', and from the *Saturday Review* compliments were handed to Mr Hardy for 'lingering in the pleasant byways of pastoral and agricultural life'.[2] Such epithets necessarily set the Wessex world well apart from the Victorian middle-class drawing-room, from which unconventional woman-farmers and 'ignoble strife' were now safely distanced.[3]

Bathsheba caused trouble nonetheless, and critics complained. Henry James was one. She was 'inconsequential, wilful and mettlesome', he remonstrated, 'and we cannot say that we either understand or like her'.[4] The *Observer* liked her even less:

The first interview between Troy and Bathsheba represents the latter in so odious a light, if women in whatever rank of society are supposed to retain any trace of modesty and reserve, that we confess we do not care one straw about her afterwards, and are only sorry that Gabriel Oak was not sufficiently manly to refuse to have anything more to say to such an incorrigible hussy.[5]

Without detecting the anomaly, this critic protests in the present tense on behalf of the modesty and reserve of women-in-whatever-rank-of-society, and continues in the same breath to criticise Hardy's 'incorrigible hussy' for offending against contemporary values. In other words, moral criticism advances a strictly Victorian ethic while the imagination holds fast to a romance of the Golden Age.

In general, if there were unsuitable elements in *Far From the Madding Crowd*, critics put these down to the ineptitude of the chronicler, to his infidelity to the genre: his 'gross impro-babilities' of characterisation; his not 'quite trustworthy' presentation; that it was doubtful whether 'Mr Hardy's pictures may be trusted'; that 'the only things we believe in are the sheep and the dogs'; that Bathsheba is 'not to be admired as [Mr Hardy] would seem to intimate'; and that he fails to elicit 'our confidence in the truthfulness of many of the idyllic incidents of rustic life'.[6]

Misgivings apart, the notional 'Pastoral' did provide an escape-route as well as an escape-world. And the emphasis stuck. Even twenty years later, in the 1890s, critics were still insisting upon Hardy's fidelity to the genre. Locating his sphere by neat sleight of hand, an affronted reader of *Tess* accuses him of parading his heroine 'like a horse dealer'[7] – an equine turn of phrase designating his 'proper' sphere in a single stroke. Proceeding to a closer examination of *Tess*, the writer adds that Hardy,

is too apt to affect a preciosity of phrase which has a somewhat incongruous effect in a tale of rustic life; he is too fond ... of making experiments in a form of language which he does not seem clearly to understand, and in a style for which he was assuredly not born. It is a pity, for Mr Hardy had a very good style once, and one moreover excellently suited to the subjects he knew and was then content to deal with.[8]

This persistent focus upon the Pastoral obfuscated much that Hardy 'knew and was content to deal with', which was not to do with cows and sheep. In effect, it obscured his actual aim manifest in the constancy with which he returned to his satire of London society begun in *The Poor Man and the Lady*.[9]

Hardy's contemporary readers were – if not themselves members of London society – mainly urban and middle-class and, no doubt, well-disposed to the values and practices of London society. They were also given, according to the mood of the nation at this time, to nostalgic dreams of a rural England that was lost, or that they feared had been lost, under the overspread of industrialisation. Hence their special affection for Hardy's pastoral world. However, by the 1890s, with Wessex heroines marrying middle-class doctors, mayors and the sons of clerics, there seems to have been small justification for confining Hardy to the 'barnyard'[10] of his texts, or the peasant's cottage of his purported origins of life. Both he and his characters were indisputably entrenched in the modern world, as critics of Tess were made uncomfortably aware – fears abounding that she endangered 'the moral fibre of young readers'.[11] The psychological necessity of setting a distance between Thomas Hardy and the Victorian 'drawing-room', was, ironically, the most eloquent testimonial to the social relevance of his novels.

It was the advent of *Far From the Madding Crowd*, and Bathsheba's advent in particular, that first set the distance – or, rather, the critic's need for one. At about this time and with this novel Hardy began to alter his stratagem, phasing out the proprietary narrator and developing alternative literary devices to embed, on the one hand, the less judicious aspects of his treatment of sexuality within the deeper structures of the text,[12] and to incorporate, on the other, the role of moraliser into the character of one of the principals. The success of the new literary stratagem lies in the greater coherency of the work, but the absence of the proprietary narrator at certain points in the text undoubtedly caused trouble with readers.

Take, for example, the (offending) meeting between Bathsheba and Troy (*FFMC*, pp.186–90), which I have summarised indecorously, as follows: The heroine is walking home alone through the woods, in the dark. She passes someone on the narrow path so closely that she feels the heat of his male body. Then she discovers that her gown has become entangled in his soldierly apparel – his spur – and disentanglement involves a certain amount of touching and handling of his person (and vice versa) and a certain amount of bending over 'for the performance'. In the meantime, her unaverted eyes have taken in this 'young and slim' soldier (*FFMC*, p.187), whose flirtatious overtures during the scuffle have disturbed and embarrassed her. And excited her. Thus, as the protracted course of her delivery from 'captivity' is concluded, instead of walking home demurely in a dignified assertion of womanly pride, she breaks into a run. Arriving home flushed and 'panting', she sets about quizzing her maid as to who the mysterious stranger might be, and finally ascends to her bedchamber, not to kneel in penitent, maidenly prayer but to relish sweet, retrospective frissons of delight.

The cause of all the trouble is body contact between the sexes, and, no doubt, Bathsheba's unconstrained delight in the event. The sensuality of the rendering is nowhere countermanded by a moralistic aside and the reader is left with no guidelines, no moral edification whatsoever. The Victorian critic did step in to redress the balance, to deplore what Hardy had not deplored, but for many readers the sheer delight of the moment must have passed without a single twinge of shame or guilt.

The role of the critic has not changed in so far as many still harp on Bathsheba's sexuality as a matter to be deplored.[13] Perhaps it would be fitting then, to begin this revisionary analysis of *Far From the Madding Crowd* with a fresh look at the incident Victorian critics most deplored – Bathsheba's maligned first interview with Troy. Judged purely on the basis of literary skill, this is Hardy's prose at its finest. It evokes sexuality poetically, yet the whole remains psychologically realistic: the soft, feminine folds of the woman's dress pierced through by the man's projecting blade suggests (and prefigures) not only the act of love-making, but as a material representation of inner, intangible desires, the erotic seizure now taking hold of his two young lovers.[14]

The work environments and interior settings chosen for the intimate meetings between Bathsheba and the farmers Bold-wood and Oak, openly contrast the nature settings Hardy chooses for her erotic encounters with Troy: meadows, woods and fields, as a mirror to Bathsheba's sexual temperament, have precisely that fresh, open-air quality that Hardy sees in her own nature. Bathsheba's youthful desire is for nothing more natural (nature-like) than to express her vibrant sexuality. On the threshold of sexual maturity, her impulse is to explore and experiment freely. The embryonic Eve in her nature invokes no sin-laden Edenic archetype, but, rather, in affinity with the Eve (Greensleeves) who features in Hardy's poem 'Voices from Things Growing in a Churchyard', she is the 'pure-woman', so beloved of the author, who would give herself up to Hellenistic joy and voluptuousness to be

> Kissed by men from many a clime,
> Beneath sun, stars, in blaze, in breeze,
> As now by glowworms and by bees ...[15]

This is the Bathsheba of Hardy's opening passages, the 'fair product of nature' (*FFMC*, p.5), who, taking up her looking glass, perceives for herself that warm creature aglow with the soft heat of her sex. Her feminine sensuousness prompts first a parting of lips then a roseate tumescent glow. A dawning is clearly taking place and not only in the morning skies; but while Hardy's appreciative gaze rests upon Bathsheba's open-eyed wonder and soft arousal, a second observer, the clandestine Oak, sees things a little differently. He promptly assumes vanity in place of sensuous self-delight.

This disjunction between form and feeling is emphasised by the contrast between the external, material world of objects, the physical expression of things, and the internal, essential world of feeling and sensation. Bathsheba had first been observed by both Oak and Hardy settled 'on the summit of the load' of her domestic paraphernalia; a motionless, mono-chromatic figure set amid a configuration of household pos-sessions and comatose cats. The scene is empty of manifest feeling and movement, or, rather, free manœuvrability: 'The only sound in the stillness was the hopping of the canary up and down the perches of its prison' (*FFMC*, p.4). But appearances are deceptive: behind the visible world a latent energy stirs. Bathsheba turns, and as she is 'moved', so Hardy is moved to evoke the fullness of her vitality. Gazing at her reflected image taking life from her animate being, Bathsheba smiles. Clearly she is what she feels and seems what she is, and in wonder at the realisation,

She blushed at herself and seeing her reflection blush, blushed the more. (*FFMC*, p.5)

The impact of Bathsheba's auto-eroticism, clearly lost on Oak but not on Hardy, is now hastily, and it seems to me, protectively screened by the mellow, interpersonal comment that the 'picture' is a 'delicate one' – a phrase that hints at intimacy but subtly defuses it by the suggestion, through 'picture' of pure aesthetic appreciation. Then, in recognition of the indelicacy of the 'delicate' and after a fumbling preamble ('What ... whether ... nobody knows'), Hardy adjusts the narrative stance to permit Oak a hearing whose conventional perspective will colour things a little differently. 'Woman's prescriptive infirmity' and Oak's 'cynical inference' (*FFMC*, p.5) of woman's vanity now tailor the narrative to a more circumspect fit. But the mirror does not lie and neither will Hardy. Bathsheba is indeed a 'fair product of nature' and artifice, vanity, have no place here:

There was no necessity whatever for her looking in the glass. She did not adjust her hat, or pat her hair, or pull a dimple into shape, or do one thing to signify that any such intention had been her motive in taking up the glass. She simply observed herself as a fair product of Nature in the feminine kind ... (*FFMC*, p.5)

And relished it.

Oak's participation in this scene is vital. Just as the proprietary narrator's moral rectitude injects moralistic overtones into *A Pair of Blue Eyes* so Oak enacts a similar role, but with, I think, considerably more strategic plotting on Hardy's part. It is critical to the success of the novel that the 'conventional' hero should carry both unconventional heroine and unconventional author into the respectable Victorian drawing-room. Hardy assists the process, not by invoking a proprietary narrator but by transferring the role of censor to Oak. The very personification of censor, Oak now observes this 'bed-room' scene from a moral vantage point, properly separated from the subject of his interest by a metaphorical boundary (hedge), and in the manner of the censor too, he scrutinises the unsuspecting woman with an inquisitorial eye and then announces with high moral seriousness: 'She has her faults /... and the greatest of them is /... Vanity' (*FFMC*, p.7).

As a figure of decorum and an observer of appearances, Oak's mode of regard differs substantially from Hardy's. I want to emphasise this point because critics overlook it entirely and tend to assume that the 'vanity' charge, and Oak's moralising in general, reflect Hardy's own point of view. This is not so. Hardy establishes, for Oak, a contrasting perspective, indeed an openly conflicting perspective, from the very outset of the novel. And no sooner does he establish it than he reinforces it. Bathsheba's self-delight and natural ease of self-perception, as Hardy sees it, changes instantly to embarrassment and unease under Oak's scrutiny, as he forces her awareness of 'the desirability of her existence' to turn to 'self-consciousness' (*FFMC*, p.19) under his rude stare. In other words the natural manner has now become an unnaturalness of manner as the viewer shapes the view and, by his mode of regard, shapes the viewed.

Oak's perspective then, most readily discernible in his judgemental, censorious role, openly conflicts with Hardy's sense-impressionistic point of view. Bathsheba's ability to 'frame' and reconstruct feeling as form in a manner analogous to the artist's engagement with self-portraiture has a virtuosity that only Hardy, as artist, would value in this context. He reserves for Oak, by contrast, a narrow point of view: the 'cynical inference' which 'was irresistible ... as he regarded the scene, generous though he fain would have been' (*FFMC*, p.5). It is, however, Oak's role as spy which clearly distinguishes his perspective from Hardy's. This is not a role Hardy either chooses or needs to choose for himself, endowed as he is with the creator's knowledge of his creation.

Establishing this set of clearly defined perspectives, which will prove crucial to a close interpretation of his text, Hardy achieves several ends. First, Oak introduces a moral perspective that will permit readers predisposed to his point of view access to a text which treats (injudiciously) with female sexuality. Second, by means of his unobtrusive abalienation of Oak-the-spy/censor, Hardy makes room for an 'alternative' Oak to materialise: a figure less idealised but more psychologically plausible than the 'worthy' of received interpretations. And finally, Hardy retains for himself, not only an oppositional stance, but also the 'odium' that might otherwise heap solely on Bathsheba were he to have allied himself with Oak. Human and imperfect as she is to her author, she is not the agent of disorder in *Far From the Madding Crowd*.

As moral watchdog, with not a few cynical preconceptions where women are concerned, Oak arrives on the scene, but not before he has been encountered as the noticeably amorphous figure of the novel's opening passages, the man of 'misty views' who stands 'in the scale of public opinion' as a person 'whose moral colour was a kind of pepper-and-salt mixture' (*FFMC*, p.1). This is purposeful and schematic: 'public opinion' or 'what-is-said' is set, at various points through the text, against 'what-is-done' to form a structural dialectic of considerable importance to Hardy's latent motif of 'ignoble strife'. As he, himself, warns:

In making even horizontal and clear inspections we colour and mould according to the wants within us whatever our eyes bring in. (*FFMC*, p.16)

Hardy is referring specifically to Oak's limitations of vision, but given the use of the present continuous tense and the strategic narrative 'interrupter', it seems reasonable to suppose that he is also addressing the reader. Oak's subjective moulding of his world is not, after all, so very different from the critic's unfailing tendency to light upon the flute-playing shepherd in this tale in order to reinforce the sense that the idyll is in truth the 'reality' in perspective. If we allowed our 'eyes to bring in' the dramatised evidence we would 'see' that the musician is not a feature of the natural landscape at all but, rather, enclosed in a dark, Ark-shaped hut. Moreover, his music issues forth in muffled, constrained cadences divested of resonance and clarity:

not floating unhindered into the open air ... muffled in some way ... altogether too curtailed in power to spread high or wide. (*FFMC*, p.10)

This is surely a parody of a Pastoral scene – if not, what do we make of Hardy's play on the phrase 'nowhere to be found in nature'? Musical sounds to be found nowhere in nature cannot be other than not-natural, non-pastoral. It seems to me that the deflation of the idyllic, the melodic and the rhapsodic is intentionally subversive and purposefully parodic.

The man whose flute-playing loses its natural clarity is the same man who loses his flock to careless husbandry and who forces Bathsheba to an unnaturalness of self-consciousness and shame. He does not belong to the Golden Age. As flute-playing shepherd, he sits, not 'under thatched hurdles as they did in old times' (*FFMC*, p.23), but in a modern mobile workshop, where, incidentally, he will shortly become suffocated, just as his fluty emissions are now, as Hardy says, 'muffled'.

As befits this industrious man, money matters materially 'colour and mould' his world. Later revived by Bathsheba in the smoke-filled hut, he thinks immediately about cost! ' "Ah, the hut!" murmured Gabriel. "I gave ten pounds for that hut." ' (*FFMC*, p.23). As the exact amount is meant to indicate, this is no small investment. If Hardy's account of wage-levels, in *The Dorset Labourer*,[16] is correct, it equals a labourer's wages over twenty weeks. The investor's 'sustained efforts of industry and chronic good spirits' (*FFMC*, p.11) have enabled him to obtain a financial loan, to lease a sheep farm of some hundred acres, and to invest his borrowed capital in two hundred sheep. At an even more prosaic level, his omitting to take out insurance coverage against accidental losses and his acquisition of a 'wrong-headed' sheepdog prove to be false economies involving more than the forfeiture of capital gains. But ambition, opportunism, and the prospect of emigrating to California (*FFMC*, p.462) – the Victorian emigrant's dream venue for making a 'fast buck' – sufficiently motivate Oak towards his goal of prosperity, and his economic status steadily improves. As Hardy emphasises (but his critics do not) Oak has no intention of shepherding flocks in perpetuity. Behind the scenes he is doggedly stocking up; not even the anguish and frustration of unrequited love disturbs this pattern. It is not Oak but Bathsheba for whom profit-making palls when love is lost.

She kept the farm going, raked in her profits without keenly caring about them, and expended money on ventures because she had done so in bygone days. (*FFMC*, p.388)

Efficiency remains unimpaired (an important point), but the heart has gone out of things for Bathsheba. The love-lorn Oak, by contrast, is at the very same moment strutting about,

'coming it quite the dand. He now wears shining boots with hardly a hob in 'em, two or three times a-week, and a tall hat a-Sundays, and 'a hardly knows the name of a smock-frock. When I see people strut enough to be cut up into bantam cocks, I stand dormant with wonder and says no more!' (*FFMC*, p.390)

Appearances are all important: he has improved upon his earlier display of one useless but impressive-looking silver watch, now publicly to sport a top-hat and new shining boots. Yet, privately in the seclusion of his home he pares his own potatoes, mends his own stockings and presumably doffs the smock frock to keep the 'dand' unspoiled. Parsimony or mere habit may urge Oak privately to hoard his income whilst publicly assuming an affluent air, but avarice would undoubtedly have suggested itself to Hardy (and to his Victorian readers also had they been looking in this direction), since custom dictated that even low-income households gave domestic employment to the yet more needy poor – the exemplar, in Hardy's novels, the impecunious Giles Winterborne and his faithful retainer, Robert Creedle, in *The Woodlanders*.

Conservative, thrifty and sternly resolute, Oak has all the makings of a successful businessman. And this is precisely how Hardy presents him in his prime. A sharp eye firmly fixed on the money-market, Oak now strikes a remarkably good bargain with Boldwood:

It was eventually known that Gabriel, though paid a fixed wage by Bathsheba independent of the fluctuations of agricultural profits, had made an engagement with Boldwood by which Oak was to receive a share of the receipts – a small share certainly, yet it was money of a higher quality than mere wages, and capable of expansion in a way that wages were not. (*FFMC*, p.390)

Where Bathsheba and Boldwood absorb agricultural losses, Oak's share of the receipts takes account only of the profits, and this at a time when, as far as Hardy's readers were concerned, the home market was being severely threatened by wheat imports and first signs of the economic depression of the 1870s were setting in.

Oak's instigation of these proceedings, his shrewd account-
ancy, and his eventual takeover of Boldwood's entire holding,
is not in any way incompatible with a 'talent' we have already
encountered. Before deciding to protect Bathsheba's ricks from
storm-damage, Oak coolly reckons their value:

Seven hundred and fifty pounds in the divinest form that money can
wear – that of necessary food for man and beast. (*FFMC*, p.286)

Then with two wheat-ricks covered,

Two hundred pounds were secured. . . . He mounted the third pile of
wealth and began operating. (*FFMC*, p.290)

Oak's sense of his own manhood, his sexuality, is so closely
linked to his mercantile mentality that in the moment of costing
his lover's ricks he also evaluates her worth as a woman. Or
rather, he devalues her to enhance his chivalric sense of acting
in a worthy cause:

Should the risk be run of deteriorating this bulk of corn to less than
half its value, because of the instability of a woman? 'Never, if I can
prevent it!' said Gabriel.
    Such was the argument that Oak set outwardly before him. But
man, even to himself is a palimpsest, having an ostensible writing,
and another beneath the lines. It is possible that there was this golden
legend underlying the utilitarian one: 'I will help to my last effort
the woman I have loved so dearly.' (*FFMC*, pp.286–7)

According to Victorian readers the 'golden legend' supervenes. Yet Hardy, it appears, feels otherwise. Is this noticeably
guarded recapitulation of Pastoral romanticism designed to
mute Oak's materialism? The key word is 'palimpsest'. The
writer effaces the original impression to make room for a second,
and although the act of inscription, effacement and over-print-
ing is, by allusion, Oak's, it too closely bears upon the act of
writing itself to hold the single meaning. Whether or not the
'golden legend' underlies the utilitarian, Hardy now inscribes
it on the surface text, presumably to blur the hard edges of
Oak's cost-accountancy assessment of the rural economy and
his equally grim sexual prejudices, which precipitate him rather
too fast and furiously into the world of patriarchal capitalism.
    Hardy's efforts to keep this aspect of Oak's characterisation
under control are not eased by the peculiarly male logic which

prompts Oak to equate a potentially unstable economy with woman's instability: 'Should the risk be run ... because of woman's instability?' In justice to Bathsheba, Hardy makes it patently obvious that the threat to her wheat-ricks arises from her husband's instability: he is at this moment drinking her labour-force insensible.

The associative links Oak makes instinctively between capital and hearts, profits and love, woman and property, are subtly grounded in the text, but whereas they exclude him from Arcadia there is no clamour. Hardy has slowly but surely dispensed with the 'shepherd' long since, who is first replaced by the bailiff, then the shareholder and, finally, the farm manager turned property owner. The progression away from rustic innocence and sylvan idylls towards a distinctly bourgeois capitalistic existence is, thus, nowhere obtrusive but everywhere foreshadowed, as for instance, at the very outset of the novel where Oak's cash-nexus consciousness is presented as the very index of his 'animus':

Love, being an extremely exacting usurer (a sense of exorbitant profit, spiritually, by an exchange of hearts, being at the bottom of pure passions, as that of exorbitant profit, bodily or materially, is at the bottom of those of lower atmosphere), every morning Oak's feelings were as sensitive as the money-market in calculations upon his chances. (*FFMC*, p.26)

And without ado: 'I'll make her my wife, or upon my soul I shall be good for nothing!' (*FFMC*, p.27)

Oak's proposal of marriage is embarrassingly miscalculated. Delighted at the prospect of acquiring a sweetheart, Bathsheba is taken completely by surprise by the notional precipitation into humdrum domesticity: 'a snug little farm' and a caretaker husband for life, 'always ... there ... whenever I looked up, there he'd be' (*FFMC*, pp.33–4). But the phrase which resounds here, long beyond the moment of its utterance, is Bathsheba's 'I *hate* to be thought men's property in that way' – a phrase Hardy anchors poetically to actions and images signifying as metaphors of threat, psychological retreat and impeded flight. We are reminded of it in the predatory nature of her suitor's approaches, whose encroachment upon her 'territory' seems forcibly to close her in. 'Creeping round the holly bush to reach her side' his manner appears so thrusting,

that he seemed to be coming, by the force of his words, straight through the bush and into her arms. (*FFMC*, p.35)

A little earlier he had snatched at her hand,

prettily extended upon her bosom to still her loud-beating heart. Directly he seized it she put it behind her, so that it slipped through his fingers like an eel. (*FFMC*, p.31)

As Oak's attempt to seize the hand (in marriage) is countered by Bathsheba's unmistakable gesture of withdrawal, so his thoughts turn promptly upon the desirable little property he *does* own: 'I have a nice, snug little farm. . . . A man has advanced me money.' This statement of means, evidently a statement of intent, urges Oak to take the cue from his own words immediately to advance himself once more: 'He went forward and stretched out his arm again.' (*FFMC*, p.32)

The pattern of manœuvring advance and retreat, is clear, but this is no lyrical rendering of courtship dance. Associations between the acquisition of monetary advances and property and the taking of the woman in marriage so infiltrate Oak's dialogues and so inform his gestures that Bathsheba, sensing the gain on herself, retreats, not only from the man but from the marriage bid itself, which forebodes total possession of her person.

If her suitor mistakes her actions for gestures of enticement, her author does not. 'Advance' and 'threat', the semantic stresses foregrounded, keep before the reader a constant reminder of the more profound implications of the scene:

Seeing his advance take the form of an attitude threatening a possible enclosure, if not compression, of her person, she edged off round the bush. (*FFMC*, p.32)

The figurative language, 'enclosure', 'compression of her person' – prefiguratively, bondage – gathers additional force from the vigour of Hardy's closely attuned narrative and dense detailing of natural objects. They come together evocatively in the image of the stunted, woody growth of the holly bush. Oak, regarding the 'red berries . . . that seemed in his after life to be a cypher signifying a proposal of marriage' (*FFMC*, p.33), has his thoughts firmly centred upon the 'fruit' of his proposal. But

Bathsheba, focusing upon the stunted growth of the shrub, assimilates to her consciousness not the fruit outcrop but the woody, truncated stem as she utters a 'terrible wooden story': her critique on marriage (*FFMC*, p.34).

Bathsheba's later experience is that marriage does stifle and compress her existence. It robs her of control of her estates, nullifies her legal existence, and renders her man's property into the bargain.[17]

In *Far From the Madding Crowd*'s microcosmic Victorian world the inescapable fact of male dominance and privilege is rigidly maintained. The privileges extended to Oak are not at any point extended to Bathsheba. Capital is made freely available to him as an inexperienced new investor, without qualification, supervision or restriction. Yet, Bathsheba, self-evidently capable of managing a profitable concern even under the duress of marital breakdown and Troy's depletion of her resources, owns no legal means for recouping her losses as a married woman whose husband has sole control over her estates. First contending with sex-discriminating pressures to which Oak is not, of course, subjected, Bathsheba then has to face the 'legal effects of her marriage ... upon her position'. Her tenure as James Everdene's successor is now threatened by Troy's legal ownership of her entitlement, by his desertion, and by his jeopardising of her good name (*FFMC*, p.383). She had earlier won the confidence of Everdene's trustees entirely in her own right, as Hardy takes pains to bring to our attention. Her uncle's testimony before his death attests to her

cleverness ... her vigorous marshalling of the numerous flocks and herds which came suddenly into her hands before negotiations were concluded, had won confidence in her powers. (*FFMC*, p.383)

[Although] there had originally been shown by the agent to the estate some distrust of Bathsheba as James Everdene's successor, on the score of her sex, her youth, and her beauty. (*FFMC*, p.382)

In contrast, Oak's sex, youth (or inexperience) and, no doubt, physical good looks, are nowhere brought to bear upon capability. Ironically, despite the disadvantages of being female, young and beautiful, Bathsheba's success as a single-woman-farmer is undone only when she takes on a male partner; that is, she marries. One way or the other her fortunes are jeopardised. As she had earlier forecast in a different context but with prophetic wisdom nonetheless, she would inevitably 'be had' some day (*FFMC*, p.32).

Legal and sexual discrimination apart, as surely as Bathsheba attempts to maintain her independence and prove her talents, so Oak attempts to subdue and reduce her. And it is this more insidious form of subjugation that Hardy treats most comprehensively in *Far From the Madding Crowd*. There is bitter irony indeed in Bathsheba's rejection of marriage on the grounds, as she tactfully puts it to Oak at one point, of her own independent nature: 'I want somebody to tame me' (*FFMC*, p.35). We infer, of course, that the voluptuous girl is actually pleading for a more virile suitor, but that she should light on the word 'tame' when in reality he owns all the 'corrective' methods for breaking her spirit entirely, is bitterly ironic.

The pressure upon her to be married, and all that that signifies in terms of dispossession of her identity and entitlements, comes in the first instance from Oak. But it is his intrusion upon her privacy, his encroachment upon the space in which she tests and evaluates her sensory experience of the world, which most insidiously robs her of judgement, free-will and self-determination. In spying upon her he steals her freedom.[18] And this has far-reaching consequences. Oak's espials and subsequent humiliation of her, lead indirectly to her tragic mismatch with Troy, with whom she had engaged primarily, at the level of private, lighthearted sexual exploration without guilt or shame or fear. These last Oak induces in her by rapid stages as he preys upon her in her private haunts to bring her under public scrutiny. As she says later, in a moment of bitter desolation, 'a watched woman must have very much circumspection to retain only a little credit' (*FFMC*, p.418). It is Oak who has driven her into this corner.

His points of espial are various. From behind hedges, through the crevices of sheds and field-huts, and less clandestinely but just as penetratingly, from behind the bland, unassuming countenance of his own moon face, he pruriently stares, probes and exposes. From these concealed vantage points he prises Bathsheba from her privacy to draw her out into the open where her exploratory activity will, of necessity, become restricted and censored.

At first he simply watches as, thinking herself alone, she takes out her looking-glass and appraises herself as a 'fair product of Nature'. He subsequently casts his judgement publicly, but it is his later efforts to humiliate her following such espials which compound the theft of her selfhood and liberty. Following hard upon the looking-glass scene (*FFMC*, p.5), Oak spies again. This time intentionally and, as Hardy puts it, as 'Milton's Satan first saw Paradise' (*FFMC*, p.15) – implicated we might suppose in demonic attempts at usurpation. Little appears to be gained from this espial until, eavesdropping on Bathsheba's conversation, Oak learns that she has lost her hat. He will find it! It will gain him an expedient introduction to the woman he covets.

Later, crouching in his hut in another attempt at spying, Oak clutches to himself the article he has found and will restore to its owner – appropriately, that precise article of woman's clothing that most denotes decorum: her hat! Peepholing through a crevice he watches the spectacle of Bathsheba engaging in yet another of her unorthodox activities: riding her horse in outlandish abandon, bareback, legs astride, or alternatively spread-eagled over its flanks. The gymnastic sensuousness of the unsuspecting woman freely riding set in dramatic opposition to the hunched, intent figure grasping the mislaid item no decorous woman should be seen without, and which he has taken such pains to retrieve, compounds the opposition Hardy has already established in the earlier scene. The 'fair product of Nature' is yet again to be judged by the puritanical censor.

Policing the woman's space does not effect a theft all the while it goes unnoticed. Thus, Oak sets out to proffer the hat and a little information with it. Squatting in wait behind the diminutive hedge, he slowly ascends to confront the startled girl, his 'face rising like the moon behind the hedge' (*FFMC*, p.19), as he rivets his stare so penetratingly upon her person that he seems to irritate 'its pink surface by actual touch' (*FFMC*, p.20). Her discomfiture rouses him and reddening at his impertinence he announces, bluntly: 'I found a hat.' Clumsy as he is, Oak, with shaming thoughts in his mind, is bound to embarrass and shame Bathsheba. And he does. Dramatically positioned in the manner of a signpost with one hand proferring the article of decorum while both eyes are cast in the direction of the plantation (scene of outlandish abandon), and 'with an aspect excessively knowing with regard to some matter in his mind', he promptly tells what he has seen. The mobile gymnast is immobilised on the spot. Prophetically, Oak's words 'fix' her in a straightened posture:

misgivings bringing every muscle of her lineaments and frame to a standstill. (*FFMC*, p.21)

The theft is compounded:

A perception caused him to withdraw his own eyes from hers as suddenly as if he had been caught in a theft. (*FFMC*, p.21)

Hardy makes his point with keen poetic suggestiveness. First he prefaces the scene with an objective view of Bathsheba's self-delight which, we are told, fails in being offensive:

There was a bright air and manner about her now, by which she seemed to imply that the desirability of her existence could not be questioned; and this rather saucy assumption failed in being offensive, because a beholder felt it to be, upon the whole, true ... (*FFMC*, p.19)

But then Oak brings her under his own offensive stare and instantly:

Recollection of the strange antics she had indulged in when passing through the trees was succeeded in the girl by a nettled palpitation, and that by a hot face. It was time to see a woman redden who was not given to reddening as a rule; not a point in the milkmaid but was of the deepest rose-colour. From the Maiden's Blush, through all varieties of the Provence down to the Crimson Tuscany, the countenance of Oak's acquaintance quickly graduated. (*FFMC*, p.21)

In creating a colour link here between the blushes of shame (Crimson Tuscany) and Bathsheba's earlier scarlet glow' (*FFMC*, p.5), Hardy implicates Oak in an act that more than shames. It violates. The subtle progression/ingression of 'From ... through ... down' renders palpable and emphatic the sense of sexual wounding, of penetration and appropriation the more portentous for the manner in which Bathsheba first loses her name and then her particularity. 'The girl' is depersonalised to the indefinite ('a woman') then to the stereotypical (a 'milk-maid') before finally ending in the possessive case as 'Oak's acquaintance'.

In justice to his heroine's sense of deep injustice, Hardy affirms that Oak's

> want of tact had deeply offended her – not by seeing what he could not help, but by letting her know that he had seen it. For as without law there is no sin, without eyes there is no indecorum; and she appeared to feel Gabriel's espial had made her an indecorous woman without her own connivance. (*FFMC*, p.22)

Despite her later (too-late) defensive cry to Oak that she will not allow any man to criticise her private conduct, Bathsheba is painfully aware that she has been deprived of that right. Her rage is the rage of one stripped of power; Oak's 'placid dignity', by contrast, evinces an unruffled assumption of owning it (*FFMC*, p.155).

Free self-expression circumscribed, liberty checked and privacy isolated, self-consciousness now begins to unsettle Bathsheba's winning 'bright air' and spontaneous manner of self-delight. Captive to Oak's censure, and the psychological condition of approval-seeking that subjects woman to man, she is now compelled to turn increasingly to Oak to test out the measure of her standing within the community – a community from which he holds himself aloof but whose loyalties to her, which she had well-earned, she had never, prior to Oak's advent, ever thought of questioning. But now exposed to his reproachful eye and driven to re-enact her exposure like an innocent caught out in a secret joy forbidden by a guilt-ridden world, she provokes repeated confrontations with the censor to test out how much she is at risk. The greatest risk, however, is to her autonomy and self-hood. Censure brands with guilt and fear where once her instinct had been 'to walk as a queen' in full possession of all her powers (*FFMC*, p.103).

Oak's induction of guilt and fear in Bathsheba, his compulsion to straighten her to conformity, to render her the 'thoughtful ... meek, and comely woman' (*FFMC*, p.153) so esteemed by himself, is as morally unjustifiable to the modern mind as it was morally right, proper and just to Victorian 'Oaks' of puritanical persuasion, for whom guilt and shame were acceptable psychological states through which woman should pass on the road to virtue. As an effective means of controlling and subordinating woman, guilt and shame served the interests of a society in which male supremacy was, at all costs, to be maintained.

If Oak, in his rustic guise and vigilante method of shaming voluptuous womanhood (which in itself may have endeared him to the critic) was welcomed by contemporary readers as a morally edifying character, Bathsheba was not. At the same time, the plethora of critical assumptions idealising Hardy's Wessex points to a more complicated response. First and foremost, it suggests that Hardy's refusal to endorse Oak's behaviour and actions – he may be benign as shepherd but not as spy – and his unwillingness to censure the self-delighting, sexually responsive Bathsheba, was perceived if not fully grasped by his contemporaries despite the sway of approval for Oak's methods of subjugation. Equally, non-specific charges of incongruity and inappropriate characterisation testify to the critics' discomfiture. It is not simply that Bathsheba expresses views on marriage which the liberal feminist of the day, lobbying for support for the Married Woman's Property Bill,[19] would have expressed (if at all) far more decorously. Rather more problematical is the felt support she receives from her author on this issue. His floating images of compression, enclosure and theft shape an association, a complicity even, between author and heroine that defies easy detection. The one specific charge levelled by the *Observer* in furious denunciation of the 'hussy', hints at the nature of the problem. A hussy she may have seemed in her luxuriant maidenhood, but as deserted wife, desolated widow and, finally, the dutiful Mrs Gabriel Oak, Bathsheba cannot logically be so termed. In a manner of speaking, the critic has reserved the right to retain the maiden for further 'punishment' (by condemning her, in polite terms, as a woman of loose morals). Evidently Hardy has not rewarded readers, to their satisfaction, with a convincing thematic line of woman's wrongdoing, punishment and redemption. What he has done instead is to ensure that there will be no complacent acceptance of Bathsheba's 'reformation'. He does not approve it and does not endorse it as improvement.

In the light of this, how much weight should be given to the much-quoted homily in which readers, looking for a happy ending, tend to invest?

This good-fellowship – camaraderie – usually occurring through similarity of pursuits, is unfortunately seldom superadded to love between the sexes, because men and women associate, not in their labours, but in their pleasure merely. Where however, happy circumstances permit its development, the compounded feeling proves itself to be the only love which is strong as death – that love which many waters cannot quench, nor the floods drown, beside which the passion usually called by the name is evanescent as steam. (*FFMC*, pp.468–9)

There is a good case for arguing in favour of a superimposed narrator here. The sermonising tone, the Old Testament borrowing,[20] and the euphuistic rhetoric point not only to something approaching a creative void, in Hardy, but also to a rather self-conscious effort to set holy writ to do the task he, himself, would not choose to do. But it is only by weighing this piece against the literary devices, narrative structures and discourses elsewhere in the novel that the measure of its declared commitment or otherwise may be determined.

Hardy's favoured artistic medium, as he said more than once, was the dramatic mode; he classified his verse as 'dramatic monologues', 'dramatic anecdotes', or poems 'dramatic or personative'. That his immediate poetic impulse in prose also tends towards dramatic forms is evidenced by his early drafts. The earliest version of the shearing supper, for example, is composed, almost entirely, of dramatic dialogue and action; descriptive or discursive commentary is entered in the form of extended marginalia and amendation. Here, I think we discover the authentic Hardyan voice, and here, too, we may uncover his allegiances – his close identification with Bathsheba and, consequently, his impulse to mourn her loss of vitality, sexual verve and bounding self-delight.

For example, a lexicon of pain – 'suffer', 'torturing sting', 'agonising', 'wounded' – infuses Hardy's narration as he observes Bathsheba in the dark days preceding her marriage to Oak (*FFMC*, p.464). A sense of injury shapes, and is shaped by, his own felt pain at her decline, although situation and event scarcely seem to warrant this accentuation. In the event, Bathsheba is but a lonely widow ruefully contemplating the departure of her trusty friend and business transactor. This might inspire epithets of frustration, despair and sorrow.

Instead, her deeper psycho-sexual wounding lingers on in Hardy's creative imagination to ground itself in his text most tellingly. And just as tellingly, the following unbidden comment enters his concluding dialogue: Bathsheba 'never laughed readily now' (*FFMC*, p.476). This coda-esque lament expresses more than is apparent at first sight. Raising implications beyond the immediate, reaching back to the very beginning of her story, it embraces more than the subdued spirit it here portends.

Hardy relies heavily upon the natural object metaphor to provide him with a language of female sexuality that is not of the fastidious, fey, 'lilies-and-lace' category. In keeping with his heterodox views – that a voluptuous woman is a fair product of nature, fit and healthy in body and mind, neither degraded by her sexuality nor mentally or morally degenerate – he relies upon wholesome, 'natural' objects to evoke her healthy sexual appetite.

A woman's mouth is not only the most natural and apt, but also the most legitimised symbol of her sexuality. More precisely, in that lips may be used to represent the sexual expression of desire, receptivity, passion, in other words a complex of sexual characteristics, the more apt figurative term is synecdoche – meaning that the part represents the whole. Hardy perceives it in this way: the mobility and expressiveness of Bathsheba's mouth is for him the very register of her 'anima' – her psycho-sexual constitution, her spiritual vigour, her inner luxuriance. As the index of female sexuality this oral symbol captures his poetic imagination forcibly. By placing focus upon shape, colour, mobility, he explores to the utmost the synec-dochic function of lips as labia which serve, throughout the text, set either in imagistic clusters or in semantic repetition, to pattern the cyclical nature of female sexuality and, more particularly, the lowering or heightening of receptivity. Take, for example, Hardy's application of enlarged, even cosmic ascriptions to her lips:

When Bathsheba was swayed by an emotion of an earthly sort her lower lip trembled: when by a refined emotion; her upper or heavenward one. (*FFMC*, p.155)

Emotional intensity variously earthy, sensual, refined and exquisite trembles the lip-brim of the orifice. The hemispherical allusion here, and a touch of Gothic elsewhere – 'exact arch' and 'pointed corners' – conjure a larger-than-life image.

Something in the exact arch of her upper unbroken row of teeth, and in the keenly pointed corners of her red mouth when, with parted lips, she somewhat defiantly turned up her face to argue a point with a tall man, suggested there was potentiality enough in that lithe slip of humanity for alarming exploits of sex, and daring enough to carry them out. (*FFMC*, p.102)

Stylistic and poetic usage of the oral symbol in Hardy's œuvre is noticeably consistent. Elizabeth Jane, in *The Mayor of Casterbridge*, one of his sexually most tepid heroines, is effectively without 'lips' (they are mentioned, I think, once). Tess's renowned mobile, peony mouth, by contrast, is suggestive of a flowering sexual nature which imagistically recalls – texturally (tissue) tonally (crimson) – the reference to gossamer tissue in connection with her defloration in the 'Chase' episode. Alternatively, Eustacia's palpable, and seemingly fixed, state of sexual tension is appropriately met by Hardy's highly elaborate reference to the 'cyma-recta or ogee' moulding of her lips.[21]

Bathsheba's incapacity for spontaneous laughter, or obmutescence – the muting or silencing of her utterances – as indicative of a lost vigour, a lost capacity for joy and sensation, may be traced to its origins by examining Hardy's use of, and reliance upon, oral symbolism. Consider, for example, the metaphoric play on Bathsheba's lips in her relationship with Boldwood; in particular, as they feature in his erotic fantasies. The middle-aged celibate, obsessed with the crimson, globular shape glowing suggestively down at him from Bathsheba's valentine in his darkened room, conjures images of the valentine's sender. He muses:

Her mouth – were the lips red or pale, plump or creased? – had curved itself to a certain expression ... the corners had moved with all their natural tremulousness: what had been the expression? (*FFMC*, p.113)

The reality is chastening – or would be, were Boldwood less obsessed with his fantasies. For at this eventual meeting Bathsheba's sexual distaste signally expresses itself as prohibition, closure:

all the motion she made was that of closing her lips which had previously been a little parted. (*FFMC*, p.145)

But it is, predictably, Oak's proximity to Bathsheba that urges Hardy to focus upon the parting and contracting of female lips. Oak's repressive effect upon her is reflected in the motion of compression and restraint: she greets him variously, 'without parting her lips to any inconvenient extent' (*FFMC*, p.15); 'compressing her lips to a demure impassivity' (*FFMC*, p.25); and contracting her mouth 'to an inoffensive smallness' (*FFMC*, p.34). These images accumulate and logically culminate in 'the close compression of her two red lips' (*FFMC*, p.156), as the sexual guilt and shame he has induced take the place of innocent delight in her own desirability.

In the erotic seizure that engulfs her as Troy dips 'his mouth downward upon her own' and kisses her for the very first time, ecstasy and sexual shame commingle with her sense of having 'sinned a great sin' (*FFMC*, p.218). That she should experience her first kiss with such guilt-ridden torment is a painful reminder of the degree to which her nature has suffered puritanical 'compression' at Oak's hands. And Hardy, who cannot openly condemn Oak, steers the narrative awkwardly through a purge of equivocations, eventually, to lead out from a safe narrative distance towards a celebration of Bathsheba's innocence. Her love, he declared (now in open opposition to Oak), 'was entire as a child's, and though warm as summer it was as fresh as spring' (*FFMC*, p.220).

Having established, then, a synecdochic scheme from the outset – introduced, in the first instance with parting lips and concluding at the last with closure – Hardy restricts use of the device as Bathsheba's repression grows. From the moment of Troy's kiss and her stunned sense of 'sin', the mobility and expressiveness of her mouth no longer features in his discourses. The incidence of semantic repetition is pruned right back from the numerous references to her mouth and lips in the first half of the novel, before her marriage with Troy, to, thereafter, merely three![22] As this physical image, no longer in focus, 'dies' in the author's imagination, so too Bathsheba is felt to suffer loss of life. In so far as her lips latterly lose colour and lustre – 'there she sat, her mouth blue and dry' (*FFMC*, p.445), which is as close to a moribund image as might be evoked in this context – so the sense is of a wasting away. The drift tends in one direction only: 'entombment' or 'burial'.

But Hardy could not afford her the heroic stature that a tragic ending would endow. Not only were readers clamouring for happy endings but Bathsheba's unconventionality, so much more radical and so much more in evidence than Elfride's had been, clamours for judicious camouflage at this critical stage of Hardy's career. Accordingly, she is conjured back to life, 'revived' and married off.

The very taut poetic structures of the novel testify in themselves to Hardy's deeper concerns. Oak's activity of espial unobtrusively links with denial, with the prohibition placed upon Bathsheba's growth to self-knowledge, which, as prefigured in the proposal scene, ultimately leads to the total enclosure of her space that Oak's wedding ring signifies. The significance of encirclement collaborating with a world of threat and theft is painstakingly elicited at diverse points throughout the text, as Hardy details her decline from glowing vigour to enervation and obmutescence – the muted utterance. It is this poetic close detailing, this thoughtful, imaginative attention to her inner life, that bring us close to the Hardy who needs and wants to give recognition and voice to Bathsheba's sorrow, pain and loss – to her truncated feminine life.

The extended metaphor of threat and enclosure – the boundaries of Oak's world and Bathsheba's encirclement – comes together in Hardy's treatment of sexuality throughout the novel, to include male sexuality as well as female. The link forged between Troy's sexuality and his spur is, of course, but elementary symbolism: Hardy elaborates further. Maximising the metaphorical potential of the blade or weapon, Troy's ritualistic method of penetration with the sword becomes his sexual 'offensive' motivated by desire for conquest. This, in turn, becomes the 'wounding' of his bride, first, by her defloration, and second, by the injury he inflicts to her self-esteem and reputation.

Hardy goes further still. Each male suitor is furnished with a killing weapon or a cutting blade. Moreover, each enjoins Bathsheba to his own action in handling the same. She is thus drawn, inexorably, into the web of male brutality and sexual domination that constitutes the darker world of *Far From the*

Madding Crowd. A woman's sphere, as Hardy perceives it, is no secure, buttressed domain as so earnestly mythologised by the more optimistic Victorian: it is pitted with traps and falls.

The extended metaphor of sexual threat and endangerment, here aligned to the killing weapon and cutting blade, may be outlined as follows. Troy's weapon in the first instance is his spur. This in isolation serves to indicate his method of controlling the creature he would dominate and subdue. In the broader context, the spur enters the order of symbols that includes his sword and Boldwood's gun – weapons used in the sexual offensive. The episode of the ensnaring spur is closely followed by Troy's sword display, and this exhibition of the larger weapon, as it were, drives the metaphor home. Roused and on the offensive, he displays well, demonstrating acute lunging cuts, lacerating a strand of hair from Bathsheba's head. Following the metaphor through to its logical end, artful flourishes, the showy, braggadocio style, the postures of the braggart, do not, however, augur well in love-making terms. Virtuosity is one thing, tenderness and responsiveness quite another.

Troy is killed by a blast from Boldwood's shotgun. This aptly mirror's the older man's attempt to take possession of Bathsheba by a moral coercion which erupts emotionally, unlike Oak's dogged browbeating, in volcanic bursts from this mentally unbalanced celibate who, as Hardy bluntly puts it, 'had no more skill than a battering ram' (*FFMC*, p.393). Ironically, the young cavalry sergeant, for all his martial skills, is not to be the victor in the one and only 'real-life' skirmish in his career. The parallel to this demonstration of failure in judgement, perception and awareness is not difficult to find: Troy, as lover, fails Bathsheba.

Oak, on the other hand, wields, appropriately, a distinctly utilitarian tool, but a wounding blade no less – as Hardy dramatises vividly in the 'Shearing' scene. Just as Troy had displayed his skills with the sword, and had lacerated a tress of hair from Bathsheba's head, so Oak now displays his skill with the shearing blade and, in so doing, extends the lacerating act beyond erotic foreplay to physical penetration. Again Bathsheba is conjoined to the action, to participate in and become intimidated by the man's manipulation of his cutting blade. Straddling the nervous she-creature about to be shorn, Oak begins by lopping off 'the tresses about its head . . . his mistress quietly looking on' (*FFMC*, p.168).

> 'She blushes at the insult,' murmured Bathsheba, watching the pink
> flush which arose and overspread the neck and shoulders . . . a flush
> which was enviable, for its delicacy, by many queens of coteries, and
> would have been creditable, for its promptness, to any woman in the
> world. (*FFMC*, p.168)

With no prior knowledge that the subject of this piece is in fact a ewe, the reader might conjure a variety of imaginative scenes. But it seems doubtful that a sheep-shearing would be one of them. With characteristic skill Hardy lights upon a suitable subject and turns it to his own ends – subtly shaping the reader's reading as, upon Oak's sexual possession of Bathsheba, his own imagination turns.

Her very real fear is that the soft flesh will be wounded by the blade she is now 'critically regarding'. But Oak's

> skilful shears, which apparently were going to gather up a piece of
> flesh at every close . . . never did so. (*FFMC*, p.168)

Not yet! The hero, blissful in Bathsheba's proximity, continues to perform with an expertise that draws her fullest admiration:

> Full of this dim and temperate bliss, he went on to fling the ewe over
> upon her other side, covering her head with his knee, gradually
> running the shears line after line round her dewlap, thence about her
> flank and back, and finishing over the tail. 'Well done, and done
> quickly!' said Bathsheba. (*FFMC*, p.169)

The implications of this scene, Oak's bliss, Bathsheba's evident relief at his speedy painless execution, reinforced by Hardy's imagery, are evocatively sexual. As the man bares the tender flesh to view with the virgin girl beside him awaiting completion of the task, so:

> The clean, sleek creature arose . . . how perfectly like Aphrodite rising
> from the foam should have been seen to be realized – looking startled
> and shy at the loss of its garment . . . never before exposed . . . white
> as snow, and without flaw or blemish of the minutest kind. (*FFMC*,
> p.169)

As defloration images begin to surface in the text, Hardy concludes the analogy by pointing to the mark of identity now about to be branded:

'B.E,' is newly stamped upon the shorn skin ... (*FFMC*, p.169)

And 'Aphrodite ... leaps, panting' away.

But the climax of the shearing scene is yet to come: Hardy's symbolic prefiguration of a 'consummation' which will, of course, bring Bathsheba to Oak already 'wounded'. Boldwood enters the scene, draws Bathsheba away, whereupon Oak, losing interest in his task and struggling instead to keep the couple in view, lets his blade slip:

> In endeavouring to continue his shearing at the same time that he watched Boldwood's manner, he snipped the sheep in the groin. The animal plunged; Bathsheba instantly gazed towards it, and saw the blood. 'O, Gabriel!' she exclaimed, with severe remonstrance, 'you who are so strict with the other men – see what you are doing yourself!' (*FFMC*, p.171)

In terms of literary aesthetics this episode provides a perfect climax, encapsulating 'ignoble strife' in various forms. First, there is Oak's compulsion to watch. He must spy! And spying, he wounds, in this case the she-creature in his care, but the analogy is clear. Then there is the question of self-interest diminishing dedication and impeding skill. Tender and heedful as he is under Bathsheba's admiring eye, out of it he wounds the struggling creature pinioned beneath him. This is a mutilating act that aligns him with Troy, in fact – with Troy's lunging at Bathsheba and adroitly lancing, not a shorn groin, but a lock of her tresses, but without drawing blood. Oak's maiming, then, his cutting Bathsheba down to size, inflicts a wound as injurious as any inflicted by Troy. And finally, since it is the 'wounded' woman Oak eventually claims who is at present subject to his constant chafings, the fact that her diverted attention provokes him to wound, confirms the picture we have unveiled of an Oak intent upon domination. Thwarted, he will draw blood.

So it is that upon Bathsheba's vulnerability, her pain, her passion, Hardy's sympathies turn and turn again. The centre of caring feeling and intense emotion is quintessentially the flow between author and heroine, even at the last, where Bathsheba is but a ghost of her former self. No longer freely riding out, no longer exploring the world about her – the cities, the market-places, the world of work and men – no longer resourcefully participating in the life of her estate, but instead, joylessly auditing book ledgers in the reduced space that is now her confined domain, Bathsheba's fearless spirit is finally broken. 'Properly' dependent, she is bewildered by the prospect of 'having to rely on her own resources again'. 'Properly' subjected she feels 'she could never again acquire energy sufficient to go to market, barter and sell' (*FFMC*, pp.459–65). Oak's efforts to mould her into the 'thoughtful ... meek and comely woman' who will neither rebel nor challenge his authority, have not been in vain.

According to this revisionary reading, there is every sense that Hardy has a very different perception of Oak from the picture handed down to us by critics. By the same token, Bathsheba's perpetual exposure to the world of male violence, her unknowing proximity to something dark and brutal in Oak's world, draws us into a deep, shadowy region of *Far From the Madding Crowd* where the Hardy, who so dearly loved the voluptuous Tess of his later novel, lovingly dwells. His vibrant, self-delighting, energetic heroine whose resourcefulness and strength sustain a family property, a labour force and a farming community, blossoms into womanhood, ventures into business, into marriage, into the world of men, and is nullified. And Hardy is the lone mourner.

3

ELEMENTAL FORCES:
The Return of the Native

The world of freedom and action Hardy's greater heroines would shape for themselves disintegrates as rapidly as the man-made world superimposes upon them its own curbing shape. With the advent of adulthood and a fully awakened sexual consciousness, every exploratory move towards self-discovery, self-realisation and sexual understanding, meets with obstruction in a male-dominated world intent upon highranking the docile woman over the daring, the meek over the assertive, the compliant over the self-determining, the submissive over the dynamic. There is no area of exploration, whether occupational, sexual or merely developmental, that does not, eventually, conflict with the dominant male will to dispossess woman of autonomy, identity, purpose and power. This becomes an increasingly important part of Hardy's critique – from Henry Knight's nullification of Elfride's needs and desires to Sue Bridehead's fight against the tyranny of man-made institutions. He would have had no hesitation at all in joining with J.S. Mill who argued for a liberated world in which

each individual will prove his or her capacities in the only way in which capacities can be proved – by trial; and the world will have the benefit of the best faculties of all its inhabitants.[1]

In Hardy's view, it is evident that the world would *not* have the benefit of the best faculties of its inhabitants because half of it, the female half, is denied the right to prove them.

While he was writing *The Return of the Native* in the mid- to late-1870s, he may well have had such thoughts in mind, for he was reading the works of a woman he greatly admired, whom he regarded as one of the 'Immortals' of literature, and who also happened to be highly unconventional – in fact, an openly and defiantly liberated woman. He was reading George Sand[2] and, taking notes from her novel, *Mauprat*, he comes across the following:

Men imagine that a woman has no individual existence, and that she ought always to be absorbed in them; and yet they love no woman deeply, unless she elevates herself, by her character, above the weakness and inertia of her sex.[3]

Hardy's attention now turns to a woman, Eustacia, whose husband certainly feels she 'ought always to be absorbed' in him, and whose 'individual existence' should, according to 'men's imaginings', most certainly be mediated by his desires.

Hardy's greater heroines are not, in his original conception of them, confined to a domestic domain beside the proverbial hearth but are persistently recalled to the world of men and work. There is no sphere, in Hardy, designated woman's realm. But Eustacia, unlike Bathsheba, Tess and Sue, is very much a prisoner in her world which she roams restlessly, night and day, yearning for freedom, action, passion – a yearning manifest in the burning fires she sets by night as beacons of her desire.

It is part of Hardy's purpose in *The Return of the Native* to expose the anger and frustration suffered by the intelligent mind and energetic body restricted to an unvarying, unchallenging, isolated existence. Thomasin's domestic world, with all its conventional trappings, throws Eustacia's into relief by contrast; the estranged solitary woman belongs to no circumscribed world, least of all Thomasin's, in the sense of settling in it, becoming habituated to it or wishing to remain in it. Where Thomasin enacts the exemplary, dutiful, submissive, forbearing wife, Eustacia burns with 'smouldering rebelliousness'.

To be loved to madness – such was her great desire. Love was to her the one cordial which could drive away the eating loneliness of her days. And she seemed to long for the abstraction called passionate love more than any particular lover. (*RN*, p.79)

The rapt joy of passionate love, of erotic bliss, of the translucent sublime – great desires indeed, and far removed from

Thomasin's world of low expectations and makeshift mon-ogamous marriage.

Eustacia's tense and frustrated sexuality is also far removed from Bathsheba's self-delighting, auto-erotic passion, but it is no less expressive, no less palpable, no less physical. In *The Return of the Native*, Hardy turns again to the natural-object metaphor covertly to evoke the sexual nature of his heroine. But here the poetic device points to the interactive, reciprocal potential in the sexual relationship and, by extension, to the equal force of Eustacia's desire. Take, for example, the her-maphroditic image of the 'mollusc' (perhaps the most arcane of Hardy's natural-object metaphors), which functions to couple the lovers Eustacia and Wildeve as they wander off to make languid love in the twilight of the heath.

Their black figures sank and disappeared from against the sky. They were as two horns which the sluggish heath had put forth from its crown, like a mollusc, and had now again drawn in. (*RN*, p.99)

Reinforcing the sense of mutuality, reciprocity, and sexual equivalence which the hermaphrodite (mollusc) image intro-duces, Hardy invokes here the metonym 'horns' which serves aptly in its significant plurality – twinned erectile pro-tuberances – to suggest sharpened appetites and sexual arousal in *both* his lovers.

Hardy takes the concept of mutuality further still, and imag-istically reinforces the latent 'force' of Eustacia's nature (*RN*, p.173) by rendering her physically sturdy, potentially comba-tive: her mouth is 'cut as the point of a spear'. Clym, in complement, is introspective, passive, soft. 'The beauty here visible' in Clym's face is meditative, not quite 'thoughtworn', a look, Hardy writes, born of 'placid pupilage' (*RN*, pp.161–2).

This woman of 'Tartarean dignity' – an 'Artemis, Athena, or Hera' (*RN*, p.77) – has none of Clym's placidity. Rather the reverse, she is constantly restless, perpetually on the move, endlessly roaming. Her confined and confining world so deprives her of sensory experience that her impulse, when walking on the heath, is to pass her thick skeins of hair through the thorny gorse, the 'prickly' tufts of 'Ulex Europeaeus' (*RN*, pp.75–6); and her need to ache and suffer in love expresses her deprivation at an even deeper level, in algolagnia – in taking pleasure in pain. 'Give us back our suffering,' cried Eustacia's peer in life, Florence Nightingale, 'for out of nothing comes nothing. But out of suffering may come the cure. Better have pain than paralysis.'[4] These could be Eustacia's own words. She too demands remission from the enervated life, the enforced seclusion of her days. To Wildeve she protests:

I should hate it all to be smooth. Indeed, I think I like you to desert me a little once now and then. Love is the dismallest thing where the lover is quite honest. O, it is a shame to say so; but it is true! ... my spirits begin at the very idea. Don't you offer me tame love, or away you go! (*RN*, p.96)

She longs for exquisite pain, sublime erotic anguish. Her spirits *begin* at the very idea. It is a challenging, not a tame lover that she needs. She wants him vulpine, athwart, to match her own intensity of feeling – an intensity palpably felt in the 'Ah!', 'Ah', 'O's of her articulations with Wildeve (*RN*, pp.95–6) and the 'O!', 'O', 'O's of those with Clym (*RN*, p.244). Eustacia craves sensation, and predictably cannot conceive of adequate objects for her desire. How could she imagine adequacy? She has been starved of what she calls 'life': 'life – music, poetry, passion, war, and all the beating and pulsing that are going on in the great arteries of the world'. (*RN*, pp.333–4)

Yet Eustacia is not merely 'romantical nonsensical', as her ful vision – 'seeing nothing of human life now, she imagined all the more of what she had seen' (*RN*, p.78) – and a firm grasp of reality: 'Nothing can ensure the continuance of love', she tells the romantically inclined Clym:

You have seen more than I, and have been into cities and among people that I have only heard of, and have lived more years than I; but yet I am older at this than you. I loved another man once, and now I love you. (*RN*, p.232)

Her fundamental acceptance of non-exclusive love, of serial monogamy scarcely equips her for the conventional world to which Clym subscribes, and to which he would have her conform.

Stressing her alienation still further, Hardy tells us her 'celestial imperiousness, love, wrath and fervour', are 'somewhat thrown away on netherward Egdon' (*RN*, p.77). On Olympus, we are told,

she would have done well with a little preparation. She had the passions and instincts which make a model goddess, that is, those which make not quite a model woman. (*RN*, p.75)

Hardy is careful to make the distinction, by negation, between model goddess and model woman: the model woman (represented here by Thomasin) exhibits submissiveness not imperiousness, docility not fervour, amiability not anger, demureness not passion. The model goddess clearly belongs to a different world:

Had it been possible for the earth and mankind to be entirely in her grasp for a while – few in the world would have noticed a change in the government. There would have been the same inequality of lot, the same heaping up of favours here, of contumely there, the same generosity before justice, the same perpetual dilemmas, the same captious alternation of caresses and blows that we endure now. (*RN*, p.75)

The 'model goddess', then, would effect no change in a mortal world. Presumably, if we are to follow Hardy, her descent from Olympus into the modern world, from the Hellenic polytheistic into the Christian monotheistic world, would find her at some considerable disadvantage. For, according to the Hellenic mythological tradition, originating with Kronos, of containing the forces of order and disorder within a pluralistic governing structure, the balance of power between the sexes is equally distributed, and the strong, the powerful, the brave and the heroic count among their number as many females as males.

That Hardy does not attempt to reconcile Eustacia as an Olympian with the everyday world, that her 'passions and instincts' remain unrealised as well as unrealisable on netherward Egdon, brings me to what I regard as a central motif in this novel: the opposition between the Victorian world of the book's principal characters and the Hellenic spirit embodied in both Eustacia and Egdon's Atlantean brow itself.[5]

This disjunction is powerfully evoked by the contrast between Hardy's personification of the Egdon heights, on the one hand, and the life of its inhabitants on the other. Egdon's highest elevation, which takes the form of Rainbarrow, is shaped from an imaginative amalgam of three Barrows, which the author has unified and centralised within his landscape, where in actuality they are spatially separated and peripheral to the heath. Geographical heights naturally lend themselves to images of elevation, high ideals, transfiguration, and to embody these concepts Hardy accords his Egdon heights fine 'architectural' proportions. But first, he conceives a stratified artefact of geological foundations upon which the imprints of humanity are superimposed: the Bronze Age burial mound and the Roman road respectively. The particularised epoch grounds the imaginative concept in physical reality, so to speak, but, in fact, both participate in the timeless spirit of Hellenism: the one signifies humanity's commemoration of the immortality of the spirit, and the other humanity's desire and capacity to broaden horizons, to forge new frontiers.

These features are essential to Egdon's composite character and to its ascendant quality. 'Almost crystallized to natural products by long continuance' (*RN*, p.7), the Barrow, on the one hand, projects the brow of Egdon 'above its natural level', and the ancient highway, on the other, 'traverses from one horizon to another' – leading on and out.

But the most important feature of this part-anthropomorphic, part-monolithic landscape is the manner in which all elements and forces interact and reciprocate. Egdon has a spectral presence signifying, in its balanced proportions and harmonious relations, an embodied ideal nowhere to be matched by the inequitable, discordant world it overreaches.

The time for action, for change, for humanity to draw a richer existence from the 'vast tract of unenclosed wild' cocooned by membraneous sky and vegetative earth, has been preternaturally prolonged:

> when other things sank brooding to sleep the heath appeared slowly to wake and listen. Every night its Titanic form seemed to await something; but it had waited thus, unmoved, during so many centuries, through the crises of so many things, that it could only be imagined to await one last crisis – the final overthrow. (*RN*, p.4)

The temporal setting is midcentury and revolution is in the air.[6] The great seats of Europe and Eustacia's Paris are in the process of overthrow, or are already overthrown, and folk speak retrospectively of decapitated kings and the Napoleonic wars (*RN*, p.124). The modern capital ideologically anterior to Hardy's Egdon is not London but 'the French capital – the centre and vortex of the fashionable world' (*RN*, p.128): a city riven by crises and political turbulence. Egdon too has seen 'the crises of so many things', and it too contains its own turbulence:

Intensity was more usually reached by way of the solemn than by way of the brilliant, and such a sort of intensity was often arrived at during winter darkness, tempests and mists. Then Egdon was aroused to reciprocity; for the storm was its lover, and the wind its friend. (*RN*, p.5)

To the modern mind 'adrift on change, and harassed by the irrepressible New' (*RN*, pp.6,7), Egdon generates a reassuring sense of endurance aligned, we are told, with humanity's pioneering 'slighted and enduring' spirit.

Hardy's reference to the heath's 'Titanic' form has already introduced the Hellenic motif, the notional opposition to the Modern World. But it is not until we encounter the 'modern' Clym with his monotheistic God, his deterministic outlook, his passive acceptance of his fate, that the opposition becomes fully apparent. Despite his affection for the heathlands that are barely visible to his increasingly failing sight, the placid Clym is patently incompatible with the Titanic force and grandeur of Egdon's Atlantean presence. Or, as we are later told, he is 'of no more account (to it) than an insect ... a mere parasite of the heath' (*RN*, p.326).

What, then, do we infer from this incompatibility between the 'native' and his environment? Michael Millgate suggests that:

Both the allusion to Greek tragedy and the evocation of setting are presumably intended to elevate the central story, to project its narrative and thematic patterns as in some sense reflective or representative of permanent elements in human experience at all times and in all places.[7]

But to juxtapose this 'desert tract of pre-civilisation' is, Millgate argues, 'to jar credulity and promote continuous unease'.[8] Hardy, I would argue, intends the clash.

It happens thus: the clash, or opposition lies between Hellenistic polytheism and the pursuit of happiness, of Greek joyousness – and Christian monotheism and the pursuit of godliness, of self-redemption through self-denial. Now, the Titanic construct, or Egdon paradigm, as I will call it, with its very physical characteristics, its 'bossy projections' (*RN*, p.13) complementing its 'rounds and hollows' (*RN*, p.4), not only embodies reciprocity (its 'female' and 'male' characteristics complementing each other), but it is also noticeably unrestrained and sensuous, noticeably turbulent and embattled, and noticeably well-endowed with strong human passions. Most important of all, it is pagan. This is not Clym's world, but it may well be Eustacia's.

To complete the symmetry and unity of the construct Hardy names its uppermost reaches 'Atlantean' and places upon its peak the heroine, herself of Greek extraction, who now features as the 'perfect, delicate, and necessary finish' to the whole. In keeping with the 'architectural demands of the mass', classic forms are inscribed upon its physical outlines. Hence, with 'Atlantean' signifying the presence of atlantes (male), the complementary figure of the caryatid (female) is required, so to speak, to complete symmetrical form:

There the form stood, motionless as the hill beneath. Above the plain rose the hill, above the hill rose the barrow, and above the barrow rose the figure. Above the figure was nothing that could be mapped elsewhere than on a celestial globe. Such a perfect, delicate, and necessary finish did the figure give to the dark pile of hills that it seemed to be the only obvious justification of their outline. Without it, there was the dome without the lantern; with it the architectural demands of the mass were satisfied. The scene was strangely homogeneous, in that the vale, the upland, the barrow, and the figure above it amounted to a unity. (*RN*, p.13)

The opposition between Greek and Modern, between unity and disunity, between parity and disparity has yet to be fully dramatised. This is instigated by the modern heathdwellers' displacement of the classic figure from the Atlantean brow, and is later compounded by her fragmented existence on the heath. But first 'Humanity appears on the scene 'Hand in Hand with Trouble' (as Hardy entitles Chapter Two) to inaugurate a temporal change from timeless past to present-day while also consolidating the theme of opposition. The first figure to appear seems innocuous enough, although, as it later transpires, he is

the neglectful guardian of the orphaned heroine. He is, therefore, one of those 'hand in hand with trouble'. The second
figure, Venn, the reddleman who trades in red ochre for the
marking of sheep,[9] is readily recognisable as an alien intruder
by virtue of his lurid blood-red raiment. No sheep, after all,
graze on Egdon. Although there is little, at this stage, to indicate
the nature of Venn's true role, Hardy's initial clues are both
apt and prefigurative. For this intruder and moral watchdog
from the civilised world who later secretes himself in the hollows
of the heath to spy on Eustacia, now stirs irritation and unease in
his companion, Captain Vye, by making five separate, secretive,
visits to peer inside his van, where the concealed Thomasin,
after the abortive wedding ceremony with Wildeve, lies in an
exhausted sleep. Venn's actions are plainly provoking:

Possibly these two [Venn and Vye] might not have spoken again till
their parting, had it not been for the reddleman's visits to his van.
When he returned from his fifth time of looking in the old man said,
'You have something inside there besides your load?' (*RN*, p.10)

Despite his manner of teasing out five previews, the reddleman
divulges nothing, leaving Vye to draw his own conclusions – to
discover what turns out in fact to be common knowledge about
the girl from 'Blooms-End' (*RN*, p.12). And what the reader
discovers from this minor instance of 'trouble' is that Venn
enjoys creating it. This will culminate in less minor troubles, in
more destructive deeds, notably in his attempts to bring down
Eustacia – the 'displacement' (*RN*, p.101) which ends in her
tragic death.

Mainstream criticism holds Venn to be a benign agent of
order within the community. This interpretation depends
heavily upon the reader's need to order Hardy's world, to locate
a recognisable regulating force within it, and to assign the locus
of order to the moral watchdog who, mirroring the Victorian
puritanical conscience, fulfils the role of censor.

Venn's activities have been seen, by critics, as appropriate to
a moral universe in which woman's irregular sexual activity
needs to be checked. However, this reading at best reflects the
exegetical pursuits of the critic and, at worst, over-simplifies
Hardy's very complicated schema here. Since Venn features
centrally in this schema, and since the Egdon paradigm presents

the only alternative *weltanschauung* (in terms of sexual relationships), in the entire range of the Wessex novels, I think it is important to examine his true role and function as the moral watchdog in *The Return of the Native*'s troubled world.

As officious intruder, troublemaker and Eustacia's demoraliser, Venn is clearly visible as the furtive stalker who persistently tracks her down in order to catch her out in actions he disapproves. And, as Hardy subtly indicates, he serves no one's interests but his own.[10]

Strongly urged by a desire to trap the 'rare' creature and to curtail her freedom, Venn rationalises his persecution of Eustacia as activated by a desire to protect Thomasin's interests. But he deceives himself:

His first active step in watching over Thomasin's interests was taken about seven o'clock the next evening, and was dictated by the news which he had learnt from the sad boy. That Eustacia was somehow the cause of Wildeve's carelessness in relation to the marriage had at once been Venn's conclusion on hearing of the secret meeting between them. It did not occur to his mind that Eustacia's love-signal to Wildeve was the tender effect upon the deserted beauty of the intelligence which her grandfather had brought home. His instinct was to regard her as a conspirator against rather than as an antecedent obstacle to Thomasin's happiness. (*RN*, p.93)

Venn's interference is not only shown to be misconceived, it is also obliquely disapproved by Hardy here, who, in speaking of Eustacia, allows soft, sympathetic tones to colour his narrative ('the tender effect') but who, in speaking of Venn, reverts to polite severity: 'His instinct was to regard her as a conspirator against rather than as an antecedent obstacle to Thomasin's happiness.' There can, of course, be no protection of Thomasin's interests all the while her self-appointed guardian gets his facts wrong; but obsessed with his mission he sets out to track Eustacia, not for a few hours, not for a day, but for five consecutive nights. Success comes 'a day-week' after her previous meeting with Wildeve; but while he is spying on the lovers Venn is frustrated by a cross-wind, which interferes with his eavesdropping. It is at this point that his compulsion to meddle is exposed by Hardy for the totally unprincipled thing it is. To overcome the cross-wind, Venn decides to creep up in disguise on the unsuspecting pair:

He took two of these (turves) as he lay, and dragged them over him till one covered his head and shoulders, the other his back and legs. The reddleman would now have been quite invisible, even by daylight; the turves, standing upon him with the heather upwards, looked precisely as if they were growing. He crept along again, and the turves on his back crept with him ... it was as though he burrowed underground. (*RN*, pp.94,95)

Where Gabriel Oak, in his espials, squats in shadows or peers through crevices, Venn, like the veritable demon of old who, it was held, mined under the earth for treasure, creeps along 'as though he burrowed underground'. This allusion shapes Hardy's discourse most tellingly to demonstrate Venn's true nature, without stripping him entirely of his superficial guise of respectability.

In his creeping and crawling spying activities Venn reveals a malevolent underside which Hardy does not cloak but, rather, continues, in gradual stages, to expose. Venn decides to confront Eustacia with his knowledge of her movements and Hardy, with a keen sense of what is fitting, has him choose a Sunday morning 'for an interview ... to attack her position as Thomasin's rival either by art or by storm' (*RN*, p.101). The Sabbath is clearly the most appropriate day for a little demonic intervention. Contravening custom and goodwill, Venn also chooses to arrive at a time when 'folks never call upon ladies' – that is while they are still in bed (*RN*, p.102). He is not, of course, perturbed by his own intrusiveness, rather he seeks to perturb, no doubt pruriently relishing the thought of his name being carried into the private quarters of the young woman as yet undressed, whom he fully intends to strip of dignity.

When eventually she greets him, he uses no 'art' whatsoever but rude and rending 'storm'. He begins by referring to her lover, Wildeve, not by name but with a vulgar jerk: 'he jerked his elbow to south-east – the direction of the Quiet Woman' (*RN*, p.103). Whereupon, distressed, but holding fast to her dignity, Eustacia coolly enquires if he is speaking of 'Mr Wildeve'. This merely prompts yet another insulting reference, this time to herself as 'This other woman' Wildeve 'has picked up with', and yet another as Venn proceeds to tell the 'pickup' that her lover has no intention of marrying her, implying that she may be fit for sex but not for wife.

Venn's most pitiless blow, though, is his disclosure of his espial. Just as Oak sought to shame and humiliate so Venn now does the same. He lets it be known that he has been watching her; that he knows a good deal about her movements; that he has seen her with Wildeve at their last meeting, the evening they had wandered off hand in hand, into the dusky twilight of the heath:

It was a disconcerting lift of the curtain, and the mortification of Candaules' wife glowed in her. The moment had arrived when her lip would tremble in spite of herself, and when the gasp could no longer be kept down. (*RN*, p.105)

Eustacia's emotional distress speaks volumes. Clearly, she fears Venn has witnessed far more than just the holding of hands.

This is just the moment he has been waiting for, the moment for engineering her displacement. He will come to her aid; he will find her a position in Budmouth; she can become a widow-lady's 'companion'. Venn may shame her, may degrade her, may humiliate her but he cannot dupe her. Seeing, instantly, his ploy to have her reduced yet further – to the menial position of unpaid serving-woman – she turns on him angrily and snaps back that she will not go.

Humiliating the proud girl may gratify Venn, but it does not urge her departure. On the contrary, even as he persuades himself that his mission is to rid Egdon of her presence, if she had fostered the remotest longing to escape, he effectively robs her of it now.

As a rule, the word Budmouth meant fascination on Egdon. That Royal port and watering-place, if truly mirrored in the minds of the heath-folk, must have combined, in a charming and indescribable manner, a Carthaginian bustle of building with Tarentine luxuriousness and Baian health and beauty. Eustacia felt little less extravagantly about the place; but she would not sink her independence to get there. (*RN*, p.108)

'Sink' is exactly the word. Venn's projection of her servitude in perpetuity has left its mark.

Clearly Venn does not operate as a benign regulating force. Perpetually meddling and perpetually failing to get his facts right, he is also responsible for passing Clym's inheritance into the wrong hands. This small interference leading to large consequences takes place in the gambling scene. Here, 'confusion' and 'vice' are well foregrounded as the addled Christian, the drunken Wildeve, and the officious Venn crouch, in an unlit world, around the Promethean 'dregs' of burning 'fires' generated in fits and starts from a collection of much abused glow-worms. And that it should be Clym's inheritance which will shortly be misappropriated, who is himself later to be found crouching and crawling, half-blind in an unlit world – 'a mere parasite of the heath' (*RN*, p.326) – reinforces Hardy's vision of polarised worlds: this world of self-interested, joyless, punitive men is singularly at odds with the Hellenic Egdon paradigm.

'It was sometimes suggested', Hardy writes,

> that reddlemen were criminals for whose misdeeds other men had wrongfully suffered: that in escaping the law they had not escaped their own consciences, and had taken to the trade as a lifelong penance. Else why should they have chosen it? In the present case such a question would have been particularly apposite. The reddleman who had entered Egdon that afternoon was an instance of the pleasing being wasted to form the ground-work of the singular, when an ugly foundation would have done just as well for that purpose. (*RN*, p.90)

Why would this 'pleasing being' in his pleasing guise – this 'agreeable specimen of rustic manhood' – relinquish 'his proper station in life' (*RN*, p.90)? For money it seems: 'Yes I am given up body and soul to the making of money. Money is all my dream' (*RN*, p.464), Venn jests to Thomasin in Mephistophelian vein, but the jest rings rather hollow. His guise of respectability is, in truth, exceedingly thin, insured, as it is, by his 'never-failing production of a well-lined purse' (*RN*, p.89). In fact, more Mephistophelian than 'an agreeable specimen of rustic manhood', he personifies, as a 'blood-coloured figure' and a 'red ghost' (*RN*, p.87), 'all the horrid dreams which had afflicted the juvenile spirit since imagination began':

> 'The reddleman is coming for you!' had been the formulated threat of Wessex mothers for many generations. (*RN*, p.89)

And only superficially less sinister in his whitewashed guise at the last, Venn 'comes for' Thomasin as a 'ghost' of altered hue:

> [Clym] heard a slight scream from Thomasin, who was sitting inside the room. 'O, how you frightened me!' she said to some one who

had entered. 'I thought you were the ghost of yourself.' (*RN*, p.454)

Not fully reassured that it is in fact Diggory Venn 'no longer reddleman', Thomasin confesses that she could not 'believe that he had got white of his own accord! It seemed supernatural,' she says (*RN*, p.455). Telling words! For if Hardy's 'white-washing' of Venn is not supernatural, it is decidedly unnatural.

Those Wessex mothers threatening their children with the reddleman are, for Hardy's purposes, prophetic. The prophecy is fulfilled most dramatically in the shooting episode, in the chapter entitled 'Rough Coercion is Employed'. Here, having already set trip-wires to bedevil Wildeve, Venn takes the law into his own hands and, while on the one hand he tells himself that he is 'prepared to go to any lengths short of absolutely shooting', on the other, he stalks the innkeeper across the heath takes aim and fires:

Had Wildeve known how thoroughly in earnest Venn had become he might have been still more alarmed.... The doubtful legitimacy of such rough coercion did not disturb the mind of Venn. (*RN*, p.319)

The 'doubtful legitimacy' may not disturb Venn but it does Hardy. If Venn is to feature in *The Return of the Native*'s 'happy ending' an exculpatory note should be sounded at this point. There is no genuine attempt, on Hardy's part, to conceal the unnaturalness of Venn's transformation, where he becomes an overnight success with Thomasin, hitherto indifferent to his charms. Hardy, in fact, openly admits that this *volte-face* goes right against his 'original conception'. Venn, he says, 'was to have retained his isolated and weird character to the last, and to have disappeared mysteriously from the heath, nobody knowing whither' (*RN*, p.470). A token 'cleaning-up' never-theless has to take place at some point, if readers' expectations of marriage-and-happy-endings are to be met. After all, Venn is becoming, by the minute, a radically more demonic version of the Oak whom Hardy aligns with Milton's Satan early in *Far From the Madding Crowd*; although Oak does have one dogged foot in the upperworld. Accordingly, with the arrival of this 'new and most unpleasant form of menace' (*RN*, p.318), Hardy offers a token exculpatory note:

Sometimes this is not to be regretted. From the impeachment of Strafford to Farmer Lynch's short way with the scamps of Virginia there have been many triumphs of justice which are mockeries of law. (*RN*, p.319)

I use the word 'token' advisedly. For this apparent vindication of Venn is subtly undermined by the anomalous examples Hardy draws upon: Strafford was, after all, impeached and be-headed on controvertible charges of treason, and the 'triumphs of justice' executed in Charles Lynch's name gave rise to some of the most brutal injustices committed in Hardy's century.

Venn may fulfil the role of a moral watchdog equipped with punitive instincts where beautiful, rebellious women are concerned, but it is not Hardy's intention that he should be applauded for it. If we go back to the novel's opening sequences, it is now apparent that Venn's first appearance 'Hand in Hand with Trouble' has led in steady, gradual steps towards far greater troubles; but before they begin to unfold Hardy shifts the focus back to the Barrow where Eustacia is seen in cameo as the 'perfect and necessary finish' to the architectural mass. The classic form is stable, unified and balanced:

The form was so much like an organic part of the entire motionless structure that to see it move would have impressed the mind as a strange phenomenon. Immobility being the chief characteristic of that whole which the person formed portion of, the discontinuance of immobility in any quarter suggested confusion. Yet that is precisely what happened. The figure perceptibly gave up its fixity ... descended ... and then vanished. The reason for her sudden displacement now appeared ... a newcomer ... protruded into the sky.... A second followed, then a third, a fourth, a fifth, and ultimately the whole barrow was peopled with burdened figures. (*RN*, pp.13,14)

The woman, we are told, 'had no relation to the forms who had taken her place'. They intrude, bringing confusion and disorder, unsettling the spectral image of classic perfection, balance and equilibrium.

The imagination of the observer clung by preference to that vanished, solitary figure, as something more interesting, more important, more likely to have a history worth knowing than these *new-comers*, and unconsciously regarded them as *intruders*. (My italics, *RN*, p.14)

This displacement of Eustacia as an Olympian apparition,

spectrally the perfect finish to the Atlantean brow, prefigures her later demise, her displacement in Egdon's modern world 'not friendly to women'. At the same time it testifies to the destabilising agency of the modern world's inhabitants. This is an important point. Critical assumptions claiming that Eustacia is both the intruder and agent of disorder in *The Return of the Native*, are not supported by the text. Hardy was writing for and about a world 'not friendly to women' but he was not inviting its perpetuation by literary critics.[11]

Heralded by Boeotian witlessness set in antithesis to Eustacia's Olympian grandeur, the intruders, 'like a travelling flock of sheep', ascend the tumulus (*RN*, p.15), and the world now becomes one in which all perspectives are dimmed. The horizon blurs and the heath below phases out: 'none of its features could be seen now' (*RN*, p.16). As if usurping 'some radiant upper storey of the world', neither complementing its grandeur nor adding to it any 'necessary finish', the heathfolk can perceive nothing of the world they customarily inhabit. The sense is now of a gradual emergence of two distinct and separate hemispheres: the one, the upper Atlantean world, pleasing in form, finish and atmosphere, and the other, the lower 'Limbo' world – the abode of souls barred from Paradise. The polarisation of the two spheres becomes the more apparent as we are told that in the nether regions of the heath 'the muttered articulations of the wind in the hollows were as complaints and petitions from the "souls of mighty worth" suspended therein' (*RN*, p.17). The one soul of 'mighty worth' now 'suspended therein' is Eustacia. Precipitated into the 'Limbo' that is to be her Egdon existence, it is her articulations that carry on the winds:

There mingled with all this wild rhetoric of night a sound which modulated so naturally into the rest that its beginning and ending were hardly to be distinguished. The bluffs, and bushes, and the heather-bells had broken silence; at last, so did the woman; and her articulation was but as another phrase of the same discourse as theirs. Thrown out on the winds it became twined in with them and with them it flew away. (*RN*, p.61)

Hardy's polarisation of the two spheres, the Hellenic and the Modern, now becomes dramatically complete as confusion takes the place of stability: 'all was unstable': 'those whom Nature had depicted as merely quaint became grotesque, and the grotesque became prenatural; for all was in extremity' (*RN*, p.18). With stability lost and divided worlds very much to the fore, dialogues now convey division within the community: the putting-up of Thomasin's wedding banns and Mrs Yeobright's opposition to them, Wildeve's worthiness or not, and Thomasin's folly or alternatively her wisdom in accepting Wildeve's suit. Added to these minor differences (all of which devolve upon issues of class and sex) there is also talk of Christian Cantle's ambiguous sexuality and a good deal of superstitious interchange. Pandemonium is finally most appropriately dramatised by the figures of the 'whirling ... dark shapes' cavorting 'demoniac' measures in the 'boiling confusion' (*RN*, p.33). Poor addled Christian Cantle is beside himself: 'They ought not to do it – how the vlankers do fly! 'tis tempting the Wicked one, 'tis' (*RN*, p.33). And sure enough a 'long, slim figure' flames up out of the heath before his very eyes, clad in 'tight raiment, and red from top to toe'. 'For all the world like the Devil in the picture of Temptation' (*RN*, p.34) Venn arrives, summoned by the 'boiling confusion of sparks' and flying vlankers to set the seal upon a scene as profane as the earlier one had been sublime.

The heathfolk finally descend and Eustacia ascends again to 'her old position at the top'. But the prelude is over: the Atlantean brow is now invisible; Eustacia's figure is blurred by an 'incomplete darkness'; the radiant upper storey is lost to view.

This displacement motif echoes on throughout the novel. It is, for example, reiterated in prefigurative form later on where Venn's declared intention to displace Eustacia is prefaced, by Hardy, with an analogy. This introduces the high-flying courser, the rare bird from hotter climes (*RN*, p.100) which, we are told, was remorselessly tracked by a 'barbarian' who 'rested neither night nor day' until he had hunted her down and finally shot her. The analogy is clear: Venn's persecution of Eustacia, in intention as much as in act, passes well beyond a bid for power. Envy and desire are equally present here.

Venn's attempts to displace the rare, splendid woman, are paralleled in less demonic form, in Clym's overshadowing of her in marriage. Her phasing into invisibility as Clym grows increasingly blind grounds the motif in harsh, physical fact, but it is the invisibility (to him) of her pain, frustration and desire that drives her out of her mind. In this instance, events are foreshadowed by the lunar eclipse which, significantly, dims the radiant upper sphere as, in their courtship days, Clym and Eustacia meet up by night on the heath.

Moving from Hardy's microcosmic world to the macrocosmic world of the reader, this motif finds its true parallel in woman's legal, social, sexual overshadowing, in her lack of equal rights in a man-made world, in which there was no need to display the sign of the headless, silenced 'Quiet Woman' (*RN*, p.45). Eustacia's live counterpart, socially conditioned to be decorative and dumb with the aid of the cult of the 'doll-madonna', lived out her amputated life without legal existence, without political voice under the auspices of the Institution of Matrimony, for all the world to see. 'Homer's Cimmerian land' (*RN*, p.60), nowhere to be found on netherward Egdon, was nowhere to be found beyond it.

Venn, as a power-mongering bully and degrader of voluptuous womankind, typifies the punitive male censor of female nonconformity,[12] although in his personification of things demonic, he takes on somewhat melodramatic proportions. This is necessary, I think, to Hardy's rather grand scheme of polarising the two worlds, Hellenic and Modern. Clym, on the other hand, is less stereotyped. He is not so much the personification of social evils in general and male-domination in particular as, simply, an 'unseeing' native of the land. He is, even so, one of Hardy's more sympathetically drawn heroes. There are not many who, in wielding power and authority, do not trivialise and debase, or (the inverse) rarefy and etherealise, the woman they love, but Clym does struggle to meet Eustacia on her own ground. He is, Hardy says, 'before his time', 'mentally in a provincial future' (*RN*, pp.203–4), and this shows in his earlier days with Eustacia (before his vision goes) as, for example, when she argues against monogamy without fear of repression or humiliation. Her views are highly unconventional not to say anarchic. Yet, unlike Venn who, in common with many of his live contemporaries, mentally categorises Eustacia a hussy, Clym listens without sneers or disgust or condescension. Or so we might suppose, for it is with tact and diplomacy, both signs of self-assurance, that she speaks to him of her past love and then moves on to deflect him from present talk of marriage –

following his sudden announcement that she should be his wife:

'Shall I claim you some day – I don't mean at once?'

'I must think,' Eustacia murmured. 'At present speak of Paris to me. Is there any place like it on earth?'

'It is very beautiful. But will you be mine?'

'I will be nobody else's in the world – does that satisfy you?'

'Yes, for the present.' (*RN*, p.233)

Eustacia seeks to gain from Clym's responses a measure of reassurance that his return to Paris is a possibility. No doubt aware that the Victorian maid taken in marriage as man's property marries not only the man but also his way of life, she must needs canvass his intentions, his affiliations, his line of country. Her stratagem, then, is to divert him back to Paris.

'Now tell me of the Tuileries, and the Louvre,' she continued evasively. 'I hate talking of Paris! Well I remember one sunny . . . ' (*RN*, p.233)

Clym does not hate talking about Paris, as Eustacia knows only too well. His vivid evocation of the place betrays him. He is discomposed, though, by the fact that both his lover and his mother appear to know what is best for him, and this turns him, in his male pride, perverse and stubborn. Vexed by Eustacia's consuming passion to belong in Paris – a city surely redolent, to her rebellious mind, of revolutionary zeal and women-on-the-barricades – and apparently ignorant of her attraction to rebels and warriors, he taxes her with loving him,

rather as a visitant from a gay world to which she rightly belonged than as a man with a purpose opposed to that recent past which so interested her. (*RN*, p.236)

He had earlier expressed his opposition in no uncertain terms:

'How extraordinary that you and my mother should be of one mind about this!' said Yeobright. 'I have vowed not to go back, Eustacia.' (*RN*, p.234)

The tenor of this vow suggests a renunciation of the worldly, of the instinctual life in favour of the devotional, but Clym's new plan is vain and unworldly to the point of impracticality:

To argue upon the possibility of culture before luxury to the bucolic world may be to argue truly, but it is an attempt to disturb a sequence to which humanity has long been accustomed. Yeobright preaching to the Egdon eremites that they might rise to a serene comprehensiveness without going through the process of enriching themselves, was not unlike arguing to ancient Chaldeans that in ascending from earth to the pure empyrean it was not necessary to pass first into the intervening ether. (*RN*, p.204)

In short, the plan is totally unrealistic. But Eustacia is not to know this, any more than she can know that his immediate impulse to set her in Paris stirs, in his mind, illusions rather than realistic visions. Notice, for example, how inappropriate his settings are: 'Why', he says, the 'Galerie d'Apollon' would be a fitting place to live, and

the Little Trianon would suit us beautifully to live, and you might walk in the gardens in the moonlight ...

you could keep to the lawn in the front of the Grand Palace ... (*RN*, p.233)

Eustacia is now uneasy. Possibly she finds the grandiose, opulent settings hard to identify with. She is a woman, after all, with a liking for warriors and a strong yearning for 'life-music, poetry, passion, war and all the beating and pulsing that are going on in the great arteries of the world' (*RN*, pp.333–4). Revolutionary, not aristocratic, Paris would be far more to her liking. Then again, Clym's settings discompose her because they give the impression that she cares more for glamour and riches than for him:

Don't mistake me Clym: though I should like Paris, I love you for yourself alone. To be your wife and live in Paris would be heaven to me; but I would rather live with you in a hermitage here than not be yours at all. It is gain to me either way, and a very great gain. There's my candid confession. (*RN*, p.235)

This is the telling moment. Despite the sympathy of her listener Eustacia has, in some subtle way, found herself re-stated. Is it the glamour, the glitter, or is it the formality of landscaped gardens that lend a different shape to her dreams, her sense of self? Whatever the cause, she is trapped in an unfamiliar identity and in the confusion she falls back upon a culturally approved language expressing approved attitudes that completely misrepresent her. She has stalled an imminent clash of wills only to find herself precipitated into a deeper conflict as Clym takes her 'candid confession' to mean her submission to his will. And in like manner he, too, falls into conventional attitudes, patronising attitudes. Metaphorically patting her on the head, he declares that she has 'spoken like a woman'. But in so saying, in falling back upon that authoritarian manner of mixing approval with condescension, he has shifted the relationship on to a different level: not only is there a disparity in their hopes and dreams, there is now an imbalance of power.

Eustacia is caught in a double-bind. Suffering a check upon her thoughts and emotions, but knowing no language of sexuality other than that of conventional courtship, her utterances are now shaped to a false representation of her true feelings. What she cannot speak of 'like a woman' and what Hardy has to tell on her behalf, is that 'Fidelity in love for fidelity's sake had less attraction for her than . . . fidelity because of love's grip' (*RN*, p.79). She has already startled Clym with her thoughts on the non-exclusivity of love; she has frankly admitted that a cosmopolitan life would be ideal; but she has not been able to say that she has 'got beyond the vision of some marriage of inexpressible glory' (*RN*, p.81); that the marriage tie is not for her. Clym, in turn, misreads her languid manner as passive acceptance, as a 'feminine' yielding to circumstance. His modernism, his enlightenment, is in this sense more theoretical than actual. Had he been less inclined to seek a 'model woman' in Eustacia, he would have discovered a radical, a potential woman-on-the-barricades. But he turns his back on the real Eustacia just as he has turned his back on the real world – on Paris, the city of social and political revolutions – to return to his native, class-divided community; to set himself up as philanthropic teacher to a handful of Egdon eremites; to 'fain make a globe to suit him' (*RN*, p.242): to play chieftain to what he calls 'the lowest classes'.

Egocentricity and introspection, 'parasite thought', devour the vision that had once urged him to strive at 'high thinking', to become 'acquainted with ethical systems popular at the time' (*RN*, p.203). Even his philanthropic outlook is self-regarding, as his own words reveal, where vagueness of vision is prefaced by the self-referential 'I' that remains the object of contemplation.

I no longer adhere to my intention of giving with my own mouth rudimentary education to the lowest classes. I can do better . . .

I shall ultimately, I hope, be at the head of one of the best schools in the county. (*RN*, p.227)

I shall do a great deal of good to my fellow-creatures! (*RN*, p.239)

Despite the 'waggery of fate' (*RN*, p.199) which has afforded Clym a highly privileged start in life, enabling him to test his ideas, needs and skills in both London and Paris with all the social and economic freedom Eustacia has been denied, it is all wasted on him. Rightfully, given his privileged background, he sees his scope as large; but his visionary powers are small. His mother and his lover both know this and tell it. But they are overruled: the right to choose his own way of life is his male birthright, and exercise this right he will.

Eustacia's dreams are by contrast either fragmented or truncated. They could scarcely be anything else. Hardy, sensitively acknowledging the extent to which her cut-off life has moulded the deeps of her unconscious, presents even her paradisal dream as truncated – in terms of both form *and* content. There is first of all some indication that this is a dream of such splendour as to outmatch all dreams. But Hardy pieces together only its final disintegrating moments. It is as if he would stress her dislocation from her Olympian heights as too remote, too atavistic, for full recall. Then there is the armoured figure who features centrally in the dream. He disintegrates before the dreamer's very eyes and just at the point of touching. The dream of harmonious relations, prefigured in Hardy's own dream of an alternative world of reciprocity and equilibrium, shatters about the dreamer's ears and falls into fragments as she awakes.

Untimely awakened from what she calls her 'youthful dream' – the music, the pulsing, the passion – Eustacia, denied all that Clym has been so freely offered and so freely squanders, suffers bitterly at the sight of him toiling on the surface of the heath singing mindlessly in defeat,

not more distinguishable from the scene around him than the green caterpillar from the leaf it feeds on ... of no more account than an insect – a mere parasite of the heath. (*RN*, p.326)

Like an imbecile, Clym draws emotional soothing relief from his 'curious microscopic' activities (*RN*, p.296), impervious to the continuing damage to his sight. But to Hardy he is an infestation, parasitical. This is reflected in his insensitivity to Eustacia's suffering as daily he makes callous references to his life in Paris. Having decided not to return to that city, having doggedly insisted to the woman he loves that there is no possibility he will change his mind, having ignored her hopes and desires, he returns, again and again, in his stories of 'Parisian life and character' and, again and again, in the songs which had struck his fancy in Paris, to the people and places she, herself, longs to hear and touch and see.

Tormented by the mindlessness of the man and haunting strains of his songs, Eustacia turns away and weeps 'in sick despair of the blasting effect upon her own life of that mood and condition in him' (*RN*, pp.297–8). It is a mood and condition of blind egocentricity. Clym's failure to attune himself to the high thinking and ethical systems of the time, becomes, in turn, his physical blindness. And blind he certainly becomes to his own double-standard. To Eustacia's attempts to persuade him to live at a different level he explains that he needs to keep himself occupied: 'You cannot seriously wish me to stay idling at home all day?' (*RN*, p.103). What then of Eustacia condemned to idling at home all day, day after day after day?

Eustacia's displacement is now fully compounded. The rare woman, with her affinity for heights she has no means of scaling can only descend and continue descending to the last. But Hardy will not have her sink, like Clym, into a wasting decline. As befits her Olympian status she will be consumed by the elements; her death will call up a fury in the natural world; like her Wessex predecessor, King Lear, she will be stricken with wild and fretful delirium under impetuous blasts: 'nocturnal scenes of disaster' (*RN*, p.418). Having seen the spectre of her greatness Hardy must draw her back into Egdon 'as if she were drawn into the Barrow by a hand beneath' (*RN*, p.419). Lashed earthwards by streaming torrential rain which gathers up her tears in its coursing, her life down-spirals:

Between the drippings of the rain from her umbrella to her mantle, from her mantle to the heather, from the heather to the earth, very similar sounds could be heard coming from her lips; and the tearfulness of the outer scene was repeated upon her face. The wings of her soul were broken ... (*RN*, p.419)

The rare creature is finally 'winged' and brought down.

Cross-relating her descent from the Barrow, where she had provided a necessary finish to the heights, Hardy cannot permit her simply to drown. The skies must break and the Barrow must seek to draw her back to itself. Her death must become a victory over life – a mortal life that had, to her, been empty of significance and purpose. For who and what had she been? She does nothing, goes nowhere and, apart from her status as Clym's wife, she is totally without identity. Unlike Clym, who is not only familiar to everyone long before his advent, who has an identity born partly of reputation, partly of kinship to the singular Mrs Yeobright, and partly of his secure status in a world predisposed to securing status for males, Eustacia is shown by Hardy to be the sum total of male circumscriptive attitudes. To her grandfather, who inconsistently chides and neglects her, she is alternately childish and romantical, non-sensical or sportive – 'one of the bucks'. To Venn she is the fabled *femme fatale*; to the heath-folk she is a witch;[13] and to Clym, predictably, given his reversion to type, she is first goddess then whore. 'Here was action and life,' writes D.H. Lawrence,

here was a move in being on [Clym's] part. But as soon as he got her, she became an idea to him, she had to fit in his system of ideas. According to his way of loving, he knew her already, she was labelled and classed and fixed down.[14]

Clym's perception of Eustacia is circumscribed by a host of assumptions that range around the polarised stereotypes of Goddess and Whore; but Hardy's own perspective, even while invoking visions of Goddesses, emphasises Eustacia's painfully isolated, nullified existence. If (recalling George Sand's words), Eustacia's urge to better herself is obstructed by a society that denies her individual existence, then Hardy will not only deny that society its ultimate appropriation of her – neither man nor institution will hold her – but he will ensure that she remains unclassifiable, a-typical, bearing no resemblance to male cir-cumscriptions. In the 'Queen of Night' chapter, for example, she remains, throughout, an unfocused, blurred figure, the 'raw material of a divinity' (*RN*, p.75). Elsewhere, she is, invariably, shrouded in darkness, or invisible to her myopic husband, or masked as a Turkish Knight, or masked again as a veiled dancer. Or she is simply a white face at a window. She is never familiar or close. She cannot be familiar or close. She, herself, does not know who or what she is: 'How I have tried and tried to be a splendid woman,' she cries in solitary anguish (*RN*, p.420). 'Tried and tried to be . . .', to come into being. She is a soul in search of a self.

Displaced, then, from her natural position of equipoise to live out her mortal life confined, inutile, restive and angry, Eustacia is suffocated in a man-made world. In her sepulchred existence, sensitively evoked by Hardy's insistence upon her life-by-night consciousness, she is prevented from coming into being in a world that denies autonomy, identity, purpose and power to women.

And that world is to be the loser in Hardy's view. It is emptied of life with Eustacia's passing. The strong women are dead. The 'native', stripped of credibility and respect, is now rootless and itinerant, and the good Thomasin with her do-good husband has removed to the very fringe of the heath's reaches – of no account to it. Egdon is inhabited at the last by a coterie of dwellers whose capacity for renewal cannot be guaranteed. The sickly Nonesuch boy and the sexually enfeebled Christian Cantle, as the heath's youthful representatives, exemplify an etiolated life wholly alien to the vigorous, turbulent, enduring heights overreaching them.

This then is a world in which, to misquote J.S. Mill, woman's capacities cannot be proved by trial, that the world might have the benefit of all its inhabitants. And as he lived out the harmonious days of his 'Sturminster idyll', composing *The Return of the Native* in the mid- 1870s, it must have struck Hardy with singular force – note-taking from his much admired George Sand and in 1876 confronted with the shock of her death – that this was indeed a world unfriendly to women.

For he would almost certainly have read Victor Hugo's obituary, in *The Saturday Review*, on George Sand, and as he reflected upon the hostile response this drew from his compatriots, he must have felt, deeply, the injustice of their attack. *The Saturday Review* first quotes Hugo:

In this country, whose law is to complete the French Revolution, and begin that of the equality of the sexes, being a part of the equality of men, a great woman was needed. It was necessary to prove that a woman could have all the manly gifts without losing any of her angelic qualities; be strong without ceasing to be tender. George Sand proved it.... Whenever one of these powerful human creatures dies we hear, as it were, an immense noise of wings. Something is going; something is coming. The earth, like heaven, has its eclipses; but here, as above, the reapparition follows the appearance. The torch which was in the form of a man or woman, and which is extinguished under that form, reappears under that of an idea. This torch is flaming higher than ever; it will constitute afterwards a part of civilisation, and enter into the vast enlightenment of humanity.[15]

It is interesting to find in both Hugo's discourses and in Hardy's *The Return of the Native* a set of images common to both authors: the splendid woman strong without ceasing to be tender, the apparition in human form that reappears as an idea, the Promethean flame, the winging bird, the equality of the sexes principle, and even the conceptual image of 'the earth, like heaven, [having] its eclipses' which, in Hardy, takes the form of Eustacia's eclipse prefigured in her night watch with Clym.

But the reactionary *Saturday* now has its say. Launching into an attack on mutinous, rebellious women, the writer works up to a full discreditation of Sand, and concludes that,

Many women would seem to be getting tired of what they call the tame and monotonous sphere in which they are confined, and demand that the same range of active life and personal freedom should be opened up to them which is allowed to men.... It may be believed that [George Sand] flung off conventional restraints, not so much under the influence of vicious passions as of rash and presumptuous confidence.... [But] it is the harmonious co-operation of the two distinct influences of manly force and womanly tenderness and spirituality, and not the confounding of them in one common form, which keeps society sound and strong.[16]

Hardy's *Return of the Native* has the last word here. By way of a rejoinder, what the Egdon paradigm proclaims, with its embodiment of reciprocal female and male characteristics, is that it is not 'confounding' but *compounding* diverse gender attributes in 'one common form' which would 'keep society sound and strong'.

4

PASSIVE VICTIM?
Tess of the d'Urbervilles

Much is made by critics of the passive Tess who yields to circumstance and fate. They were and are voicing the nine-teenth-century liberal point of view that exonerated the fallen woman on the grounds that she was one of nature's unfor-tunates. Innately mute and trusting, passive and yielding, she suffered a weakness of will and reason and was not, therefore, responsible for her actions. These are the contours of the domi-nant cultural perspective and the language that shapes them: from Havelock Ellis to Roman Polanski it is the dumb, gentle, unthinking, passive Tess who too often survives in interpre-tation. This defeats Hardy's purposes entirely. There is no denunciation, in his entire *œuvre*, as unequivocal as his denunci-ation of the sexual double-standard in *Tess*. And I include under this heading the sexual double-standard that would not deny to the sexually active male the power of will and reason, the self-responsibility and moral integrity that is so often denied to the sexually active female. Hardy's Tess is a sexually vital consciousness and, without any shadow of doubt, to my mind, she owns each and every one of these qualities.

Victorian critics were in no doubt about her sexuality. She was, in their eyes, excessively voluptuous. They doubted, instead, her moral purity and, if they exonerated her at all it was on presuppositional grounds that voluptuousness went hand in hand with enfeebled powers of will and reason. Today, the reverse is the case. Tess has recovered her moral good sense but now has an enfeebled sexuality. Either way, she is misrepresented. What Hardy denounces, in his creation of Tess, is the popular belief – handed down to us today in the form of the 'dumb blonde' – that a voluptuous woman, a sexy woman, is intellectually vapid or morally 'loose', or as many Victorians believed, diseased in body and mind. It is, in my opinion, the combination of sexual vigour and moral rigour that makes Tess not just one of the greatest but also one of the strongest women in the annals of English literature. My aim, then, in this chapter, will be to resurrect Hardy's original strong Tess from the blurred stereotype of the sexually passive fallen woman, as critics and film-directors would have it. Indeed, from her first recognition of sexual overtures in Alex's fruit-thrusting gestures (*TD*, pp.70–1) to her ecstasy in the 'Garden' sequence, Tess expresses a fully developed sexual nature as sensitive to the needs of her impassioned lover as to her own auto-erotic powers and desires.

Here, as in *The Return of the Native*, Hardy's poetic sensibility comes into play to embed within seemingly innocuous figures of speech a language of sexuality which is neither fastidious nor fey but, rather, earthy and physical. For example, at a loss to explain to Angel how she would love him – and he is not the most perceptive of lovers – Tess instinctively draws close to the physical world of nature and sensuously rubs down the skins of the 'Lords and Ladies' (*TD*, pp.164–5); which for some perverse reason rouses in Angel the desire to teach her *history*.

Even where such figurative evocations do approach the delicate violets-and-lace, virginal/funereal lilies category of description, they remain coherent and integrated. Alec's rose pressed into Tess's breast, for instance, with the collocation of pricking thorn, blood drawn, red petals, imagistically prefigures his violation of Tess and the loss of her virginity in 'The Chase' episode.

But for Tess's own erotic energies Hardy reserves less overblown imagery. The resemblances or analogies he draws between the external world of natural phenomena and the internal world of feminine sensation evince and sustain vitality and vigour, and above all physicality and naturalness. The Tess sexually aroused by her passion for Angel is therefore centred in a world of lush fecundity, of vigorous regeneration:

Rays from the sunrise drew forth the buds and stretched them into long stalks, lifted up sap in noiseless streams, opened petals, and sucked out scents in invisible jets and breathings. . . . Thus passed the leafy time when arborescence seems to be the one thing aimed at out of doors. Tess and Clare . . . ever balanced on the edge of a passion . . . were converging, under an irresistible law, as surely as two streams in one vale. (*TD*, p.168)

In a manner not unlike the 'mollusc' imagery in *The Return of the Native*, but with a sensual, pulsing emphasis upon the hidden springs of passion, Hardy evokes sexual readiness in both his young lovers. The warm, moist season, in which buds and stalks swell, stiffen, distend and dilate, is Tess's season as much as it is Angel's. The 'sapling' which had 'rooted down to a poisonous stratum on the spot of its sowing' is now 'transplanted to a deeper soil': 'physically and mentally' Tess burgeons into life, 'never in her recent life . . . so happy as she was now, possibly never . . . so happy again' (*TD*, p.168).

Hardy extends use of the analogical metaphor further to render implicit what he may not render explicit. Tess's most important erotic scene is the widely discussed 'Garden' scene. The suggestive imagery, symbolic setting and metaphorical action have all been variously interpreted as having their common referent in the Edenic myth, but it seems to me that Hardy has devised a deliberate parody. Tess never enters the garden; she remains on the outskirts from first to last, 'behind the hedge' in an uncultivated tract of land where apple trees grow untended (*TD*, p.161). There is no central tree set 'amidst' (as there is in 'Genesis'); rather, several trees are placed on the periphery and are patently 'uncovenanted'. Nor are they fruiting (knowledge); instead, they produce blossom (nescience). In keeping with the parody, the 'Edenic' roles of the central characters are inverted. It is 'Eve' who is lured 'like a fascinated bird' and 'Adam' who lures. Already 'fallen' in that his 'performance' is flawed, Angel sounds the seductive call-note that wanders 'in the still air with a stark quality like that of nudity' (*TD*, p.161), while Tess is drawn close to the 'Garden' yet remains withdrawn from it throughout. This emphasis suitably fulfils the promise of the subtitle, 'A Pure Woman Faithfully Presented'. There is no fall, for Tess, that renders her impure, just as there is nothing to render her impure by association. In Hardy's eyes (if not in Angel's), she remains beyond the boundary of sin-laden archetypes and man-made 'Gardens' of diabolism and sexual shame.

Hardy's focus is upon untended, unfettered Nature. Angel's harp-playing lures Tess out, not into a covenanted or cultivated (man-made) garden but into the raw wilderness. Drawn by the call of his harp through a 'profusion of growth' and into close proximity to the object of her passion, Tess listens 'like a fascinated bird' – mesmerised but at the same time 'winged' for flight:

> The outskirt of the garden in which Tess found herself had been left uncultivated for some years, and was now damp and rank with juicy grass which sent up mists of pollen at a touch; and with tall blooming weeds emitting offensive smells – weeds whose red and yellow and purple hues formed a polychrome as dazzling as that of cultivated flowers. She went stealthily as a cat through this profusion of growth, gathering cuckoo-spittle on her skirts, cracking snails that were underfoot, staining her hands with thistle-milk and slug-slime, and rubbing off upon her naked arms sticky blights which, though snow-white on the apple-tree trunks, made madder stains on her skin; thus she drew quite near to Clare, still unobserved of him. (*TD*, pp. 161–2)

The seductive moment for Tess, as she moves gradually closer to Angel, moves Hardy to hyphenate the world of nature that it might lean closer to her as she now assimilates her surroundings to her own consciousness. '-Milk', '-spittle', '-slime', 'sticky blights' – the mucosa and emissions of biological sex – 'rub off' upon Tess as much from the objects in nature which wet and stain her person, as from Hardy's linguistic hyphenations. With 'damp and rank ... juicy grass',[1] bursting pollen at a touch, and upward thrusting 'tall blooming weeds emitting offensive smells', there is no sense of a fastidious, antiseptic, deodorised sexuality in Tess's world. Pungently scented (as surely it should be), burning to the senses, hot in hue – 'red and yellow' and Virgilian 'purple' – the physical world Tess assimilates to her erotic consciousness is as unadulterated as her own 'pure' nature.[2]

Psychologically realistic, too, is the vivid rendering of attraction/repulsion sensations as Tess passes from the intimately physical, elemental wilderness to draw closer and closer to transcendental ecstasy. In her abandonment to the world of sensation, voluptuously gathering nature's secretions and mucosa upon her person – the generative fluids of 'sex' – so now she unleashes her passion:

Tess was conscious of neither time nor space. The exaltation which she had described as being producible at will by gazing at a star, came now without any determination of hers; she undulated upon the thin notes of the second-hand harp, and their harmonies passed like breezes through her, bringing tears into her eyes. The floating pollen seemed to be his notes made visible, and the dampness of the garden the weeping of the garden's sensibility. Though near nightfall, the rank-smelling weed-flowers glowed as if they would not close for intentness, and the waves of colour mixed with the waves of sound. (*TD*, p.162)

Reaching her plateau of sexual ecstasy Tess soars to such a pitch of intensity that tears spring to her eyes as, at the same time, the world of sight, colour and sound fuse and dissolve in her consciousness. Fully in keeping with the intensity of her female sensation, her alternating 'waves' of orgasmic dilation, so too the lush, vegetative 'weed-flowers glowed as if they would not close for intentness', as Tess now glows, 'her cheeks on fire' at Angel's approach. Suddenly feeling exposed, she draws off to a distance to utter herself in safe, circumlocutions. She speaks of the apple blossom falling and 'everything so green' – in detumescence drawing only the 'falling off' in nature to her consciousness. Fending off Angel's probings about her 'indoor fears', which are at this moment fears of over-exposure, she cannot help but feel that the very trees themselves have 'inquisitive eyes' (*TD*, p.163). Then, as she gathers that her sexual langour is not apparent to her lover, she waxes unselfconsciously philosophical and wanes to a wistfulness – to 'sad imaginings' – as if the melting ache that lingers on has phased to bitter-sweet, post-orgasmic *triste* (*TD*, p.163).

Hardy's sensitive exposition of Tess in sexual ecstasy, the candour and poetic truthfulness of the evocation, gives forcible physical expression to a sexual consciousness refreshingly unvarnished, unprettified, and nowhere sanctified or trivialised to a delicate niceness. Ecstatic to the point of tears, Tess emerges as 'pure' as the unbound wilderness, with which she is in complete accord. As its most vital centre of energy, she absorbs, indeed celebrates, all its exuding essences, forces, sensations with a joy that the original Eve, assimilated not to nature but to man's moral law, is denied.

Sexual passion actively informs Tess's consciousness, her wisdom, her moral sense, her emotional generosity. By the same token, her heightened sensibilities kindle in her the purity of feeling which sees fit, on the one hand, to abjure the father of her child because she does not love him, and on the other, to repudiate a heaven that has no place for a newborn infant's unbaptised soul. Far from being a passive victim, Tess embodies a fierce impulse to self-determination against daunting, and ultimately insurmountable, odds.

From her repudiation of an ethic which says she should play the hard-to-get Beauty in order to win her rich 'cousin' into providing for his poor relations, to her final execution of that same violating, vulgarising 'cousin', the mutinous Tess's least impulse is to suffer-and-be-still. Is it in fact a passive Tess who, as is frequently claimed, connives at her own fate by falling asleep at the wrong moment? Textual evidence does not support this claim. The drowsy Tess is, in every respect, a thoroughly *exhausted* Tess, and Hardy takes pains to elicit in detail the sheer expenditure of energy and unremitting fatigue she endures in her efforts to keep body and soul together – her family's as well as her own.

Hardy's emphasis is upon a physical, active Tess from the very outset. Affiliated to a 'votive sisterhood', remarkable, we are told, for its survival – 'either the natural shyness of the softer sex, or a sarcastic attitude on the part of male relatives, had denuded such women's clubs as remained ... of ... their glory and consummation' (*TD*, p.40) – Tess is first seen in procession with the 'sisterhood' through the village of Marlott, whom she joins later 'with a certain zest in the dancing' until dusk (*TD*, p.46). Disturbed though, by 'the incident of her father's odd appearance' (*TD*, p.46), she decides she should return home, whereupon she takes charge of her siblings, 'six helpless creatures' in 'the Durbeyfield ship' (*TD*, p.51). Eventually she retires to bed at eleven o'clock only to be awakened one-and-a-half hours later to undertake the family's marketing requirements (*TD*, p.57). That the sixteen-year-old girl should then doze off on her journey is the most natural, the most inevitable consequence. It is not symptomatic of an innate passivity, or, as has also been claimed, a tendency to drift; nor does it demonstrate Hardy's idealisation of a somnambulistic, sexually inert female consciousness.[3] If anything emerges from his treatment of this episode, it is not that Tess sleeps at an inappropriate moment but that she suffers an appropriation of her sleep!

The labour/woman exploitative, machine-grinding world in *Tess*, its exhausting demands closely linked at salient points throughout the text to Tess's beleaguered states of being, is quite clearly a causal factor in her tragedy: the taxing demands upon her energy and resilience have immediate, palpably felt repercussions upon her faculties. Hardy's most potent emblematic image in this context is, of course, the 'red tyrant that the women had come to serve ... which kept a despotic demand upon the endurance of their muscles and nerves' (*TD*, p.372).

The 'buzzing red glutton', remorselessly grinding, bears a suggestive resemblance to the lusty Alec; man and machine alike reduce Tess to physical exhaustion and mental stupefaction:

A panting ache ran through the rick ... (Tess) ... still stood at her post, her flushed and perspiring face coated with the corn-dust, and her white bonnet embrowned by it. She was the only woman whose place was upon the machine so as to be shaken bodily by its spinning, and the decrease of the stack now separated her from Marian and Izz, and prevented their changing duties with her as they had done. The incessant quivering, in which every fibre of her frame participated, had thrown her into a stupefied reverie in which her arms worked on independently of her consciousness.[4] (*TD*, pp.380–1)

This condition of physical exhaustion inducing mental fatigue and stupefaction should not be confused with the transcendence Tess herself induces, in which she retains a sense of self, sensation and energy.

'I don't know about ghosts,' she was saying; 'but I do know that our souls can be made to go outside our bodies when we are alive.'

'A very easy way to feel 'em go,' continued Tess, 'is to lie on the grass at night and look straight up at some big bright star; and, by fixing your mind upon it, you will soon find that you are hundreds

and hundreds o' miles away from your body, which you don't want
at all'. (*TD*, p.158)

Tess's facility for transcendence, for summoning what is commonly known as an 'out-of-body' experience, is an act of will,
and not coextensive, as Mary Jacobus suggests, with the stupefied reverie of her exhaustion in labour, 'as close to sleep – to
unconsciousness – as is compatible with going about her work'.[5]
Tess in transcendence is not stupefied, not comatose. Quite the
reverse. She remains in full possession of all her faculties. She
assimilates to her consciousness the larger world of nature, its
sounds, odours, its very essences, expanding, not contracting
sensory experience, possessing, not being possessed. In such a
moment of great intensity, time too is suspended. Elsewhere
aware of how little the individual is able to control her own
existence, which is ever subject to the dictates of time and
circumstance, Tess in transcendental ecstasy suspends both.
Expanding time to fit her own 'space', her private world of
inner sensation intensified by mental transcendence to reach
beyond corporeal bounds, Tess effortlessly shapes the spatial/
temporal world to suit her own needs and desires.

It is to the life of the sensations, the intimate life of feminine
sensations, that Hardy devotes his time and attention in this
novel. The more complex and varied the evocation of these
sensations, the more immediate and palpable they become for
the reader. Hence, in allowing for the full expression of Tess's
surging psycho-erotic drives, Hardy also extends to her narrative time – time to utter, as it were, physically (as in the
'Garden' episode) the powers she had previously uttered vocally
(as above). In neither instance does he marginalise her experience by edging it into paraphrasis or reported speech: Tess
utters herself sensuously, self-expressively – by word and by
gesture, actively. Dramatic action invites visualisation. It has
impact and immediacy. Dialogue invites an exchange of ideas.
It has a confiding intimacy. Hardy offers his reader both.
Tess in transcendental bliss, then, gives free expression to that
'precious life' of which Hardy speaks but chooses not to confine
to cryptic symbol or enigmatic profile.[6]

There is plentiful evidence of an openly expressed and
expressive sexual consciousness in Tess that testifies, without

further need of justification, to her capacity to utter her sexuality lucidly, though not, of course, in the verbal sense. This would be entirely implausible for the Victorian heroine deprived, as were her sisters in life, of a lexical means of expressing sexuality. Tess utters herself by means of physical action, which in terms of sexual responsiveness most aptly articulates authentic erotic 'utterance'.[7]

The Tess perceived by Hardy is a sentient, physical being inhabiting a palpably physical world. And her capitulation to Alec, in 'The Chase', is the uttermost expression of this physicality. She is quite simply exhausted. Hardy leads up to this episode describing, in detail, the hard material fact of life as it is lived, for Tess: the miles she walks, the meals she goes without, the hours she works, the sleep she lacks, the moments of repose she is denied.

We are told, for example, that upon this particular fateful day Tess's 'occupations made her late' in setting out upon her three mile walk to Chaseborough (*TD*, p.95). From this we infer that her employers, the d'Urbervilles, who have appointed her 'supervisor, purveyor, nurse, surgeon and friend' to their 'community of fowls' (*TD*, p.88), require her to labour on Saturdays. Firmly entrenched then, in an everyday world of work, Tess walks the three miles to Chaseborough. She makes her market purchases, and then sets out to find her companions for the night walk home. While she waits for their barn-dancing to conclude, Alec intervenes and Hardy takes this opportunity to focus upon her physical condition:

> She looked round, and saw the red coal of a cigar: Alec d'Urberville was standing there alone. He beckoned to her, and she reluctantly retreated towards him. 'Well, my Beauty, what are you doing here?' She was so tired after her long day and her walk that she confided her trouble to him – that she had been waiting ever since he saw her to have their company home, because the road at night was strange to her. (*TD*, p.97)

Feeling, wearily, that her companions 'will never leave off', Tess decides she can bear to wait no longer. Alec offers to hire a trap and drive her home but despite pangs of hunger and fatigue, and the lateness of the hour, she had 'never quite got over her original mistrust of him' – so she turns down his offer.[8] Frequently infuriated, but rarely cavalier with her feelings of pride and assertions of self-will, Alec departs with the half-approving retort: 'Very well, Miss Independence. Please yourself ... '(*TD*, p.98). Shortly afterwards Tess sets off with her companions upon 'a three-mile walk, along a dry white road', and if Hardy evokes a hazy consciousness here, it is quite appropriately on behalf of the inebriates: they follow the road, 'with a sensation that they were soaring along in a supporting medium ... as sublime as the moon and stars above them' (*TD*, p.98). For Tess, by contrast, there is only hard physical reality: 'The discovery of their condition spoilt the pleasure she was beginning to feel in the moonlight journey' (*TD*, p.99). Then, following an imbroglio with the lusty Car Darch and her equally lusty compeers, Tess is provoked to a vituperative assault upon 'whorage', which leaves her 'almost ready to faint, so vivid was her sense of the crisis' (*TD*, p.101). At this point Alec reappears. Tess accepts his offer of escape and instantly gets 'shot of the screaming cars in a jiffy!' – as he crudely puts it (*TD*, p.100).

They engage briefly in a conversation that devolves not upon Tess's passive emotions but upon her feelings of anger; and from this focus upon her emotional 'burning' to her 'burnt-out' physical energies Hardy swiftly moves:

She was inexpressibly weary. She had risen at five o'clock every morning that week, had been on foot the whole of each day, and on this evening had in addition walked the three miles to Chaseborough, waited three hours for her neighbours without eating or drinking, her impatience to start them preventing either; she had then walked a mile of the way home, and had undergone the excitement of the quarrel, till, with the slow progress of their steed, it was now nearly one o'clock. Only once, however, was she overcome by actual drowsiness. In that moment of oblivion her head sank gently against him. (*TD*, p.104)

Alec naturally takes advantage of this moment. Reining in he encloses 'her waist with his arms to support her', whereupon, alert and defensive, Tess springs up and 'with one of those sudden impulses to reprisal to which she was liable she [gives] him a little push' (*TD*, p.104), and almost precipitates him into the road.

This is not dumb, passive yielding but self-determined, volatile resistance. Nevertheless, Tess is unspeakably weary. Thus, when the couple find themselves lost, with Alec's connivance, she is bedded down upon the leaves he has prepared for her and, tenderly buttoned into his overcoat for warmth, instantly falls asleep. Sleeping her body is appropriated:

Why was it that upon this beautiful feminine tissue, sensitive as gossamer, and practically blank as snow as yet, there should have been traced a coarse pattern as it was doomed to receive; why so often the coarse appropriates the finer thus ... (*TD*, p.107)

Hardy's word is 'appropriates'. The act is an act of theft, a dishonest appropriation of another's property with the intent to deprive her of it permanently. The term suffices to denote the moral nature of the act, which passes beyond sexual assault to take account of violation of rightful ownership. It is a fitting emphasis in a novel that stresses a sexual ethic that denies woman the right to control not only her own mode of existence but also her own body.

A close critical reading of 'The Chase' episode reveals a clear, untrammelled vision and an uncomfortably close focus upon this moment, for Tess, of harsh, sexual reality.[9] Hardy summons, with characteristic economy, an evocative symbolic setting, the woodland ceiling that would be, in the event, Tess's perspective: 'Above them rose the primeval yews and oaks of the Chase, in which were poised gentle roosting birds in their last nap' (*TD*, p.107). Beneath the upward-thrusting trunks and poised gentle birds a sleeping girl is ravished. Hardy's world is not clearly lit, it is spot-lit. Its spatial proportions are wide and clear (unlike Alec's, which are befogged), and its temporal focus upon the 'last nap' of the 'poised gentle roosting birds', which is by transference the gentle girl's last sleep as a virgin, is as comprehensive as it is percipient. Closely detailed too, is Hardy's account of Alec's act of penetration, the 'coarse pattern' he *traces* upon Tess's 'beautiful feminine tissue'. Expressing at once the notion of an imprint which will, at length, take the form of the infant Sorrow (trace to, father upon), as well as the sense of a tracking (tracing) object, which Alec does, of course, become, there is also the suggestion of phallic interdigitation or tracer's probe 'rooting-out' unpenetrated, hidden recesses. And finally there is Hardy's empathetic sense of Tess's experience of excoriation, the coarse scoring of her 'gossamer tissue'. The emphasis is rightly on the physical:

Tess will almost certainly bear the aching smarts of her defloration for some days, given her immaturity and sexual unpreparedness.

Tess, then, is maid no more. Some weeks later, discovering that she is pregnant, she packs her belongings and leaves. And it is at this point that Hardy draws attention to her facility for uttering sexual feeling and meaning, quite lucidly, with little more than a gesture. Alec has followed, and caught up with her along the road, but fails to persuade her to return. Needled, he demands a kiss, whereupon Tess openly insults him by turning her head 'in the same passive way, as one might turn at the request of a sketcher or hairdresser'. Alec's frustration at her mockery of his needs turns swiftly to hurt and despondency:

'You don't give me your mouth and kiss me back. You never willingly do that – you'll never love me, I fear'. (*TD*, p.113)

As he knows only too well, Tess's mannered sufferance of his kiss tells of a strongly repressed antagonism, a refusal to yield to his desire. She had rested her eyes, we are told, 'vaguely . . . upon the remotest trees in the land while the kiss was given, as though she were nearly unconscious of what he did' (*TD*, p.113). Repression is not submission. 'The essence of repression', says Freud, 'lies simply in turning something away . . . keeping it at a distance from the conscious.'[10] Tess's subtly expressive gestures and posture describe this psychological condition exactly! Distancing unwanted sexual advances she is simultaneously fully aware of how best she may repel them. There is, in passive resistance of this kind, deliberate, conscious rebellion and considerable self-control. Authentic passivity exerts no such controls.

All women, wrote J.S. Mill:

are brought up from their earliest years in the belief that the ideal of character is the very opposite to that of men; not self-will and self-government by self-control, but submission, and yielding to the control of others.[11]

All women are not Tess. Alec may have appropriated her body but her spirit remains self-governing and unyielding. Depression and despair do, even so, subdue her as she silently dwells upon her relationship with her 'cousin' and his 'trace' now enlarging in her body. But anger flames quickly enough as he renews his attempt to appropriate the 'self' she actively, persistently withholds:

She resumed – 'I didn't understand your meaning till it was too late.' 'That's what every woman says.' 'How can you dare to use such words!' she cried, turning impetuously upon him, her eyes flashing as the latent spirit (of which he was to see more some day) awoke in her. 'My God! I could knock you out of the gig! Did it never strike your mind that what every woman says some women may feel?' (*TD*, p.112)

'Dare', 'flashing', 'spirit', 'knock you out', 'strike'. Hardy's perception of the rebounding Tess shapes his language most tellingly to elicit active, physical impulses. She resists possession of her person with 'katabolic'[12] rage in defiance of Alec's attempt to gain dominion over her by undermining her utterances and reducing them to 'Everywoman' triviality.

Tess abjures the father of her child because she does not love him and will not submit to a conventional solution to her predicament: 'I have never really loved you, and I think I never can.' Then, rather mournfully,

'Perhaps, of all things a lie on this thing would do the most good to me now; but I have honour enough left, little as 'tis, not to tell that lie. If I did love you I may have the best o' causes for letting you know it. But I don't.' (*TD*, p.113)

Alec clearly does not take her meaning, but then Tess's purposeful ambiguities and cutting closure resist such a taking.

Here as elsewhere Tess throws down the gauntlet openly to challenge Alec to a battle of wills. In yet more maddened fury, she would fling it in his face. Tracking her to the arid chalklands of Flintcomb Ash, he first gibes and taunts to rouse her but then resorts to more subtle, and we sense, genuinely sympathetic overtures:

'Tess ... I don't like you to be working like this, and I have come on purpose for you. You say you have a husband who is not I. Well, perhaps you have; but I've never seen him, and you've not told me his name; and altogether he seems rather a mythological personage. However, even if you have one, I think I am nearer to you than he is. I, at any rate, try to help you out of trouble, but he does not, bless his invisible face!.... Tess, my trap is waiting just under the hill, and darling mine, not his! – you know the rest.' (*TD*, p.378)

Poor Tess. It is a melting speech. But to Alec's alarm, she rises to a 'dull crimson fire'. Hastily, he tried a different approach. A little moral coercion:

'You have been the cause of my backsliding,' he continued, stretching his arm towards her waist; 'you should be willing to share it, and leave that mule you call husband for ever.'

One of her leather gloves, which she had taken off to eat her skimmer-cake, lay in her lap, and without the slightest warning she passionately swung the glove by the gauntlet directly in his face. It was heavy and thick as a warrior's, and it struck him flat on the mouth.... A scarlet oozing appeared ... (*TD*, pp.378–9)

Intensely alert, as always, Tess now resists a more violent confrontation as Alec 'fiercely' starts up. She too springs up, but immediately sinks down again to dare him to hit her:

'Now, punish me!' she said, turning up her eyes to him with the hopeless defiance of the sparrow's gaze before its captor twists its neck. 'Whip me, crush me; you need not mind those people under the rick! I shall not cry out. Once victim, always victim – that's the law!' (*TD*, p.379)

Tess knows her man. Just as earlier she had returned to him a passive-insulting 'other' cheek, so now she returns to him 'hopeless defiance', daring him to an action he cannot perform because she has shifted an emotional confrontation to a level of mocking near-melodrama, which clearly he cannot meet in all its staginess. Tess's power over him surpasses the narrowly sexual. She knows full well that it is not just her yielding body he would own. He must and will claim her unyielding spirit, the spirit she will only yield to him in a travesty of submission by returning to him a docile, pathetic face, a face mocking, choking his needs. Bridled and aggravated, he departs.

Finding her shortly afterwards so 'whipped' and 'crushed', so utterly exhausted from her labours that she has not even the strength to speak above an 'underbreath', 'weak as a bled calf', Alec holds her with respect and kind regard (*TD*, pp.382–3). But, evidently, forcing her into submission in her inert, enervated condition would not now meet his psycho-sexual needs. The Tess he deeply desires, the woman he genuinely wants to possess, was not claimed in 'The Chase': unyielding to the last, flinging gauntlets, slamming casements (*TD*, p.404), and finally

knifing the heart that tirelessly tracks her, Tess's resistance –
passive and active – knows no bounds, other than those set by
her own will and self-responsibility.

This then is the self-determined girl whose instinct is to
dismiss the past, tread it out, put it out (*TD*, p.234)

The past was past; whatever it had been it was no more at hand.
(*TD*, p.126)

To escape the past and all that appertained thereto was to annihilate
it, and to do that she would have to get away. (*TD*, p.135)

It was impossible that any event should have left upon her an
impression that was not capable of transmutation. (*TD*, p.140)

But how to annihilate the past and make new the day, when,
in the form of Alec, it becomes very much 'at hand'? More
important still, how to transmute and actualise a renewed 'self'
from the self the world has appropriated and labelled as fallen?
One of Tess's greatest psychological dilemmas, from her first
encounters with Alec to her last enactment of the cashmere-
wrapped, 'embroidered' kept-woman, lies in resisting classification. To Alec she is Everywoman and Eve-temptress. To
Angel, predictably, she is first stereotypal Goddess and later
stereotypal fallen woman: 'ill', 'unformed', and 'crude' (*TD*,
pp.272–81). To Hardy, though, she is complex, diverse, unique:
fierce and gentle, regenerative and destructive, trusting and
suspicious, philosophical, mystical and sexy. Accordingly, in
her momentary drift into a frame of mind that passively accepts
the dueness of Nemesis, Hardy discovers in her a complex
interaction of passive and active impulses:

Tess had drifted into a frame of mind which accepted passively the
consideration that if she should have to burn for what she had done,
burn she must, and there was an end of it. (*TD*, p.128)

Notice how Tess's passive frame of mind is countermanded here
with a strong, active tonicity: the decisive, self-willed 'and
there was an end of it'. Significantly, this phrase resounds with
internal echoes of her own quickened articulations, whereas
'drifted into a passive frame of mind' has no ring of Tess about
it at all. Notice too, how her deliberations are imbued with raw
elemental energy: 'if she should have to burn ... then burn she
must.'

This strong, active impulse in Tess to confront the past, to put an end to it, and to make new the day, urges Hardy to structure her story in such a way as to reflect both her regenerative powers, her rebounding will to act, and her physical, sexual powers of revitalisation. In replacing the customary literary demarcation, 'Book', with 'Phase' ('Phase the First', 'Phase the Second', and so on), Hardy places a rhythmic, periodic accent upon her story. This mirrors her capacity for transmutation, as it also mirrors her cyclical feminine life. The shedding-of-blood phases appropriately reflect her biological cycle in that they occur at regular intervals throughout the book and are closely associated with the beginning or ending of a period in her life. But the 'Phase' demarcation of periodic changes signifies more than this, to encompass, in fact, Tess's will to self-renewal – as, for example, in the 'fly' and 'baptism' sequences. Having developmental links with the baptism scene in 'Phase the Second', the later 'fly' sequence, in 'Phase the Third', marks a stage in Tess's transition from familial dependency to independence; her second, greater move from home into the world.

Tess has determined to 'escape the past and ... get away' (*TD*, p.135). Accordingly, Hardy offers her a new landscape, a journey, and the challenge of altered perspectives as she traverses unfamiliar terrain. From the enclosed, familiar world of family and Marlott she moves out into the new and strange, where Hardy's 'spatial images of boundary and enclosure'[13] – the 'curve of the hill' over Marlott's 'interior tract of land' 'engirdled' by railways – are replaced with a 'world drawn to a larger pattern' (*TD*, pp.138,139). Focus now rests upon Tess's desire for transmutation. First, contemplating the 'environs of Kingsbere', parish of her ancestors, she repudiates her d'Urberville forebears: 'I have as much of mother as father in me!' 'She had', Hardy says, 'no admiration for them now.'

She almost hated them for the dance they had led her; not a thing of all theirs did she retain but the old seal and spoon. (*TD*, p.139)

Then, caught between two worlds, the old and the new, Tess now becomes 'not quite sure of her direction'; and it is at this most appropriate juncture, as she feels herself to be lost, that her author also 'loses sight' of her:

Tess stood still upon the hemmed expanse of verdant flatness, like a
fly on a billiard-table of indefinite length, and of no more
consequence to the surroundings than that fly. (*TD*, p.142)

In observing Tess from this distance, as a desolate figure in the
vastness – the unknown she now confronts – Hardy deliberately
introduces a note of dislocation. The sudden sense of Tess's
insignificance, and of her author's remote stance combine to
create a disquieting unease. Tess seems horribly abandoned!
This passage unnerves Hardy readers, as insistent critical
references to it demonstrate. But it is meant to unsettle us, to
arouse in us strong caring, even indignant, feelings.

The baptism and 'fly' scenes are devised, in fact, to provoke
entirely different sets of responses. In the 'fly' sequence we are
urged to sense Tess's frightening new feeling of strangeness,
alienation and loss as she embarks on her new phase – eventually
to arrive at Talbothays. In the baptism sequence we are invited
to perceive something of her powers of spiritual regeneration,
her capacity to utter herself new and free from guilt.

The baptism sequence occurs in Tess's shortest Phase,
'Maiden No More', and an important aspect of Hardy's presentation here is that her witnesses are a congregation of young
children: Tess is described as she would appear through the
eyes of a small child. This perspective is important to Hardy's
emphasis here upon innocence. Tess's defiant act of baptising
her illegitimate child, seen through the eyes of innocents, is
the purest act of grace and loving-kindness. Whether or not
Christian orthodoxy would deem her act sacrilegious, is to
Hardy irrelevant. The relevance lies simply in innocence speaking to innocence, child-mother to child-son, before an audience
of innocent children.

In the first instance, the focus is upon Tess's big words, big
gestures (she 'fervently drew an immense cross upon the baby
with her forefinger'). This emphasis clearly indicates an open-
eyed, open-mouthed audience. In keeping with this perspective,
the minister of the sacrament/big sister Tess towers hugely,
whitely, in her nightgown, an imposing figure in the eyes of her
tiny, uncomprehending attendants. In addition, this sighting
takes into account her actual physical condition: a work-worn
girl-mother with tousled hair, weary eyes, and stubble-scratches

on her wrists. Clearly, Hardy has not lost sight of the flesh-and-blood Tess even as child-like wonder infuses the scene with a sense of the marvellous – a half-ignorant, essentially open-eyed attempt to grasp the seemingly incomprehensible. Tess takes up her ministerial role:

'SORROW, I baptize thee in the name of the Father, and of the Son, and of the Holy Ghost.'

She sprinkled the water, and there was silence.

'Say "Amen", children.'

The tiny voices piped in obedient response 'Amen!'

Tess went on:

'We receive this child' – and so forth – 'and do sign him with the sign of the Cross.'

Here she dipped her hand into the basin, and fervently drew an immense cross upon the baby with her forefinger, continuing with the customary sentences as to his manfully fighting against sin, the world, and the devil, and being a faithful soldier and servant unto his life's end. She duly went on with the Lord's Prayer, the children lisping it after her in a thin gnat-like wail, till, at the conclusion, raising their voices to clerk's pitch, they again piped into the silence, 'Amen!' (*TD*, pp. 130–1)

As emblematic rite, baptism objectifies sin and guilt and enacts the release of the forces of darkness. Tess invokes this rite and utters the words of redemption over her child. Thus empowered to utter the spirit clean and new, the fallen woman/minister-of-the-sacrament is quite openly vindicated by her author. She cannot logically fulfil both roles. The one invalidates the other. Religious objections can scarcely be raised against the fittingness of her desire to mediate between Heaven and Hell, salvation and damnation, to anoint redemption upon the object of her 'sin' (permissible, if 'Romish' practice), for according to received doctrine no repentant believer is held to be irredeemable, and that has to include Tess in her 'ecstasy of faith' (*TD*, p. 131). In a sense, then, she utters her own redemption, for as surely as her 'fall' stains (in Victorian eyes), so the blessings she invokes as consecrator of the sacrament effect a token cleansing of her soul.

(Tess) with much augmented confidence in the efficacy of this sacrament, poured forth from the bottom of her heart the thanksgiving that follows, uttering it boldly and triumphantly in the stopt-diapason note which her voice acquired when her heart was in her speech, and which will never be forgotten by those who knew her. The ecstasy of faith almost apotheosized her; it set upon her face a glowing irradiation, and brought a red spot into the middle of each cheek; while the miniature candle-flame inverted in her eye-pupils shone like a diamond. (*TD*, p.131)

Hardy does not, however, intend this scene merely to 'carry' Tess into spirituality, into saintly transfiguration.[14] Rather, she turns church ritual and dogma to her own advantage and subverts both. First, Hardy introduces the subversive element with the lightly mocking comment that,

Poor Sorrow's campaign against sin, the world, and the devil was doomed to be of limited brilliancy ... (*TD*, p.131)

Then Tess, too, is sceptical:

In the daylight ... she felt her terrors about his soul to have been somewhat exaggerated; whether well founded or not she had no uneasiness now, reasoning that if Providence would not ratify such an act of approximation she, for one, did not value the kind of heaven lost by the irregularity – either for herself or her child. (*TD*, p.131)

With Tess's defiant afterthought echoing the comment on the infant Sorrow's 'campaign against sin, the world, and the devil', it becomes evident that Hardy is paying mere lip-service to an observance of Christian doctrine on the one hand, as do the lisping innocents, and making a mockery of it on the other. The concept of a sin-laden Tess and a sin-laden Sorrow is clearly risible in his eyes. Irony and scepticism point to his scorn of a cultural ideology that fosters, under the mantle of Christianity, both the myth of the fallen woman's guilt and the guilt of unbaptised innocents.[15]

Nina Auerbach points out that Hardy's Tess 'seems vindicated by her narrator from having fallen at all ... her affinities with burgeoning nature, her incorrigible will to renewal and joy seem to exempt her from the fallen woman's guilt and sorrow'.[16]

Hardy's vindication of Tess is unequivocal. He does not 'seem' to exempt her from the fallen woman's guilt but commits himself wholeheartedly to her exemption. She will and must triumph over a deterministic cultural prescription that would deny her ascendancy, both sexual and moral, after her fall. She has not earned but, rather, learned the guilt and sorrow, and Hardy (if not Angel Clare), is convinced, not only of her purity but also of her capacity for ascendancy.

In her sacramental cleansing of the infant Sorrow's guilt Tess enacts her own desire to liberate the innocent soul from damnation, to 'bury' guilt and sorrow purged of all stain. Her mediating powers kindle, in turn, her own spiritual regeneration, which, following an interregnum, a time for changing from 'simple girl to complex woman' (*TD*, p.135), urges her upon departure, upon a new phase, a new life.

The woman who usurps the male minister's role, who utters her own form of baptism, gives powerful voice to her longing to govern, to control her own existence.[17] There are echoes of this will to self-determination and self-renewal in her repudiation of her dark ancestry. But a closer parallel may be found in her insistence, to Angel, upon use of her baptismal name. Repudiating pseudonymity, she quietly asserts her own identity when Angel would condense her to a type.

She was no longer the milkmaid, but a visionary essence of woman – a whole sex condensed into one typical form. He called her Artemis, Demeter, and other fanciful names half teasingly, which she did not like because she did not understand them. (*TD*, p.170)

Re-naming, like wrong-naming, stirs a startling, if fleeting, non-recognition of self; and even if Tess had understood Angel's fanciful names she would have liked them no better for condensing her 'into one typical form'; just as she had earlier balked at Alec's depersonalising 'Everywoman' ascription. Drawing Angel away from 'visionary essences' and pseudonyms she now asks him to use her baptismal name: ' "Call me Tess" she would say askance; and he did' (*TD*, p.170). Repudiating pseudonymity, she seeks at once to 'cleanse' him of his illusive vision of her and to resist his appropriation, by renaming, of her person.

Cocooned in his fanciful world, Angel can scarcely conceive of a Tess brought into being without his creation: first he raises a pedestal and denominates her Goddess, then lowers it, renaming her an 'unconstrained' child of nature (*TD*, p.214), and finally he fashions her the unformed creature that he alone will endow with existence. He will give her his name and a new identity, his books to change her into a 'well read woman' (*TD*, pp.230–1), and he will carry her off as his property into the bargain (*TD*, p.244). She will, he says, depend 'for her happiness entirely upon him' (*TD*, p.237). Proposing marriage, Angel outlines his plans to Tess:

'I wish to ask you something of a very practical nature. . . . I shall soon want to marry, and, being a farmer, you see I shall require for my wife a woman who knows all about the management of farms. Will you be that woman, Tessy?' (*TD*, p.211)

'He put it in that way', Hardy says, 'that she might not think he had yielded to an impulse of which his head would disapprove.' The emotional economy of the proposal shapes Tess's response:

She had bowed to the inevitable result of proximity, the necessity of loving him; but she had not calculated upon this sudden corollary, which, indeed, Clare had put before her without quite meaning himself to do it so soon. With pain that was like the bitterness of dissolution she murmured the words of her indispensable and sworn answer as an honourable woman.
   'O Mr Clare – I cannot be your wife – I cannot be!'
   The sound of her own decision seemed to break Tess's very heart, and she bowed her face in her grief. (*TD*, p.211)

In a manner of speaking, Angel's premature proposal outlining the shape of things to come excludes Tess from his world. Had she not cause enough already, to prefer an alternative way of life over the bourgeois marriage he holds out, she might well have felt the 'bitterness of dissolution', in smaller measure, just the same.
   Angel is incredulous:

'Do you say no? Surely you love me?'
   'O yes, yes! And I would rather be yours than anybody's in the world,' returned the sweet and honest voice of the distressed girl. 'But I *cannot* marry you! . . . I don't want to marry! I have not thought of doing it. I cannot! I only want to love you'. (*TD*, p.212)

Angel cannot take this seriously. These are 'the dallyings of coyness', he tells himself, after all she has 'permitted him to make love to her' (*TD*, p.215). Tess, however, has been harbouring slightly different expectations, love-making being here more often accepted inconsiderately and for its own sweet sake than in the carking anxious homes of the ambitious, where a girl's craving for an establishment paralyses her healthy thought of a passion as an end. (*TD*, p.215)

This ideological gap between passion 'for its own sweet sake' and 'passion as an end', which points, on the one hand, to Tess's unconditional 'I only want to love you' and, on the other, to Angel's need for a suitable wife, suggests just how far Tess has come to a sense of her own autonomy and self-hood. Just as she will actively resist Alec to the very end, defying him with passive-resistance, mocking her own victim role, so her 'healthy passions' actively flow for their 'own sweet sake' and are by no means 'paralysed' by ambitions to marry. Thus the ideological gap, later to split the love-bond, now begins to make itself felt.

She has reason enough, after all, to suppose that loving could be an end itself. Not only have Angel's 'resolutions, reticences, prudences, fears' fallen back 'like a defeated battalion', but his ardent leaps to embrace her at unexpected moments openly demonstrate as much:

He jumped from his seat, and, leaving his pail to be kicked over if the milcher had such a mind, went quickly towards the desire of his eyes, and kneeling down beside her, clasped her in his arms.

Tess was taken completely by surprise, and she yielded to his embrace with unreflecting inevitableness. Having seen that it was really her lover who had advanced, and no one else, her lips parted, and she sank upon him in her momentary joy, with something very like an ecstatic cry. (*TD*, p.191) He stepped forward.... 'Dear, darling Tessy!' he whispered, putting his arm round her, and his face to her flushed cheek. 'Don't, for Heaven's sake, Mister me any more. I have hastened back so soon because of you!'

Tess's excitable heart beat against his by way of reply; and there they stood ... as he held her tightly to his breast.... At first she would not look straight up at him, but her eyes soon lifted, and his plumbed the deepness of the ever-varying pupils, with their radiating fibrils of blue, and black, and gray, and violet, while she regarded him as Eve at her second waking might have regarded Adam. (*TD*, p.210)

As the Eve of Genesis, at her second waking, regards Adam in his 'nakedness', so, too, Tess is seeing Angel in full erotic aware-ness of his sexuality – her 'ever-varying pupils' no doubt dilating as Angel plumbs their depths, as arousal intensifies with gazing.

Partly disabused, with Tess's aid, of his phantasmas and rarefied visions, Angel now perceives her 'real vitality, real warmth, real incarnation' (*TD*, p.190), but he still cannot credit her with an existence out of his power and control. Her refusal to marry him, he tells himself, tallies well enough with what he knows of women:

his experience of women was great enough for him to be aware that the negative often meant nothing more than the preface to the affirmative. (*TD*, p.215)

What experience of women? His near entrapment 'by a woman much older than himself' from whom he had 'escaped not greatly the worse for the experience' (*TD*, p.155)? Or his 'experience' of Mercy Chant perhaps? Falling into platitudes betrays ignorance and prejudice, but Angel, unaware of this, and rather taken with his own worldly-wisdom, assumes a lofty air:

At such times as this, apprehending the grounds of her refusal to be her modest sense of incompetence in matters social and polite, he would say that she was wonderfully well-informed and versatile – which was certainly true, her natural quickness, and her admiration for him, having led her to pick up his vocabulary, his accent, and fragments of his knowledge, to a surprising extent. (*TD*, p.216)

To a surprising extent Angel too has become wonderfully improved: he is awakened and sensitised to 'the aesthetic, sensuous, pagan pleasure in natural life and lush womanhood' aroused in him by Tess (*TD*, p.199), though what her influence might reveal about him never enters his thoughts.

In her natural lover's empathy, Tess risks suffering his imprint to trace itself upon her, albeit less tangibly than Alec's. Yet, even as outwardly she picks up his accent, vocabulary and fragments of his knowledge, inwardly she struggles with an emotional tumult of which he knows nothing, as she keeps at bay 'gloom, doubt, fear, moodiness, care, shame', which were 'waiting like wolves just outside the circumscribing light'. She had, Hardy writes, 'long spells of power to keep them in hungry subjection there' (*TD*, pp.236,237). And it is her power to keep anxiety and fear in subjection, even while yielding to the influence of the beloved, that urges her to act. She will, and must, govern inner conflict, just as she will and must exercise courage and daring in her desire for Angel. And does. Proving herself less than passive in her erotic passion,

She clasped his neck, and for the first time Clare learnt what an impassioned woman's kisses were like upon the lips of one whom she loved with all her heart and soul, as Tess loved him. (*TD*, p.231)

Later Tess recounts her wedding-night story with the same rebounding courage, 'without flinching', without shame (*TD*, p.268). 'No exculpatory phrase of any kind' enters her account, we are told. She does not even weep (*TD*, p.270). Angel is shocked beyond measure, shocked at her self-possession, at her lack of remorse for her ruin, at her lack of self-pity or self-abasement. It is he, instead, who withers and cowers. In the moment of 'fall', it is he who passively yields to emotional conflict, fear and shock.

Hardy vividly dramatises Angel's moral weakness, his fall from being the caring lover who had sworn to 'love and cherish and defend her under any conditions, changes, charges, or revelations' (*TD*, p.223), by charging and changing the world of external objects, which now becomes the mirror to Angel's nature. His mockery of a philosophy to which he had sworn allegiance – the moral reconstruction of an erstwhile Pauline ethic (*TD*, p.154) and a turn to the communistic life (*TD*, p.179) – now becomes a mockery of both the marriage vow and the woman to whom he has pledged his troth. For Tess exemplifies the very humanitarian philosophy he had sought to embrace. The world Angel repudiates now 'mocks' and is 'mocked':

The complexion even of external things seemed to suffer transmutation as her pronouncement progressed. The fire in the grate looked impish – demoniacally funny, as if it did not care in the least about her strait. The fender grinned idly.... All material objects around announced their irresponsibility with terrible iteration. (*TD*, p.270)

Angel casts a 'Last Day' judgement upon Tess just as his father and forefathers would have done before him. 'Imagination' says Hardy, 'might have beheld a Last Day luridness in this red-coaled glow', as the now-fallen Angel performs the 'irrelevant act of stirring the fire ... stirring the embers', as he leaps demonically to his feet with 'horrible laughter, as unnatural and ghastly as a laugh in hell' – brutally to disown the woman he had earlier set his mind upon owning. Mirroring his own toady-ing to an ethic he claims to have repudiated, his family jewels give 'a sinister wink like a toad's', in mockery, it seems, of their gemstone loveliness. And in like manner, the glowing embers in the hearth call up the hellish depths to which Angel has sunk. In their 'torrid waste' they peer luridly 'into the loose hair about (Tess's) brow ... firing the delicate skin underneath', as if to brand her as Angel surely does (*TD*, p.268).

For all Tess's terror in this 'hellish' scene, with Angel 'fitfully' treading the floor, his face 'withered', even his voice 'fallen' to a 'commonplace' (*TD*, p.270), she still summons the nerve to oppose him as he taxes her with bearing no mark of her sin, no mark of her shame, no sickness; 'O you cannot be out of your mind!' he rants, 'You ought to be!' 'I am not', she replies, 'out of my mind':

I thought, Angel, that you loved me – me, my very self! If it is I you do love, O how can it be that you look and speak so? It frightens me! Having begun to love you, I love you for ever – in all changes, in all disgraces, because you are yourself. I ask no more. Then how can you, O my own husband, stop loving me? (*TD*, p.271)

How can he? By annihilating her: 'the woman I have been loving is not you' (*TD*, p.271).

Tess breaks; 'Terror was upon her white face' and the beautiful expressive mouth which had once reminded Angel of 'roses filled with snow' (*TD*, p.191) is blasted: 'a round little hole'. 'Deadened ... she staggered' and seeing her collapse, Angel becomes conciliatory. 'You are ill', he tells her, 'and it is natural that you should be so' (*TD*, p.272). She is now as she ought to be, ill and distraught, and Angel is vaguely reassured. His solicitude, withheld all the while she showed no sign of illness, all the while she staunchly stood her ground, comes into play with her collapse. But it does not effect a bonding. He does not feel compassion but pity. And pity permits of distance which he does not attempt to breach.

Angel, to a far greater extent than Tess, is formed and shaped by his past. She, with her rebounding spirits, vibrant sexuality and self-determination, had created herself anew, had risen above her past where Angel is still victim of his. Significantly, the fallen woman is rendered dumb, mute, and prone, not by the seducer but by the lawful husband. The emphasis is purposeful. Hardy's denunciation of a mythology which prescribed the fallen woman sick and sickening from the day of her 'fall' comes full circle in the wedding-night scene, where, with a bitter, satiric twist, the legitimate marriage partner becomes the myth-maker's agent.

Hardy retains, then, for Tess, with her emotional generosity, sexual vitality and moral strength, the capacity to rise above her fall and, ultimately, to redeem the man who, bearing the values and sexual prejudices and double-standards of the society, fails to rise above them in the hour of need. Nor does Tess's last hour find her bereft of will, self-determination and courage. In knifing the heart of the man who so remorselessly hunts her down, she turns her own life around yet again; but this time with readiness, she says, to face her executioner.

5

PASSION DENIED:
Jude the Obscure

All of the Hardy heroines I have discussed so far oppose the notion that marriage should be the expressed goal of their sexuality. Two decades before Sue Bridehead's advent, Bathsheba, the most vociferous of Hardy's early heroines, not only protests vehemently against becoming some man's property in marriage, but also, at Oak's suggestion that she should give herself to a man for reasons other than love, she displays a purity of conscience that he clearly does not own. Confronting his coercive measures to have her wed Bold-wood because she has captivated his heart, Bathsheba responds indignantly:

I hate the act of marriage under such circumstances, and the class of woman I should seem to belong to by doing it! (*FFMC*, p.420)

Oak, unlike Bathsheba, is evidently completely unaware of the profanity lurking in his suggestion that a woman should give her body to a man because she has cost him!

Bathsheba *is* of course finally married off to a man for whom she has no sexual feeling. And, if that puts her in that class of women to which she had earlier referred, this fully coheres with Hardy's subversive intentions in this novel, which have less to do with recalling pastoral idylls of the Golden Age than with calling attention to the sexual codes and practices of the Victorian Age.

The difference in *Jude*, Hardy's last polemical novel, is, fundamentally, one of emphasis. Sue's resistance to the notion that marriage should be the expressed goal of her sexuality is of central importance to the novel, and Hardy, now adopting a more openly heterodox stance than he had felt permissible in earlier works, stands openly and defiantly behind her. In contrast to Bathsheba's muted voice as Mrs Gabriel Oak, Sue's crushing defeat as the unhappy Mrs Phillotson does not eclipse either her rebellious voice or her heartfelt principles: her ineluctable truths long outlive her tergiversation. Hardy gives one last twist, here, to the marriage-and-happy-ending denouement he had always despised as false and misleading. It is also a vindicating twist, for getting married and living unhappily ever after has to be the most appropriate of obituaries for Sue, who, in her fighting days, demands the right to broadcast the ills of marriage 'upon the housetops'.

Hardy provides, at the beginning of this novel, a prefatory perspective on marriage that introduces the element of absurdity which, for Sue Bridehead, will become cruel farce. Of Jude and Arabella's nuptials he writes:

The two swore that every other time of their lives till death took them, they would assuredly believe, feel, and desire precisely as they had believed, felt, and desired during the preceding weeks. What was as remarkable as the undertaking itself was the fact that nobody seemed at all surprised at what they swore. (*JO*, p.64)

This ironic mode of discourse has such a familiar Hardyan ring to it that Sue's articulations are thrown into relief by contrast:

If marriage is only a sordid contract, based on material convenience in house-keeping, rating, and taxing, and the inheritance of land and money by children, making it necessary that the male parent should be known – which it seems to be – why surely a person may say, even proclaim upon the housetops, that it hurts and grieves him or her? (*JO*, p.218)

Sue's campaign against the Institution of Marriage is rigorous, radical and militant. Ideologically ahead of the times as far as the feminist movement of the early 1890s goes, and more in line with twentieth-century suffragettism, she argues not only with foresight but also with a hindsight wisdom available to few educated Victorian women: that of a divorced wife. Victorian marriage codes are an anachronism to Sue. The notion strikes her as outrageous that a married woman should still be regarded as a man's property, or that sexual relationships should still require institutionalisation in a modern society pioneering in its radical quarters the dissolution of rigid role demarcations and sexual inequality.

Sue's call for total reconstruction of bonded relationships along equitable lines, what Olive Schreiner, a decade later, was to call 'a fellowship of comrades',[1] was theoretically neither revolutionary nor even new. In fact her 'voice' so frequently resounds with the over-tones of the nineteenth-century radical socialist it is surprising to find in *Jude* no mention of influences or, indeed, of readings in contemporary socialist thought[2]: Engels, for example, who claims that only with the abolition of private ownership will a new generation of women grow up, who have never known 'what it is to give themselves to a man from any other consideration than real love or ... [what it is] to give themselves to their lover from fear of the economic consequences.'[3]

Now while Sue submits to Phillotson more out of duty than fear of the economic consequences, she does fear the obligation and equally fears the repercussions should she refuse. And no doubt were Phillotson to exercise his rights to the full she might also be made to fear the economic consequences. At any rate, she is conscious of the 'torture' (*JO*, p.221) of being obliged to submit and, as she explains to Jude, she is also conscious that many women do 'give themselves to a man' from considerations other than 'real love':

Fewer women like marriage than you suppose, only they enter into it for the dignity it is assumed to confer, and the social advantages it gains them sometimes – a dignity and an advantage that I am willing to do without. (*JO*, p.268)

Social advantage or economic necessity, however it may be phrased, it is fairly evident that Sue is thinking along lines very similar to Engels' – albeit, we must suppose, unknowingly. More knowing is Hardy, despite his disclaimer that 'the purpose of a chronicler of moods and deeds does not require him to express his personal views upon the grave controversy [on marriage] above given' (*JO*, p.298). Whereas Sue appears to have acquired her knowledge and ideas by some osmotic process

unrevealed to the reader, Hardy, with his excursions into socialist thought, has not.[4]

Possibly Hardy keeps J. S. Mill to the fore, as a major influence on Sue, to soften the radicalism of her anti-marriage views
(which Mill did not hold), although he had hoped that when
he came to publish *Jude* his unconventional heroine would be
greeted by a more liberal readership ('we are educating them
in degrees', he later told Millicent Garrett Fawcett). But yet
again Hardy seems to have overestimated his critics' threshold
of toleration. In practice, middle-class women still held strong
to the liberal feminists' idealisation of marriage and their
redemptive emphasis upon woman's calling to devotional wifehood.

Even Fawcett, vociferous spokeswoman for liberal feminists,
in pleading woman's right to work, implicitly accommodates
ideology to the inequitable relation between husband and wife:

Is it not for the benefit of society that the women who have the
greatest natural fitness for marriage should marry, whilst those who
have fewer natural qualifications for the endurance and enjoyment
of the special pains and pleasures of married life, should find other
honourable and useful careers open to them?[5]

The line between an (approved) vocational calling to wifehood
and the (less approved) 'useful career' is quite unconsciously
drawn here. Further, a man may find for himself an 'honourable
and useful career', yet have the 'greatest natural fitness' for
marriage, but the woman is confined to the single, self-immolating role.

It was not until the furore over *Jude* had long since subsided
that Hardy presented his views openly to Fawcett, expressing,
in a letter, his hopes that:

The tendency of the women's vote will be to break up the present
pernicious conventions in respect of manners, customs, religion,
illegitimacy, the stereotyped household (that it must be the unit of
society), the father of a woman's child (that it is anybody's business
but the woman's own except in cases of disease or insanity).[6]

John Stuart Mill had earlier drawn an analogy between
woman's status in marriage and slavery. 'The wife,' he wrote,

is the actual bond-servant of her husband: no less so, as far as legal
obligation goes, than slaves commonly so called.

A female slave has (in Christian countries) an admitted right, and is considered under a moral obligation, to refuse to her master the last familiarity. Not so the wife: however brutal a tyrant she may unfortunately be married to – though she may know that he hates her, though it may be his daily pleasure to torture her, and though she may feel it impossible not to loathe him – he can claim from her and enforce the lowest degradation of a human being, that of being made the instrument of an animal function contrary to her inclinations.[7]

In *Jude*, Hardy addresses himself to the dual issue of woman's obligation to submit to 'present pernicious conventions' and the long-term psychological effects of this – the long-term effects of her enforced repression, subjection and degradation. Central to the 'psychical novel', he says, is the effect of casualty upon the faculties. This is 'the important matter to be depicted' (*Life*, p.204). Sue's socio-political outlook, in which she is not typical of any one faction, class or category (though critical opinion tends to differ here)[8] allows Hardy to perceive her as set-apart, unique, the 'outsider' he himself can identify with. However, in so far as she is sexually repressed, psychologically conditioned a 'loser', a 'casualty' of her class and background, she is representative of her suffragist peers who, in the public sphere at least, accommodated similar frustrations and defeats and encountered comparable destructive attitudes.

Lauded for her decorum, her respectability and the sweet reasonableness of her political agitation, the nineteenth-century liberal feminist has this much in common with Hardy's Sue. In order to achieve the most meagre of ends she had to play heavily on all her so-called 'feminine' qualities effectively to gain the male approval or patronage vital to her success. As Sara Delamont and Lorna Duffin point out,

women used the dominant ideas to obtain their own ends and . . . in order to make their ideas known (they) had to articulate them in a form which was acceptable to men.

The most successful feminist campaigners were those who managed to minimise hostile reactions by manipulating the classification system and not violating it. These were the pioneers who were able to reorganise the beliefs and values of the dominant male culture, who articulated their ideas in a form acceptable to that dominant male opinion and used the dominant ideas to achieve their own ends.[9]

The suggestion here that successful campaigning – synonymous with deferential tactics – led to a successful gaining of ends cannot go unchallenged. Despite the historian's recommendation that it was just this decorous approach which earned woman the necessary male approval in high places to ensure her imminent enfranchisement, the fact that the 'imminent' took nigh on half-a-century to arrive suggests that there was something awry in her method of political agitation as well as in the historian's approval of it.[10]

By way of contrast, American feminist tactics – the openly aggressive methods of the National Woman Suffrage Association (1890) – draw from the historian, if not open approval, at least acknowledgment of the efficacy of their militant methods. Under the leadership of Susan Anthony, we are told, the National Woman Suffrage Association 'resorted to militant tactics that had already gained the vote for women in eleven states before the First World War'.[11] Militancy, then, was not only effective, as opposed to putting the Cause into jeopardy (as some historians claim of the militancy of the twentieth-century suffragettes) but is also acknowledged as such.

The insurrection of women and establishment reaction to it is possibly nowhere better expressed in nineteenth-century literature than in J.S. Mill's 'Subjection of Women' (1869):

The case of women is now the only case in which to rebel against established rule is still looked upon with the same eyes as was formerly a subject's claim to the right of rebelling against his king.[12]

And that was treason.

There is no doubt that division within the mid- to late-Victorian suffragists' camp was an impediment to the Cause, a division or lack of solidarity which cannot be explained away, as so many Victorians tried to do, as evidence of woman's innate inability to unite with her own kind in a common Sisterhood. (Mrs Pankhurst's formation of the 'Women's Social and Political Union' in 1903, which from 1906 to 1914 undertook increasingly militant action to further the suffragette cause, surely gives the lie to that assumption.) Among the many explanations that abounded in the nineteenth century none cites woman's subordination itself to be a causal factor in her failure to achieve solidarity. Yet it seems reasonable to suppose that women displaying all the signs of their subjugation, manipulative behaviour rather than rebellion, respectability instead of nonconformity, approval-seeking as opposed to the flagrant disregard for authority the suffragettes showed, should also display correlated traits of in-group rivalry, hostility and malice. This impaired drive to combine and cooperate with peer groups accords with the findings of social historians correlating the degree of this kind of psychic impairment to the degree of repression and subordination enforced by authoritarian systems.[13]

Feminists would inevitably have run up against division within the camp for the very simple reason that they were competing for attention and sanctions from the dominant class (men in power) whom they were obliged to please, and with whom they were obliged to identify by adopting male-approved female roles. The dominant class possessed precisely those privileges and powers feminists themselves sought to possess – but sought to possess by conforming to male rule. In other words, division was not simply an organisational problem. The failure to achieve solidarity was but the outer manifestation of the division within woman herself: in abjuring her own sexuality, in adopting the respected ennobled-and-ennobling role (the Angel) she suffered a loss of identification with her own kind. She had split with her own sex.

Hardy's Sue exemplifies just such a split. Conditioned to behavioural patterns associated with enforced dependency, and motivated to compete, under a system of rewards and punishments, for attention and approval from those in authority over her, Sue instinctively employs manipulative behaviour to secure recognition of her needs. Thus she invests in an appealing little-girl role to secure her hold on Jude, especially in those moments when she feels threatened by his withdrawal of affection. He is the one male she respects, admires, and with whom she identifies. By the same token, he is the one male from whom she seeks respect, admiration, identification. But, whether he likes it or not, he is, by virtue of his maleness alone, in authority over her.

Lightheartedly enough in the early stages of their relationship, she has occasion to tease him at his prayers, but she overdoes it and irritates him. Instantly, she alters her behaviour:

'Very well – I'll do just as you bid me, and I won't vex you, Jude,' she replied, in the tone of a child who was going to be good ever after. (*JO*, p.159)

Hardy perceives that Sue's most characteristic psychological move is to slide instinctively from the little-girl role to the ennobled role when her emotional anxieties are appeased. Both are approval-seeking roles. And although the significance of this alternation of poses is lost on Jude, Hardy makes it apparent to the reader that this pattern of behaviour must and does maintain Sue in unliberated subjection. Childlike or ennobled, each directional shift gains her momentary personal satisfaction, in that she gains Jude's approval – indulgence on the one hand, reverence on the other – but at the expense of driving an ever thickening wedge of inequity between herself and her lover. Neither to submissive child nor ethereal paragon can he relate in any sexually fulfilling or mutually rewarding way. He would always have the feeling, or would unwittingly generate in her the feeling, that she is either abused and exploited or debased and degraded.

Sue shifts so unobtrusively from the one role to the other that it is clear Hardy fully intends to convey a strong sense of their interaction. They are two different personae but one and the same divided self. Part of that self is an objectified self. Both submissive little-girl and saintly idol fulfil the function of being objects of approval whilst providing Sue with a shield against her other subjective self, which fears constant rejection or disapproval. That she would disown the fearful, unlovable self and give it another identity is revealed by her unconscious use of the objective case: 'your faulty and tiresome little Sue!' (*JO*, p.161), or, the 'poor wicked woman who is trying to mend!' (*JO*, p.373). The wicked 'selves' are split off from the 'I', who is not referred to in either case. It is as if Sue is offering Jude a punishable self from which she can feel safely distanced – so intense is her fear of losing his love. Evidently she cannot regard herself as both lovable and faulty, hence the splitting of selves (the faulty self is now a third person), and hence the recourse to childlike poses when the inevitable fall from perfection in the paragon role takes place. Such is the tyranny of the ideal: perfection, unlike excellence, admits of no flaws; thus in struggling for perfection there is no escape from guilt, no relief from anxiety and fear.

Teasing, as we have seen, is Sue's ploy to distract Jude's attention away from his devotions and to herself; but he is genuinely irritated, so unconsciously she adopts a childlike posture and 'won't vex' him. Feeling, then, that she has gained some ground, she shifts once more to the ennobling role and offers to deliver Jude from the hypocrisy and humbug of what she calls his falsified biblical text. Something of her astute critical talent begins to show here; but this is obscured by her efforts to sound impressive, to sound ennobling: her language grows loftier by the minute, and inadvertently, begins to take on a pontificating tone – the very thing she is condemning. Jude is not amused:

'And what a literary enormity this is,' she said, as she glanced into the pages of Solomon's Song. 'I mean the synopsis at the head of each chapter, explaining away the real nature of that rhapsody. You needn't be alarmed: nobody claims inspiration for the chapter headings. Indeed, many divines treat them with contempt. It seems the drollest thing to think of the four-and-twenty elders, or bishops, or whatever number they were, sitting with long faces and writing down such stuff.'

Jude looked pained. 'You are quite Voltairean!' he murmured. (*JO*, p.159)

Instantly aware that she has displeased, Sue, without ado, alters her approach:

Her speech had grown spirited, and almost petulant at his rebuke, and her eyes moist. 'I *wish* I had a friend here to support me; but nobody is ever on my side!' (*JO*, p.159)

How the language changes! And so does Jude. From petulance to tears and from tears to reconciliation Sue wins him to her and, having won, declares:

I did want and long to ennoble some man to high aims; and when I saw you ... I ... thought that man might be you. (*JO*, p.160)

The ground seems firmer now. Jude is just a little pompous, evidently gratified. 'Well dear' he begins (fatherly),

I suppose one must take some things on trust. Life isn't long enough to work out everything in Euclid problems before you believe it. I take Christianity. (*JO*, p.160)

Puzzled, perhaps, by the fact that her expressed desire to ennoble seems to soften him in a way that her Voltairean discourse does not, Sue evidently grasps what is required of her: she should ennoble, not by instructional erudition, but by more 'feminine' means, by turning 'angelic' and appealing to the man's better nature:

'we are going to be very *nice* with each other, aren't we, and never never vex each other any more?' She looked up trustfully, and her voice seemed trying to nestle in his breast.

'I shall always care for you!' said Jude. (*JO*, p.160)

As their relationship develops, it becomes increasingly difficult, with Jude's approving reinforcement, for Sue to break this behavioural pattern. Increasingly, she plays on bad-little-Sue where good-little-Sue becomes inappropriate, as it does inexorably with her repeated falls from perfection. Jude responds to the negative role and accompanying bouts of self-derogation with equability and just an occasional small show of irritation – mostly when he wants to have sex with Sue, which is of course cut across by her infantile posturing.

Following her flight from Phillotson, just such a situation arises. Discovering that Jude has presumptuously reserved a double room for the night at Aldbrickham, Sue, flustered and defensive, alternates between feeling wretched and saying so – she is 'a poor miserable creature' (*JO*, p.250) – and feeling affronted and 'sitting up ... so prim!' that Jude himself is affronted (*JO*, p.251). Then guiltily thinking she should try to coax away his anger she reverts, as seems inevitable by now, to self-derogation and passes herself off as 'very bad and unprincipled' (*JO*, p.252). With self-disparagement degenerating to infantilism the cycle becomes complete:

'you shall kiss me just once there – not very long.' She put the tip of her finger gingerly to her cheek; and he did as commanded. 'You do care for me very much, don't you, in spite of my not – you know?' (*JO*, p.256)

Jude is thoroughly needled. It is a woman in bed he wants and not a truculent little girl to whom he is supposed to play the petting father:

'Yes, sweet!' he said with a sigh; and bade her good-night. (*JO*, p.256)

Despite her psychological handicaps and the unremitting pressure of Jude's desire to make claims on her, sexual and matrimonial, Sue makes an exhaustive (and exhausting) bid to emancipate herself from dependency, from the man-made laws circumscribing her bondage – a bid pre-empted from the outset by what Hardy would call the curbed mould of her temperament. He would leave the reader in no doubt as to the pernicious effects of her conditioning; how firmly she has been moulded to 'fit' Victorian standards of sexual behaviour, and how extensively the 'common enemy coercion' (*JO*, p.297) will complete the process.

Victorian marriage lines had one obvious feature in common with slave-code practice. Both institutions required the bonded party to take the master's name upon bondage. The implications of this are not lost on Hardy, and, in justice to Sue's deep resentment of the assumptions that are made about what is appropriate or inappropriate for women, he lets it be known that taking Jude's cognominal identity is not, to either author or heroine, a preferment. On the contrary, it is yet another seemingly innocuous convention that purports to endow a privilege upon woman but in truth coerces her into accepting her underprivileged status. Thus it is that in being persuaded that by rights, as Jude's ostensible wife, she should go by 'the name of Mrs Fawley' her sense of depersonalisation is so overwhelming as to turn her 'dull, cowed, and listless' for days (*JO*, p.308). These are the symptoms of clinical depression, a condition of prolonged lethargy, dispiritedness and sense of futility. Hardy makes Sue's psychological condition acutely felt and, moreover, introduces an element of textual strangeness, as if to mirror what is, to Sue, estranging in reality. A dull, cowed, and listless bride is, to say the least, impressionistically odd.

Mill's slavery analogy suggests a comparison between the sexual role of women in marriage and miscegenation. Sue would not disagree:

I think I should begin to be afraid of you ... the moment you had contracted to cherish me under a Government stamp, and I was licensed to be loved on the premises by you. (*JO*, p.267)

Sue's language says it well enough despite the fact that she cannot bring herself to utter the word prostitution. Indeed, her use of the passive tense suggests more than prostitution; it suggests a purchase that she has no say in negotiating.

Sue has learned from her experience with Phillotson that such a contracted obligation can 'involve one in ... a daily, continuous tragedy' (*JO*, p.241). A husband can absorb himself in his own activities throughout a whole evening to the exclusion of all else including his new, young, and 'unusually silent, tense, and restless' wife (*JO*, p.225); he can spend until midnight 'balancing the school registers', and then, muttering on about school committees and draughty ventilators, he can ascend to the nuptial chamber quite as if sexual intercourse with his wife were just part of the day's functions (*JO*, pp.228–9). Or, alternatively, he might sit up late 'as was often his custom, trying to get together the materials for his long-neglected hobby of Roman antiquities' when, at length, forgetting time and place, he might ascend 'mechanically to the room that he and his wife had occupied' but which is now hers exclusively, and go so far as to start undressing before, prompted by her terrified scream, he might recall she had wished to sleep alone (*JO*, p.235).

If a young bride were to assume that sexual intimacy should coincide with mutual sexual readiness, married to a Phillotson she would learn otherwise: 'What tortures me so much', Sue cries, 'is the necessity of being responsive to this man whenever he wishes' (*JO*, p.221). Unhappily, Phillotson's awareness that he has been 'taking advantage' of a young, inexperienced woman whose growth to womanhood has stopped short of sexual self-knowledge emerges all the more tardily for his chronic self-absorption (*JO*, p.239). There is very little in his behaviour to indicate *his* sexual responsiveness and a good deal to suggest that Sue is quite justified in thinking him content with celibacy. How had he wooed her after all? 'Not kissing me – that I'm certain!' she protests to Jude (*JO*, p.140). Phillotson, even so, feels it incumbent upon himself to exercise his conjugal rights. He assumes this to be an extension of his day-to-day functions and he assumes that Sue's sexual submission to him is a moral obligation. In resisting him, she is not in his eyes simply unresponsive, coldhearted, selfish or unsympathetic, but morally at fault. 'You vowed to love me', he accuses: 'you are committing a sin in not liking me'. (*JO*, p.232)

Sue, then, has every reason to question whether or not a 'legal obligation ... is destructive to a passion whose essence is gratuitousness' (*JO*, p.281). If Phillotson can transform from a sexually undemanding companion, unhabituated to kissing anything other than the 'dead, pasteboard' (*JO*, p.169) photograph of his bride-to-be, to an insensitive spouse mechanically exercising his rights and even driven to spying on his wife when not totally oblivious to her needs and desires, what would be the effect of 'legal obligation' upon the yet more impressionable, immature Jude? What too of the effect upon Sue? Just becoming aware of the shocking repercussions of years of emotional and sexual repression, she is by no means yet free from the anxieties, fears and guilt those years have wrought. How, then, could she ever remain 'proof against the sordid conditions' of the marriage contract? (*JO*, p.295).

In the matter of marriage, Hardy takes every possible step to ensure Sue a hearing. And despite the fact that she has available only a language invented by men for men (Bathsheba's point), which threatens to cast her thoughts and feelings in locutions that do not express her true meaning, that tends to place her consciousness on the periphery of a male world, and despite the fact that she has no radical feminist guidelines, no inspiring models, nor even the literature of liberation beyond Mill, she uses the language she does have available with intelligence, sensitivity and skill. Fully aware of its coercive power, she too will use it as a weapon, and does. While she cannot escape her psychological conditioning or the perpetuation of her subjugation, she can protest and rally against both, persuasively, as Jude is made uncomfortably aware.

Sue's articulate 'voice' is also significant in that it indicates the extent to which Hardy came to ally himself openly with his female protagonist. Coming full circle from the superinduced proprietary narrator who renders Elfride's story palatable to the Victorian reader, Hardy creates in Sue a heroine who not only objectifies her own behaviour but capably rationalises it. The censor has diminished in importance to become at the last, in Phillotson, a shadow of his former self. Shades of the puritanical bully are still there in Phillotson, and he is certainly quite capable of tyrannising the woman he desires and fears. But he is not, as Knight, the harsh critic lacking sexual potency who wounds what he desires sexually to penetrate; nor is he, like Venn, the self-appointed vigilante with marked voyeuristic leanings. Moreover, Sue is fully equipped to plead her case against him theoretically if not practically.

She becomes, in fact, the objective voice for Hardy's own case, his own political views. That this voice is less authentically her own than those utterances she expresses through gesture, through posture, through action, is essential. Hardy recognises that her beliefs gain credibility and power from the 'male' language she adopts, although in adopting it she limits her growth to liberation. Clarity and lucidity is one thing; patriarchal rhetoric is quite another.

This double-bind, for Victorian women, was inescapable. To be taken seriously in an age when nonconformism and militancy in women was so frequently ridiculed and belittled, Sue's erudition and rhetoric has to be flawless, as her feminist sisters in life also quickly learned:

Calmly, with impeccable logic, they methodically demolished the increasingly frenzied arguments of the opposition. The contrast in tone was so striking as to cause an observer to remark that in this debate the feminine champions of emancipation and their masculine opponents seemed to have exchanged roles. It was the men who argued heatedly, irrationally, and emotionally; the women who responded coolly, rationally, and logically.[14]

Although Sue's tendency is to regress into the infantilised roles of the child-woman reliant upon solicitude and approval, she runs no risk of having ascriptions such as 'empty-headed' or 'frivolous' pinned on her as did many of her unfortunate peers in life, deprived as they were of skills in the arts of reason, logic and rhetoric. And of equal importance, in Victorian eyes, she generates an air of distinct sexual fastidiousness, which for entirely different reasons also ensures her credibility and power. As a sexy woman may be 'dumb' to a twentieth-century Hollywood-bred public, to Victorians, long habituated to associating voluptuousness with organic malfunction and mental instability, she would lack moral as well as intellectual force.

Millicent Garrett Fawcett's apologia in her Introduction to Mary Wollstonecraft's *Vindication*,[15] which enjoins the reader not to permit the author's 'irregular' (unmarried and sexually active) life to detract from the moral seriousness of her work, provides an apt illustration of just how deeply such attitudes had become entrenched in the culture. An open exposition of a sexually passionate nature in Sue would then threaten to diminish her political 'voice' and Hardy is clearly very sensitive to this difficulty.

It is possibly largely due to her voluptuousness that Bathsheba failed to engage her live contemporaries in the anti-marriage question. Certainly no Victorian critic found her views on the subject worthy of mention. So too Eustacia, whose erotic longings to be loved-to-madness, and moreover loved-to-madness not by one man but by many, have led critics to trivialise her as adolescent and puerile. And, of course, Tess's lush sexuality thoroughly upset contemporary readers for whom the synonymity of voluptuousness and purity was nothing short of a Hardyan hoax. These sexy heroines clearly disturbed readers to the point where the ethical and moral issues they present or represent became hard to take at face value, although few could actually dismiss their threat to the status quo.

Sue is superficially the least sexually responsive of all Hardy's great heroines. She cohabits with three men in the course of her young life but remains in ignorance of her sexual needs with each. She never suspects for a moment that her 'craving to attract' (*JO*, p.365) is not gross, not deserving of punishment, not unnatural, but quite simply sexual longing seeking sexual fulfilment.

Her most intense sexual response appears to be revulsion, which many readers might have taken as a sign of her high-mindedness. However, in probing the deeper complexities of her psyche, Hardy discovers dormant powers which, in manifesting intense revulsion, testify less to an insipid sexual drive than to deeply repressed sexual impulses.

Hardy must have been struck by the paradox when the vociferous critic, Mrs Oliphant, attacked Sue for making 'virtue vicious by keeping the physical facts of ... life in constant prominence by denying ... them ... the fantastic *raisonneuse*, Susan, completes the circle of the unclean.'[16] After two decades of circumnavigating and encircling Mrs Grundy, then to have his female protagonist accused of keeping the physical facts of life in constant prominence by denying them! Rightfully, Oliphant finds Sue preoccupied with sex, and typically she finds this not only unclean but incompatible with a reasoning intelligence assumed, in this instance, to be 'fantastic'.

Sue does keep the physical facts of life in constant prominence, and this heightens her consciousness of a woman's right to sole control over her own body. Erotic love, she argues, cannot be given 'continuously to the chamber-officer appointed by the bishop's licence to receive it' (*JO*, p.213). Nor should lovers be 'actuated by a dreadful contract to feel in a particular way in a matter whose essence is voluntariness' (*JO*, pp.221–2). Sue's staunch efforts to intellectualise, rationalise and politicise an issue which she dare not confront in all its sensuousness and intimacy provides Hardy with an excellent platform upon which to air the related questions of the social and psychological conditioning of women and their sexual exploitation in marriage. No voluptuous Bathsheba, Eustacia or Tess would do as well. Sexual fastidiousness or repression strikes the perfect note for exposition of a coldly austere convention which still sanctioned in the 1890s (by custom not by law) what Phillotson calls the 'right and proper and honourable' act of putting erring wives 'virtuously under lock and key': an act he cannot bring himself to perform despite the apparent rectitude and propriety of the deed (*JO*, p.240). But Hardy makes his point well enough. It may not be the mawkish schoolmaster's intention to take his wife by force or to confine her in one of those spider-infested closets she prefers to her husband's bed, but Sue, feeling herself to be entirely at his mercy, has no guarantee of this. How could she possibly be assured that the coldly chastising husband of her early married days will not become more pitiless yet? He does, after all, show more concern for disturbing the maid than for soothing her distress on the night of her self-incarceration. And as Hardy makes plain, she lives her days, as well as her nights, in unrelieved fear, guilt and anxiety. Making constant appeals to Phillotson's better nature, carefully avoiding raising the emotional temperature beyond a man-ageable level, she lives in daily dread of the absolute authority he has over her.

From her protestations, heavily imbued with the phrases of officialdom ('licence', 'chamber-officer', 'contract', 'government stamp', 'on the premises'), her sense of resentment and oppression in the face of male authority communicates itself as a revulsion for all things male-dominated or bureaucratic. This emphasis together with the manner in which the language of officialdom judders not only upon Sue's delicate sensibilities but also within Hardy's own discourses (as in the extract below), indicates that he intends a measure of his critical attack upon marriage to fall upon its secularisation: its assimilation to a male governing order less concerned with holy rite than with patriarchal might.

The secularisation of marriage in Victorian England brought with it more than depersonalising officialese. With the trappings of bureaucracy came a heavy emphasis upon duties, obligations, rights and privileges which regimented human values into rules. In *Jude* it is Sue, of course, who registers the alienating effect of all this as she detects in the language of nuptials of a brutalising,coercive legalese shockingly at variance with lovers' tender vows. Carefully she examines the crudities of the rubric:

As she read the four-square undertaking, never before seen by her, into which her own and Jude's names were inserted, and by which that very volatile essence, their love for each other, was supposed to be made permanent, her face seemed to grow painfully apprehensive. 'Names and Surnames of the Parties' – (they were to be parties now, not lovers, she thought). 'Condition' – (a horrid idea) – 'Rank or Occupation' – 'Age' – 'Dwelling at' – 'Length of Residence' – 'Church or Building in which the Marriage is to be Solemnized' – 'District and County in which the Parties respectively dwell'.

'It spoils the sentiment, doesn't it!' she said on their way home. 'It seems making a more sordid business of it even than signing the contract in the vestry.' (*JO*, p.290)

Whereas a touch of the Fielding frolics tail-ending into confusion and muddle attends the acquisition of marriage licences in early Hardy, there are no such touches in *Jude*. The Arabella/Jude nuptials are not rendered serio-comic but satiric, and the Jude/Sue ventures are just plain grim. With its contractual emphasis placed solely upon terms, the terms most profitable to the bond-holder, in contrast to the simple exchange of promissory oaths under the old practice of betrothal and simple church ceremonial, matrimony has become, in Sue's eyes, less a mutual undertaking than the legitimisation of a 'sordid business' granting one individual authority and power over another.

Bitter and cynical as this attitude may appear to be in one so young and untutored in the social evolution of marriage and the family, the modern historian would support it in principle if not with the same rancour. The evolution of the family among the middle classes from 1770 to the mid-nineteenth century is marked, Lawrence Stone tells us, 'by a strong revival of moral reform, paternal authority and sexual repression'.[17] And as the linguistic terms in Stone's citation from *The English Matron* (1846) reveal, the members of the Victorian household take on a subtle resemblance to offenders in a penal institution:

the government of a household, for the sake of all its inmates, should be a monarchy, but a limited monarchy; of all forms, a democracy is most uncomfortable in domestic life.[18]

Stone claims that this was moderate advice, that it was interpreted in a more authoritarian fashion to incorporate a new ideal of womanhood involving 'total abnegation, making the wife a slave to convention, propriety, and her husband'. And where Hardy's Sue makes the link between the new family type and the laws of property and inheritance, Stone likewise associates it with 'the upper level of the urban bourgeoisie and professional classes. To this extent there is certainly a connection with the spirit of capitalism.'[19] The trend towards a re-inforced hierarchical order in the capitalist industrial society, which gave 'one class practically all the rights, and the other class practically all the duties',[20] was reflected in the smaller political unit, the family: total authority rested in the patriarchal head from whom all lines of authority descend. The family unit in Hardy reflects just such a trend. The male-dominated households of Swancourt, Clare and Melbury, for example, show a close structural similarity to hierarchical societal structures in a way that his matriarchies do not. The largesse practised by Bathsheba neither instigates nor perpetuates class-division, whereas under Parson Clare's authority the household begets not only class prejudice but hypocrisy into the bargain. Nor does Paula Power, unlike Melbury and Swancourt, cement division within the community; and where Ethelberta's household exemplifies the most anarchic of domestic systems, regulated by the principle 'from each according to her ability, to each according to her needs', autocratic rule and internecine division are absent and interdependence, self-help and mutual co-operation very much in evidence.

But if the patriarchal household in Hardy is the organ of class- and sex-division, and if Sue is a casualty of just such a household, the evidence Hardy provides is very rudimentary. Mr Bridehead, whose role in Sue's life is the more significant for his absence (he never actually makes an appearance in *Jude*), has not only taught his infant daughter to hate and reject her departed mother, but in turn rejects the mother's daughter. Following Sue's decision to live with her student friend in London, he cuts her off and makes no further appearance in her life. He does not attend her wedding, nor is he beside her as she lives through the tragedy of her dead babies. Yet he lives and works in Wessex where, presumably, there is newspaper coverage of his grandchildren's deaths.

All we can infer from this is that if Sue fears her own sexuality this probably originated in her infancy in being taught to hate her mother and in identifying with the father who both hates the mother and rejects the mother's daughter. And if, to follow the implications of this, Sue's behavioural pattern of approval-seeking can similarly be traced to early conditioning, we may also infer that her dependency upon the punitive father figure (Phillotson) is a means of restoring the lost parent, whose disapproval and withdrawal by no means lessens his hold upon the rejected child.

However Mr Bridehead's influence on his daughter is interpreted, Sue can only be right to question the imbalance of power that results from assigning it solely to the male partner in marriage. This necessarily distorts the structure of a union, if only by placing unnatural pressures upon both partners to fit individual nature to role, rather than role to individual nature. That Sue relates all this to the effect it may have upon her own, and Jude's, impressionable, developing sensibilities testifies to her remarkably sensitive, prescient intelligence: she is the most fitting of Hardy's heroines to be accorded a political voice.

Bathsheba had feared her ultimate subordination in marriage. Sue fears the more – fears exacerbated by her sensitivity to the social formation, the indifferent, dismissive touch of the patriarchal State. This is considerably more obtrusive in her world than in Bathsheba's, who encounters no Training School Committees, no School Inspectors, no School Boards, and no urban Police Forces. The encroachment of the machinery of

State, of the Law and its male representatives in *Jude*, does not, as Hardy conceives it, justify its own intrusiveness.

In the inquiry into Phillotson's divorce, for example, directed by a government body which holds that 'the private eccentricities of a teacher came quite within their sphere of control', Hardy shows, forcibly, that there is no moral justification for their interference. The forcible element takes the form of a token 'battle' on the schoolmaster's behalf. This takes place in the schoolroom itself, and comprises 'a curious and interesting group of itinerants ... a generous phalanx of supporters, and a few others of independent judgement' who break in on the official meeting to 'express their thoughts strongly' to a committee comprising the 'respectable inhabitants and well-to-do natives of the town' (*JO*, pp.258,9). The 'battle' scene, narrated with unconcealed relish as dignitaries scuffle with assorted itinerants, is Hardy demolition at its mischievous best:

This generous phalanx of supporters, and a few others of independent judgement, whose own domestic experiences had not been without vicissitude, came up and warmly shook hands with Phillotson; after which they expressed their thoughts so strongly to the meeting that issue was joined, the result being a general scuffle, wherein a blackboard was split, three panes of the school-windows were broken, an inkbottle was spilled over a town-councillor's shirt-front, a churchwarden was dealt such a topper with the map of Palestine that his head went right through Samaria, and many black eyes and bleeding noses were given, one of which, to everybody's horror, was the venerable incumbent's, owing to the zeal of an emancipated chimney-sweep, who took the side of Phillotson's party. (*JO*, p.259)

The anti-establishment spirit which moves Hardy here bears closely upon the broader issue raised in *Jude* of the encroachment of institutionalised values upon individual liberty.[21] The question arises as to what extent an authoritarian society invites a transfer of moral responsibility from the individual to the authority determining the 'well-being' of those in its charge. Such an abdication of moral responsibility characterises the Christminster crowd awaiting the arrival of processioning dignitaries (*JO*, p.338), when Jude, protesting at a cab-driver's cruelty to his cab-horse, is silenced by the strong arm of the law. Order must be maintained at all costs, not in the interests of one abused dumb animal who may be beaten to death before the eyes of the crowd, but in the interests of the dignity and solemnity of the occasion.

Jude's sense, here, of frustration and impotency in the face of authority, accentuates a fundamental theme in *Jude*: the overriding of humanitarian concerns – the violation of basic human rights within the society generally and within the institution of marriage in particular. The very term 'Institution of Marriage' itself resounds somewhat chillingly in an Institution-bound age which subsumes remedial and punitive establishments such as reformatories, mental and penal institutions under the same heading, but reserves 'Association' for the denomination of *voluntarily* grouped bodies.

Sue's finely tuned sensibility picks up the subtle conformations of language, the very physical effects of language, although she is barely aware of the extent to which these conformations exert a moulding influence upon her consciousness. She is as susceptible to the 'word' (the 'letter that killeth'), as Tess is suggestible to the lurid biblical texts painted on field-gates. Such a susceptibility can offer unexpected insights, generate new understandings, open up vistas in the imagination, and generally sensitise thought and feeling. But for Sue there is this very real danger: her susceptibility is partly born of a need to appropriate words, a verbal armoury, in order to gain the hearing, the 'voice', the ascendancy she deserves. Her need is as deep as her intelligence and frustration with the world are strong. But she becomes dangerously over-reliant upon what Hardy calls her learned language. This assumes a dominance – in a sense a male dominance – superseding her own consciousness, ultimately to reshape it against her own interests.

It happens thus. The child who knits her little brows and glares round tragically as she conjures up images of the 'ghastly, grim and ancient Raven ... on the Night's Plutonian shore' (*JO*, p.119) is the same girl who later shocks Jude by admitting to a sneaking liking for 'ghastly stories of saints, dead limbs of gibbeted Gods!' (*JO*, p.157). This is also the woman who finally subjects herself physically to the ghastly, grim act of offering herself in sexual repulsion to Phillotson. The reversion is psychologically conditioned: Sue now identifies with an image of herself that was confirmed in her childhood as acceptable.

Raised by her father to 'hate her mother's family' (*JO*, p.118) – which would lead to hating her mother in herself – the infant Sue, made constantly aware of her shamelessness, has at least one identity she can superimpose over her bad, hated, feminine self. The pixillated girl possessed of imaginary furies and spectral terrors – 'you could see un a'most before your very eyes' (*JO*, p.120) – has clearly mesmerised her elders with a poetic performance which expresses some of her repressed passion, dread and fury but couched in the language of morbidity and martyrdom. So impressive is her performance in its impact and pathos, that it passes through anecdote into perpetuity, together with Sue's identification with the central character, herself: a little oddity glowering tragic glares, an object of admiration and pity.

This is but a single aspect of a highly complex nature. Hardy has not troubled, though, to chronicle such matters for no purpose. Consequently, when we discover in Sue a facility for being 'always much affected at a picture of herself as an object of pity' (*JO*, p.309), or when we are disconcerted by her impulse to act out her ghastly terrors in front of Phillotson, or when we are perplexed by her need to provoke Jude to stupefaction and pity, we have no reason to find her unstateable or unintelligible, as Jude claims she is.

When Sue reverts at the last to the grossest form of subjection, having physically steeled herself for the task by purging body, mind and spirit, 'I've wrestled and struggled, and fasted and prayed, I have nearly brought my body into complete subjection' (*JO*, p.403), she takes on her infantilised role with a vengeance. Step by step, she regresses to total dependency upon Phillotson, the 'punitive' father figure, to beg forgiveness, punishment, pity. She had longed in her derangement for 'something to take the evil right out' of what she calls her 'monstrous errors' and 'sinful ways', and as she takes psychological refuge in self-disgust, so real-life grim and tortuous terrors block out the pain of the far greater real-life horror of her murdered babies.

Significantly, it is the newly invoked biblical 'word' which precipitates this final regression. Sexual self-disgust and frustration crave intensity of sensation, even painful sensation, as Sue seems to intuit – with her need to purge her body. And biblical texts abound with physical images of struggle, suffering and torment. They are, moreover, in prescriptive, punitive terms, but a short step away from the officialese that had enthralled and repelled her in her fighting days. Her reversion is physically, sexually and emotionally a passage back to child-hood, a way back to the self-image created in infancy. The images generated from ghastly stories act as verbal cues prompting half-forgotten memories of cathartic dramatisations in youth. The childhood identity, the approved self-immolating role, is now recovered. The terrors externalised by acting out self-pity and revulsion carry 'safe' associations for Sue because they recall the socially approved dramatisations of her youth. Such a regression is retreat under cover. But it is the only means available to Sue, in danger of total personality breakdown, of gaining a hold on her identity, of gaining a hold on a self which in its infantile sexlessness and hatred of its femaleness had won the hearts of those standing in judgement upon her.

To one perplexed member of an earlier order in *Jude*, the kindly Mrs Edlin, the troubling marriage question is, however, no trouble at all.

I don't know what the times be coming to! Matrimony have growed to be that serious in these days, that one really do feel afeared to move in it at all. In my time we took it more careless; and I don't know that we was any the worse for it! When I and my poor man were jined in it we kept up the junketing all the week, and drunk the parish dry, and had to borrow half-a-crown to begin housekeeping! (*JO*, p.380)

Such insouciance places Sue's anxieties and high seriousness on a different plane and in a different light. Hardy presents, in this new contribution to the debate, so contrasting a view of marriage that the sociological standpoint he has now introduced deserves a long overdue critical appraisal. Times have changed: 'Nobody thought o'being afeard o'matrimony in my time', says Mrs Edlin (*JO*, p.297). And it is the nature of that change which Hardy invites his readers not once, not twice, but thrice to consider (*JO*, pp.297,380,412).

Class, epoch, a changing socio-political climate and an altered consciousness are the major differentiating factors. Mrs Edlin, belonging to a class and clime unencumbered by institutions, formal ceremonies, rights and obligations, which engaged and disengaged with espousals with relative ease, is not of Sue's generation. She is a member of the same order as the widow of Hardy's anecdote in *The Woodlanders*, whose husband returns unexpectedly after an absence of twenty-four years:

one night he came home when she was sitting by the fire, and thereupon he sat down himself on the other side of the chimney-corner. "Well" says she, "have ye got any news?" "Don't know as I have," says he; "have you?" "No" says she, "except that my daughter by the husband that succeeded 'ee was married last month, which was a year after I was made a widow by him", "Oh! Anything else?" he says. "No," says she. (*W*, pp.390–1)

Anything less like a Sue/Jude situation could scarcely be imagined!

The more relaxed attitudes that characterised early nineteenth-century rural, working-class family life, had, we are told, much to do with a more flexible familial structure. A significant feature of this was the absence of an authoritarian figurehead – or as Edward Shorter explains:

One might plausibly argue that in the course of the eighteenth century population growth decapitated the authority of the lower-class family by creating so many children that the parents had nothing to pass on to their extra-numerous offspring, and hence no control over their behaviour.[22]

We can safely assume that Mrs Edlin and her counterpart from *The Woodlanders* are descendants of this class and clime. Unlike Sue and Jude they have not been exposed to, or conditioned by, the sexual ethic of the rising Victorian petit-bourgeoisie.

If the rural working-class family exercised less strict, authoritarian control over its young (to which the Arabellas, Fanny Robins, Marions, Izzies, and Rettys of Hardy's Wessex world all testify) the authority of the petit-bourgeois family remained inviolate, managing

to preserve the sense of family tradition which said that children would follow in the footsteps of the father. To be sure, young men of middle-class origin responded to a new Zeitgeist of gratification by sleeping with prostitutes; but these liaisons posed no threat to the family. What we know about middle-class daughters suggests that they stayed pure before marriage. Thus the authority of the middle-class family over its offspring remained inviolate, and, as a result, middle-class youth, however sensitised by change, did not actually break out of the web of familial custody and control.[23]

If 'Nobody thought ... of much else but a cannonball or empty cupboard!' (*JO*, p. 297) in Mrs Edlin's married days (by which I take her to mean the Napoleonic wars and the effects of the Corn Law tariffs respectively), the modern consciousness, as Hardy presents it in *Jude*, is less preoccupied with battle campaigns and the corn exchange than with the might and right of the patriarchal state. The use and abuse of power and authority touches the lives of Sue and Jude in manifold, intimate ways, as it had never touched the life of the Edlins. 'Abuse' looms large and takes the form, in their consciousness, of the 'common enemy coercion': the body politic whose institutionalised values compress individuals into stereotypes, their relationships into fixed structures, their very lives into pre-shaped moulds from which there is no easy breaking.

Perceiving that her frustrated wish to be released from the marriage contract is not one of the natural tragedies of love, 'but a tragedy artificially manufactured for people who in a natural state would find relief in parting!' (*JO*, p.224), Sue levels her criticism at state and institution as agents of the 'artificially manufactured' tragedy.

Divorce does not, of course, occur to her since she has no right, under the prevailing laws, to petition for one. Despite the much lauded Matrimonial Causes Act of 1857, Victorian Divorce Laws continued to uphold the archaic principle of one law for the rich and another for the poor and women: 'The position of women and poor people being not improved by the 1857 Bill'.[24] To divorce Phillotson Sue would have had to provide evidence of her husband's 'incestuous Adultery, or of Bigamy with Adultery, or of Rape, or of Sodomy or Bestiality, or of Adultery coupled with such cruelty as without Adultery would have entitled her to a Divorce *a Mensa et Thoro*, or of Adultery coupled with Desertion, and without reasonable excuse, for Two Years or upwards' (I quote verbatim from the 1857 Statute). Alternatively, according to the 1878 amendment, she would have had to prove 'aggravated' assault (that is, gain a conviction) within the meaning of the statute 24th,

25th Vic., c.100. Sue, then, has no grounds for divorce. Neither incompatibility nor mental cruelty were admissible grounds.

Phillotson, on the other hand, does have adequate grounds, and here the double standard becomes glaringly obvious. Although both agree, eventually, to separate (albeit unlawfully in the divorce context since collusion technically invalidated the plaintiff's case), Sue has no legal grounds for divorce whatsoever, whereas Phillotson may sue on the most facile of grounds: that his wife has refused his request to stay after, as the schoolmaster puts it, 'I said I had forgiven her' (*JO*, p.263). Phillotson then divorces Sue on the basis of her refusal to continue to cohabit with him compounded with an accusation of adultery, which going unchallenged is evidently deemed proven by default (*JO*, p.329).

What Hardy does not mention but does tacitly acknowledge is the husband's additional entitlement to claiming damages against the co-respondent. A wife had no such entitlement. The schoolmaster's suit nominating 'Phillotson versus Phillotson and Fawley' legally defines Jude as co-respondent (*JO*, p.265); there is no reason for Hardy to say more for not only would this contingency have been common knowledge to his readers, but Jude's poverty would have made a suit for damages against him useless. The detail, '. . . and Fawley', is enough to yield up the significant point that Sue is the 'property' appropriated and Jude the appropriator of the 'property', for which he could be asked to pay.

Unlike the offending Marriage Laws, which are felt to grate without relief upon the individual consciousness, the Phillotson-versus-Phillotson-and-Fawley proceedings roll on as part of the impersonal machinery of State, rumbling interminably in the background of the novel. Reaching their 'consciousness but as a distant sound, and an occasional missive which they hardly understood' (*JO*, p.265), the whole business, while perplexing, seems completely mechanical. The more so to Sue who finds the circumstances of the Decree Absolute quite artificial: 'Are we – you and I – just as free now as if we had never married at all?' 'One thing is certain,' Jude replies blandly, 'however the decree is brought about, a marriage is dissolved when it is dissolved' (*JO*, p.266).

Jude is, of course, principally concerned with physically

possessing Sue: 'Well my dearest,' he says at the first opportunity, 'the result of all this is that we can marry after a decent interval' (*JO*, p.267). Sue is not so sure that this is the result. There appears to be the very reasonable doubt in her mind that to dissolve a legal contract *ex cathedra*, so to speak – that is without her written or verbal consent – is not necessarily the same thing as being released from a promise, which requires the oath-giver to consent, not only to its making and keeping, but also to its breaking. And as far as she is concerned, her agreement with Phillotson was to their separate lives – not to her re-marriage to Jude.

Sue's feeling of unreality at being free and seemingly never married at all is partly due to the very physical effect upon her of the marriage contract – that it gives the husband rights of ownership over his wife's body. These are not effects, in the psychic dread and revulsion they have induced, that *can* be spirited away by legal decree. She does not feel free. Nor as Phillotson's benighted wife does she ever feel in possession of herself in the smallest degree. Indeed, so ingrained in her is the sense that she is totally unprotected, unbefriended – 'a woman tossed about, all alone' (*JO*, p.214) – that her entreaties for a separation are based solely upon the notion of a simple renunciation of the promissory oath, and not upon legal considerations at all: 'We made the compact, and surely we can cancel it – not legally of course, but we can morally' (*JO*, p.232).

Simple renunciation of the promissory oath would, in fact, have been more than adequate had not prevailing marriage laws dictated otherwise. Sue's attempt to work towards a mutually acceptable arrangement, an agreement to separate on amicable terms so that, as she puts it, 'then we might be friends, and meet without pain to either' (*JO*, p.232) suggests a most satisfactory solution. The divorce decree, by contrast, requires that the female partner be appointed the guilty party, and her lover likewise. A far from amicable solution.

Sue's solution, which no contemporary law would sanction, is noticeably progressive: collusion and incompatibility are both now considered reasonable practice and grounds respectively.

To all intents and purposes, as Hardy perceives it, there has been little improvement over the years upon the barbaric method of wife-selling as practised by Henchard in *The Major of Casterbridge*.[25] In effect one ritualised procedure has been substituted for another but without changing the fundamental principle of male privilege. Once upon a time a man might auction his wife, custom not law sanctioning the procedure, but in Sue's world he might dispose of her on a more favourable basis: woman still has a price on her head and man receives the secular law's blessing in the event.

Hardy's characterisation of Sue with her sexual repressions and inhibitions, her lack of that sensuality, sexual luxuriance and physical self-delight that Hardy sees as the birthright of his strong women, strikes a note of severity into this, his most polemical attack upon Victorian sexual codes and practices and their institutionalisation in marriage. This marked severity not only adds tonicity to his attack, it also permits him a clear, dispassionate focus upon the mind and psycho-sexual make-up of a highly intelligent young woman prone to neurasthenia and subjected to unremitting stress. Were Sue endowed with a voluptuous sensuality, to which Hardy would (surely) be tempted to defer at times, the emotional temperature of the novel would lose its hard edge of bitter repression, its sharp focus upon the harsh codes that govern the lives of women struggling for independence, for autonomy, for ways and means of governing their own lives. Seeking to sustain this focus, Hardy deflects attention from Sue's volatile presence, resisting her allure, resisting the gentle ardour he displays with Tess who so captivates his imagination that he is moved to reach out to the soft, mushroom-skin of her forearm, or into the glistening red interior of her mouth. With Sue he averts his glance, countering nearly all impulses to render her in terms of warm, physical immediacy. It is upon Arabella instead that he rests his gaze. From the 'fine, dark-eyed girl' of the opening chapters, with her 'round and prominent bosom, full lips, perfect teeth, and the rich complexion of a Cochin's egg' (*JO*, p.44), right through to the hymn-singing matron at Kennetbridge Fair, Arabella's form is the object of Hardy's ranging, appreciative eye.[26]

It is solely through Jude's ascetic eyes that the ethereal, sexless Sue is apprehended, although by establishing alternative sightings, conflicting perspectives, notably Arabella's and his own, Hardy ensures that a proper distinction is drawn between the respective points of view. The distinction is an important one. We are drawn, on the one hand, to a close understanding of Jude, whose fantasies about the sexless 'ennobled' Sue have their roots in a culturally conditioned fear and guilt about sexuality. On the other, we are invited to glimpse, for evaluative purposes, the less conjectural Sue who prefigures Jude's circumscriptions. This is not a Sue that Jude perceives nor is it indeed a Sue who ever achieves self-knowledge, self-realisation. But it is a Sue that both Arabella and Hardy perceive to be nascently sensual, more corporeal than ethereal, and not, as Jude would have her, 'a phantasmal, bodiless creature, one who . . . has so little animal passion' (*JO*, p.268).

The assimilation of Sue to Jude's Christminster phantasma – his dream of a nourishing world in which the 'Alma Mater' of his fantasies will cherish her lost 'beloved son' – is predicated by Hardy at the very outset. From his first sexual encounter with Arabella it is evident that it is not just upon Christminster and Sue that Jude projects his 'yearning . . . to find something to anchor on, to cling to' (*JO*, p.30). Orphanism and, presumably, maternal deprivation have wrought in him a desperate need for a reassuring, nurturing love object which he might idolise, to which he might cling, on which he might become completely reliant. His overtures and responses to Arabella are telling. The 'dark-eyed' compelling creature who holds him to the spot against his intention excites in him an erotic passion and, simultaneously, a passive, child-like dependency. His virility is not held in question – on the contrary, as he dwells upon his encounter with Arabella he is erotically aroused to a readiness which no amount of mental application to Greek studies and hands guided to the temples will slacken:

In the gliding and noiseless current of his life . . . he felt as a snake must feel who has sloughed off its winter skin, and cannot understand the brightness and sensitiveness of its new one.

He would not go out and meet her, after all. He sat down, opened the book, and with his elbows firmly planted on the table, and his hands to his temples, began at the beginning. (*JO*, pp.48–9)

To no avail! No amount of urging hand and mind to the

Testament will harden the spirit against the roused flesh – or as Hardy suggestively puts it:

In short, as if materially, a compelling arm of extraordinary muscular power seized hold of him – something which had nothing in common with the spirits and influences that had moved him hitherto. (*JO*, p.49)

Ready and able he may be, but Hardy's use of the passive tense here implies a contradictory response in his sexual make-up which will shortly surface in his relationship with Arabella.

Accordingly, arrayed in his best clothes, Jude now strikes away over path and field in Arabella's direction where, upon arrival, he announces himself by knocking on her door with the 'knob of his stick' (*JO*, p.50). All this phallic posturing notwithstanding, he now presents himself to his lover as something rather different, as an utterly puerile young man!

As earlier, when he had sensed that he should toy with this voluptuous gratifier of his needs and 'assert more sportiveness' (*JO*, p.47), so again he decides to play at pleasing her. But not in any galvanising or virile sense, or even as a companionable peer, but in an infantile way that places Arabella in the dominant role and himself in the role of something resembling an agreeable little boy playing at being grown-up. He talks silly talk – the 'commonest local twaddle' (*JO*, p.50). And when their long walk creates a thirst it is Arabella who takes the initiative and suggests tea. And when that is not available, it is she who suggests beer. Jude meanwhile, is alternately gazing and moping and showing himself to be naive and helpless at every point.

It seems inevitable that his first sexual experience, which reinforces his need for feminine solicitude but does not develop in him an active, assertive sex-drive, should leave him ill-equipped to cope with Sue. Whereas she can readily fulfil the roles of loving cousin, fond kin, and companionable woman – all familiar, socially approved roles – she remains as yet sexually unawakened, sexually immature, and Jude's manner of alternating between adulation and condescension simply leaves her brittle and nervous and unaroused. Had Sue only the most tentative of sexual longings, Jude must surely have robbed her of them from the outset by high-ranking over her and above the sex act for which she is, he insists, too finely tuned and ethereal.

Even on the night when they come, for the first time, to make love, Jude so persistently distances Sue that the moment of consummation becomes unwittingly abased by the mode of its undertaking. Insisting upon making a verbal declaration of his desires, first in a hectoring manner that both minimises the sensuality of the moment and maximises its awkwardness, then with supplicating gestures, which may invoke pity but not sexual arousal, Jude at no point approaches Sue without a barrage of words. Small, affective intimacies, tender embraces, soft caresses, lingering kisses – these Sue might well have been able to answer. Instead, she is harangued:

All that's best and noblest in me loves you, and your freedom from everything that's gross has elevated me, and enabled me to do what I should never have dreamt myself capable of . . . It is all very well to preach about self-control, and the wickedness of coercing a woman. But I should just like a few virtuous people . . . to have been in my tantalizing position with you these late weeks. (*JO*, p.275)

How can Sue yield now out of any other feelings than guilt and responsibility, and a frightening sense that at all costs she must not appear 'gross' (sexually passionate) lest she lose that noblest and best love?

Does Jude ever take seriously, or indeed, take at all, her aggressive/defensive postures? Her sudden animal starts and flights? Her self-confessed impulse to kick? (*JO*, p.224) Her advance/retreat testing activities, her enticement/rejection seduction moves are all signals inviting sexual recognition. But they draw a response in Jude only in so far as they seem to him to add to her mystification. Whereas he can read Arabella clearly – she is after all a classic text so to speak – Sue requires a good deal of translation. She has long since been required to restate herself, to repress her sexuality and to riddle herself with contradictory signals. Predictably these fail to signify with Jude, whose regard for the 'other sex' as 'beings outside his life and purposes' (*JO*, pp.46,47) has scarcely provided him with anything more than the most superficial of insights into the psychological complexities of sexual relationships. He has, moreover, clear preconceptions about the woman he will love, and that Sue could be anything other than the 'phantasmal, bodiless creature' of his vivid imaginings does not enter his head.

He traps her in this image from the very first moment. As he gazes at her illuminating texts in an Anglican bookshop so she seems to personify the very essence, the very atmosphere of Christminster, *his own* atmosphere, he thinks! He has already shaped a rather curious kin relationship with the city as if, at last, he has found a portion of the world which belongs to him:

Yes, Christminster shall be my Alma Mater; and I'll be her beloved son, in whom she shall be well pleased. (*JO*, p.43)

He now draws himself not into the life of the people but into the designs and forms of inanimate things:

Not as yet having mingled with the active life of the place it was largely non-existent to him. But the saints and prophets in the window-tracery, the paintings in the galleries, the statues, the busts, the gurgoyles, the corbel-heads – these seemed to breathe his atmosphere. (*JO*, p.92)

Not the active life but inanimate relics inspire the dream, and moving from dream city to dream woman, Jude then enters the bookshop containing,

Anglican books, stationary, texts, and fancy goods: little plaster angels on brackets, Gothic-framed pictures of saints, ebony crosses that were almost crucifixes, prayer-books that were almost missals. He felt very shy of looking at the girl in the desk; she was so pretty that he could not believe it possible that she should belong to him. Then she spoke ... and he recognized in the accents certain qualities of his own voice; softened and sweetened, but his own. (*JO*, p.95)

Framed by saints and angels, breathing 'his atmosphere', 'his voice', Sue, the beloved incarnate, is formed in Jude's own likeness, fashioned by his own desires, belonging 'to him ... his own ... his own'.

As the 'more or less ... ideal character about whose form he began to weave curious and fantastic day-dreams' takes a hold on his imagination, so her appearance takes on 'little plaster angel' likenesses: her china-doll-like eyes, 'liquid untrans-lateable eyes', and her lips which 'take life from some words just spoken', transform her into an animated effigy, a marionette, a doll-woman (*JO*, p.96). She is in no sense fleshly, no 'complete and substantial female animal', as Jude perceives Arabella (*JO*, p.44). Rather she is a vibrant presence, 'all . . . nervous motion', a guiding light, 'a kindly star, an elevating power', and more conversably, 'a companion in Anglican worship, a tender friend' (*JO*, pp.96–97). This rapid mental progression from lofty 'star' to companionable 'friend' blurs the distinction between the unattainable and the attainable, the ethereal and the real, the unknowable and the knowable. And indeed Jude's tendency to blur such distinctions imprisons Sue in a fiction of his own making. Her stellar quality supervenes in his imagination to eclipse all sense of her flesh and blood presence.

With Jude removed from the Christminster scene, Hardy now introduces Sue from a contrasting vantage point – his own entirely: there is no other observer in view. And this is no ethereal, sainted Sue but a very physical Sue with feet and hands and a restless, active body. 'Light-footed', she sets out on her afternoon's holiday, her atmosphere now organic nature and her previous sepulchred surroundings significantly distanced – 'left behind' (*JO*, p.100). And no plaster angels now, but rather pagan statuettes, which she first fingers, then clasps, then purchases (after some un-spiritual price-bargaining), and finally proceeds to carry home. Perceiving with some nervousness how very large and how very naked they are, and how their whitish substance rubs off on her body, she wraps them up in 'huge burdock leaves, parsley, and other rank growths' gathered from the hedge, in order to bear them home undetected (*JO*, p.101).

This is the first of what I would call Hardy's alternative sightings. And the Sue perceived here is no phantasma, nor is she ethereal, nor is she engaged in any kind of 'sweet, saintly . . . business'. Instead, she bears home her 'heathen' load (*JO*, p.101), wraps it up yet again, but this time in homespun brown paper lest the dreadful Miss Fontover should pounce on its impious contents, and spends the rest of the evening in a state of restless physical excitement. In a 'great zest for unpacking her objects' she finally stops fingering them and unrobes them – placing them candlelit upon her chest of drawers – and after a restless attempt to read Gibbon, alternately flinging herself on the bed and jumping up again, she unrobes *herself* and spends the remainder of the night 'tossing and staring' at her naked, pagan figurines.

As this textual separation of perspectives and voices makes clear, it is not Hardy who idealises Sue, not he who perpetuates her mystification, her sexlessness. It is Jude and Jude alone whose erstwhile sense, in Arabella's proximity, of being 'whisked ... back to a milk-fed infancy' (*JO*, p.131), now becomes a more conscious 'childlike yearning for the one being in the world to whom it seemed possible to fly' (*JO*, p.131). His cousin Sue will become his Alma Mater.

It is of course Hardy who situates Sue in the closed, sepulchred spaces of Anglican bookshops and the Cathedral Church of Cardinal College; surroundings conducive to Jude's need to nourish dreams of the beloved ensphered by plaster angels and psalmic chantings. But it is Jude, not Hardy, who fixes Sue in these confining, enclosed spaces. Hardy, by contrast, follows her out into the 'field' and back into the 'bedroom' where, with girlish nervousness she takes a self-conscious, tremulous glance at her newly awakened sexual consciousness.

It is a very shortlived glance or exploration. Sue is rapidly drawn into Jude's orbit and thereafter Phillotson's, and there are no more assays of this kind. 'All that's best and noblest' in Jude's love for her is sustained by his belief in her 'freedom from everything that's gross' (*JO*, p.275), and Sue, at her 'best and noblest', represses her sexuality accordingly. (She cannot even bring herself to reveal to him the reasons why Miss Fontover stamped upon her statuary. Jude never discovers that they were offensive not for their Popish-ness but for their Pagan sensuousness.)

Learned talk now becomes Sue's most effective weapon and her most effective shield. Heavily investing in this, in the belief that in commanding her learned language she is 'mistress of herself' (*JO*, p.176), she is aware that Jude, lulled into pacific contentment by her sweet baffling talk, is completely charmed by her remoteness.

If Jude needs to read Sue in this way Arabella does not. And although Jude's perspective is central and Arabella's peripheral, hers gains considerable force and credibility by virtue of receiving Hardy's support, in the sense that her penetrating insights and objective appraisals are supplemented throughout the text by his own. Her 'readings' become an amplification of his, both providing a variant interpretation of Sue.

Arabella is cast in a variety of roles: seductive maid, discontented wife, unscrupulous lover, respectable matron, hot-gospeller, fun-loving barmaid. But as Sue's interpreter she is consistently reliable. This is her one immutable role – curiously, a role that has never been appraised by critics.

In terms of narrative function, Arabella's point of view fulfills two related objectives for Hardy. First, it retains critical distance. Arabella's 'feminine' last judgement upon Sue juxtaposed to the authorial voice balances a perspective in favour of woman's intimate knowledge of woman. And second, as a corollary to the first, by drawing upon Arabella's sharp intuitive powers from the vantage point of woman-perceiving-woman unfettered by sexual ideologies and preconceptions, Hardy seeks to ensure that readers do not fall into the trap of reading Sue as Jude reads her. His is but one, limited point of view. Arabella's contrasting view, her sheer physicality and sexual vitality giving her a perceptual advantage over Jude, invites us to explore Sue's sexuality as he clearly fails to do.

Despite Arabella's living down to the low standards that are expected of her within the life of the novel, conditioned to expect the least of her capabilities to be the best she can achieve, she is nonetheless a woman of untapped potential. Her sexual energies are, it seems, the outward expression of latent dynamic, creative urges in need of an outlet, but however unbridled her sexual appetite and however unrefined her habits, her sexual vitality sharpens, in Hardy's view, her perceptual acuity, her discerning judgement, and her sharp intuition. These remain consistently, demonstrably, keen. In common with most of Hardy's strong women, and, for all her unappealing qualities I would count Arabella among them, sexual vigour combines with an acuteness of all the senses, to sharpen insight, to fire alertness and to quicken intelligence.

Arabella's lonely isolated existence in a roadside cottage, caring for a vegetable garden, a single pig and Jude, is clearly miserably unfulfilling for a woman of adventurous and enquiring mind. But she applies herself to the task in hand with spirited vigour and competence. She has a fine markswoman's eye: her missile at Jude in the chitterling episode scores an immediate hit! She has a discerning palate: detecting additives in adulterated ale after the briefest spell as barmaid. And from her farming experience as a young girl she has acquired skills in pig husbandry which draw approval, if not from the reproachful Jude, at least from the professional slaughterer. Not least are her Thespian talents. Hardy describes with undisguised relish the 'extraordinary spectacle' of her performance in front of the Sunday walkers at Alfredstone: 'bonnet-less, her dishevelled hair blowing in the wind, her bodice apart, her sleeves rolled above the elbows for work, and her hands reeking with fat' (*JO*, p.76). She enacts with perfect timing the serio-comic role of the abused, slatternly maid. Jude, needless to say, is not amused.

Timing is Arabella's forte. She prepares her dramatic exit from her unsatisfactory life with Jude opportunely, and with a flourish that would do credit to any Verismo heroine of the day. She extracts no promises or provisos, nor does she provoke any long-drawn out scenes or recriminations. Sue's exit from Jude's life, modelled upon the more conventional conjugal pattern of rejection, punishment and humiliation, is, by contrast, a painfully destructive affair. Mortified, stripped of all dignity and purpose, Jude loses not only the woman he loves and values but his own self-esteem into the bargain.

Although it is not Hardy's purpose to invite us to care for Arabella, it is primarily by setting the novel's emotional temperature at such a mercurial high that he intensifies, at her expense, the sense of Sue's and Jude's exquisite passions and frenzied emanations. These tend to supercharge the text to the exclusion of most else.

As a voluptuous, sexually active woman, Arabella has, of necessity, to be phased into the background so that her perspective on Sue, later in the novel, might not be discredited by the Grundyist. Thus, in her interpretive role she appears on the scene, successively, as a respectable married woman, a matronly widow, a chapel-goer, and finally, as Jude's lawful wife. Hardy thereby ensures that she holds her own well enough, and despite the anxious efforts of her prime detractors (Jude and Sue) to set themselves up by putting her down, we are never given reason to doubt her judgement as a truthful reporter of all she witnesses. Unlike Sue, who makes as many riddles out of mind as out of body, Arabella scorns the language of men. She shows no sign of dependency upon creed or doctrine and is noticeably free from prejudice or zealotry. The single exception is her brief alliance with the Chapel-going set, and even this Hardy turns to her advantage. Arabella is no sooner the sanctimonious prude than the new guise is discarded and her native honesty breaks through; her efforts at self-salvation utterly fail. What does emerge from the Chapel incident is an exposition of her total lack of self-deception and pretension. This is all the more apparent for its contrast with Sue's struggle to confront the self, remain true to the self, and to make herself responsible for her own actions. Desire and will conflict in Arabella, but piety, while it may look good, does not feel good to this earnest hymnist who protests.

'Do what I will, and though I sing hymns wi' all my strength, I have not been able to help thinking about 'n; which I've no right to do as a chapel member.'
    'Can't ye fix your mind upon what was said by the London preacher to-day, and try to get rid of your wandering fancies that way?'
    'I do. But my wicked heart will ramble off in spite of myself!' (*JO*, p.325)

Unlike Sue in her affliction, driven to locate the source of her 'wickedness' in the 'Curse of Adam' (*JO*, p.356), Arabella abdicates not a whit of responsibility to any external force. We are aware, of course, that Sue, as the tormented heroine caught in the crossfire of that 'deadly war', is trapped in a far wider net. Even so, Arabella's spiritual void does demand a certain courage, something of the courage of the existentialist orphaned from the all-caring, all-loving Divinity. Her confrontation with the self, unbound by any form of external saving grace, manifests a strength of thought and action that the oppressed Sue struggles desperately to own. Moreover, had Arabella succumbed to what Hardy describes as 'the serene heights of a soul conscious ... of spiritual ... superiority' (*JO*, p.324), we might trust to her faith but not at all to the integrity of her thoughts and feelings: 'Feelings are feelings! ... I won't be a creeping hypocrite any longer.' (*JO*, p.326) Hardy's immediate impulse at this stage is to countermand the impression Arabella gives of smug self-righteousness in her 'serene heights' at the Kennetbridge fair. It is significant that he leaves no temporal or spatial gaps in his narrative which might allow readers to consolidate negative feelings towards her. Instead, he rapidly shifts his focus from the hostilities between the women to Arabella's delightful candour, and her admission of sexual desire for Jude. 'I do dream sometimes o' nights', she confides, 'quite against my wishes' (*JO*, p.325). And we are won!

Arabella alternately confounds and disarms us. The scene of Jude's death is notable. With her total lack of reverence for death-bed conventions she flies from the 'beautiful corpse' to the yet more beautiful day that beckons, to return at the last to speak heartfelt, reverent 'truths' on Sue's behalf. Truths that the lovers had been barely able to acknowledge for themselves. For all Sue's swearing to this and that cult or creed, Arabella suggests, she was no 'sweet saintly Christian', no 'phantasmal, bodiless creature', no 'Alma Mater' and no heavenly 'star', but a flesh and blood creature with womanly needs and a deeply passionate heart. Widow Edlin, suggesting Sue has now found peace, is rebutted by Arabella:

'She may swear that on her knees to the holy cross upon her necklace till she's hoarse, but it won't be true!' said Arabella. 'She's never found peace since she left his arms, and never will again till she's as he is now!' (*JO*, p.423)

Earlier, observing Jude and Sue walking together at the Wessex Agricultural Show, Arabella's jealousy gives way to intense curiosity as she tries to determine the depth of their intimacy – the true nature of their relationship. At first she is bitterly envious:

As far as they themselves are concerned they are the only two in the show. I should be ashamed of making myself so silly if I were he! (*JO*, p.302)

With what Hardy here calls her 'sharpened vision', she progresses, however, to a closely analytical view, communicating her thoughts as, simultaneously, she watches the lovers from a distance. The more she watches the more convinced she becomes, for reasons entirely of her own, that the undemonstrative Sue of first impressions is a woman of far deeper feeling than might be suspected.

See how he looks round at her, and lets his eyes rest on her. I am inclined to think that she don't care for him quite so much as he does for her. She's not a particular warm-hearted creature to my thinking, though she cares for him pretty middling much – as much as she's able to; and he could make her heart ache a bit if he likes to try. (*JO*, p.302)

From being 'inclined to think that she don't care' to sensing that Sue's heart could be made to 'ache a bit', Arabella registers a whole complexity of feeling in Sue that catches not only at her contradictoriness but at the dormant passions underlying the contradictory signals. It is most subtly and sensitively done, and as we follow her very thought processes in flux, as we listen and watch as she listens and watches, we cannot doubt her ability to report back her findings with absolute accuracy to readers to whom Sue is temporarily unobservable. Had Hardy simply recorded her final observation without preamble, her insights into Sue's nature would still signify in their abbreviated form, but they would lose much of their impact and meaning. It is the process of careful observation, cognitive adjustment and psychological understanding at work, not the commentary in itself, that invites us to trust in Arabella's judgement and wisdom.

The Sue that she perceives is then a vulnerable but self-camouflaging woman harbouring smothered or latent passions under a composed exterior. Arabella goes even further: 'She don't know what love is – at least what I call love! I can see in her face she don't' (*JO*, p.303). This more we then learn. Sue is still sexually unawakened, not yet orgasmic, not yet generating those subtle sex signals that surge from the erotic body of the woman to the erotic body of the man. Jude, we know, is responsive enough to Arabella's erotic signals, what Hardy calls woman's 'unvoiced call', and it is evident that Sue's 'call' is inaudible here. Unlike Arabella, she exerts no riveting or melting effect upon her lover. All told, there is a noticeable lack of sexual intimacy in this one major scene offering a glimpse of the interregnum between the consummation and dissolution of the cousins' turbulent relationship.

The scene of the Wessex Agricultural Show is one of those rare but critically important occasions in *Jude* where Hardy 'watches' Sue in the company, as it were, of Arabella, co-ordinating his point of view with her own. She has spent a large part of the day idling after the lovers; as they enter the horticultural tent, she is still in their proximity, but it is now Hardy's turn to speak:

In the meantime the more exceptional couple and the boy lingered in the pavilion of flowers – an enchanted palace to their appreciative taste – Sue's usually pale cheeks reflecting the pink of the tinted roses at which she gazed; for the gay sights, the air, the music, and the excitement of a day's outing with Jude, had quickened her blood and made her eyes sparkle with vivacity. (*JO*, p.306)

Like the episode of the naked figurines, this is a picture of a young woman of decidedly physical presence who reacts to her surroundings in a decidedly sensuous manner. The immediacy and impact of her sensations is evidently too vivid, too vital for Hardy to resist. His account abounds with physical images, sensory impressions: taste, touch, scent, sight, sound. The narrative shifts from the initial mood of stillness and repose, conveyed by such words as 'lingered' and 'reflecting', to an accelerated rhythmic pace: the shorter, staccato notation of 'the tinted roses/at which she gazed;/for the gay sights,/the air,/the music ...' The heightened pace, here, approximates to Sue's catch-in-the-throat breathless excitement; and as these words heave and cluster, from 'pavilions' and 'enchanted palaces' to 'gazed', 'gay', 'eyes' and 'vivacity' – from the first 'lingering' to the last 'quickening' – so the sense is of a palpitating, live, sexually aroused woman. She moves into Hardy's consciousness, she stirs his vision, she moulds his discourse.

This is not the Sue we usually see. It is as if Hardy must, just once or twice, draw out her repressed soul from its confined interior spaces to release it back into the wider arena of the organic, natural world where it surges into life. Certainly Arabella, who had accurately perceived in Sue a fractiousness, a 'fidgety' nervousness (*JO*, p.303), an appearance of sexual frustration, is now eaten away with curiosity to see how Jude will respond to his sensuously aroused companion. For what she had also seen,

was Sue detaining Jude almost against his will while she learnt the names of this variety and that, and put her face within an inch of their blooms to smell them. (*JO*, p.306)

We infer then that Jude, detained almost against his will, is not fully given up to the moment. He is not drawn, as Hardy is drawn, to the voluptuous Sue, nor does he see her as Hardy sees her. Arabella, by contrast, sees what Hardy sees, shares his insights, and although he now alters the narrative drift to accommodate her point of view there is no disjunction in perception.

Arabella's observations now take the form of a single perfunctory phrase sandwiched between the dialogue which passes between the lovers. The narrative method neatly approximates to her mood and quashed feelings as they are now set against Hardy's own which had been delivered in poetic effulgence. At the same time the simultaneity of their shared vantage points flows from the narrative with ease. Sue puts her face 'within an inch' of the rose blossoms and tells Jude:

'I should like to push my face quite into them – the dears!' she had said. 'But I suppose it is against the rules to touch them – isn't it, Jude?'

'Yes, you baby,' said he: and then playfully gave her a little push, so that her nose went down among the petals.

'The policeman will be down on us, and I shall say it was my husband's fault!' Then she looked up at him, and smiled in a way *that told so much to Arabella.* (*JO*, p.307) (my italics)

But does it tell so much to Jude? What Arabella has perceived with her 'sharpened vision' and what Hardy has evoked even more fully, is not apparent to Jude at all. Quite unconsciously he steers away from the upturned, glowing face to propel Sue back into her dark interior spaces of mind, away from her warm, vibrant world and back to interrogatives:

'Happy?' he murmured.

She nodded.

'Why? Because you have come to the Great Wessex Agricultural Show – or because *we* have come?' (*JO*, p.307)

The spell is broken. The woman who had shed her defensive armour just long enough to experience her body as a vehicle of rich, ecstatic sensation is plummeted back into her old familiar role. She must explain herself again!

You are always trying to make me confess to all sorts of absurdities. Because I am improving my mind, of course, by seeing all these steam-ploughs, and threshing-machines, and chaff-cutters, and cows, and pigs, and sheep. (*JO*, p.307)

Here as elsewhere Sue reverts to talking 'vaguely and indis-
criminately' to prevent her interlocutor 'talking pertinently'
(*JO*, p.235) – as the list of proliferating objects signifies: mechanical objects and beasts far removed from her heightened
plane. With Jude's demand for verbal explanations she is once
more back on the barricades, and for the moment any tactical
defence will do. Detecting in him a resistance to her mood, to
her physical excitement which remains in want only of his
reciprocal response – a soft kiss, a warm embrace – she falls
back upon a barrier language as if in unconscious recognition
of his need to invoke in her a cool intellectual response and to
banish her warm physicality from his consciousness. If her words
seem more imbued with irony than seriousness her subsequent
abstraction as she drifts into a discourse upon 'Greek seriousness'
and 'Christminster luminaries' soon dispels that impression.
Sadly, pathetically, the now withdrawn and distanced Sue is
to Jude the more appealing figure. He rests 'content with a
baffle from his ever evasive companion' (*JO*, p.307).

In this brief episode a remarkable amount is happening.
Hardy 'sees' Sue, Arabella 'sees' Sue, Jude 'sees' Sue – and sees
the least. On one earlier isolated occasion and in a sexually
alert frame of mind following a night with Arabella, he had
actually registered Sue's physical presence, the shape and form
of her body: 'the delicate lines of her profile, and the small,
tight, apple-like convexities of her bodice' (*JO*, p.196). More
customarily, he has so great a need to shape her according to
his imaginings that he fails altogether to register her sexual
presence. Typically, on the night when she arrives with her
river drenched clothes clinging wetly and rather suggestively,
I would think, to her small body, Jude looks at her in purely
aesthetic, abstract terms. Her hands seem to him as 'clammy
as a marine deity' and her wet clothes cling 'like the ropes upon
the figures in the Parthenon frieze' (*JO*, p.15).

So too at the Agricultural Show. With 'Greek seriousness'
now upon her lips and 'content' upon his face, the pattern is,
by now, a familiar one. As Sue becomes discomposed, alienated
from her 'self', from her lover, so Jude remains unseeing. She
glides, so to speak, back on to the 'frieze', and fades from gay
animation to lifeless withering – or so Hardy subtly conveys in
his re-invocation of the hermeneutics of her 'blossoming'. For

just as the roses, pink blooms were earlier linked with her flushed cheeks (tumescence), so now, as she is drained of 'quickened blood' those same blossoms, we are told, will wither. Or in the words of little prophetic 'Time', all will be 'withered in a few days!' (*JO*, p.301). Hardy evokes, then, in this episode, a Sue less ethereal than exhilarated, less frigid than refrigerated, and less wanting in sexual responsiveness than in a sexually responsive lover. In other words, this is a Sue that conflicts quite openly with Jude's ideal. Sexless she is not. Sexually frustrated she may be.

This is suggested elsewhere, notably in the post-nuptial scene, where the couple are breakfasting after their first night as lovers. Hardy here exploits to the full the dramatic significance of gestures and actions. Were we to read this scene without due awareness of resemblances, as an evocation of a 'morning after' scene without interpreting what kind of 'morning after' or 'evening before' is being dramatised, it would be one of the most pointless scenes in the novel. As it happens, it is one of the most revealing. Most telling are moods. Jude, we discover, is in buoyant mood 'gaily' making plans for marriage. Sue, by contrast, is subdued and preoccupied: 'A glow had passed away from her and depression sat upon her features' (*JO*, p.276). This is hardly the manner of a woman in post-orgasmic repose, rapt in tender bliss. Moreover, Jude not only acts 'gaily' but also relaxes 'placidly' – clear symptoms of an easeful frame of mind and body. Sue, on the other hand, neither gay nor relaxed, returns Jude's kisses 'in a way she had never done before' – at first sight an ambiguous phrase, but less so if we take into account her mood of dull depression. This points to dutiful compliance rather than sexual responsiveness. In keeping with her chastened mood, contrite and meek, Sue is now bound upon a course of 'strange and unnecessary penance', leaving Jude with the melancholy thought that she is a bird 'caught at last' who shows sadness in her smile (*JO*, p.277).

The pattern of behaviour Hardy evokes not only points to, but enacts, Sue's lack of sexual fulfilment with Jude. These morning gestures mimic the act of lovemaking itself – subtly, poetically, convincingly. The active/passive conjunction of high/low temperature emotions as they are filtered through Jude's behaviour, his gestures and expressions – his initial elevation and subsequent placidity – approximates to coital excitement and post-emission repose respectively. By the same token, where Jude's behaviour mimics the heightened emotion/ low tension ease of sexual activity, so Sue's meekness, contriteness and wistful sadness – all non-kinetic emotions – mimic her repressed, inhibited response to lovemaking. For, if we recall, she had been won the night before by coercion – by the needy Jude's frustration, irritation and vociferous recriminations. Having been thus won, she subsequently experiences no physical release, through lovemaking, of emotional tension. Jude's pledge of faith in her lack of 'grossness' preordains, not free sexual expression but fear and constraint. She beds him out of guilt and anxiety – powerful repressors upon the female erotic drive.

In much the same mood of conflicting feelings, but now secure in her mind that she has established a sexual claim on Jude, Sue sets off to visit Arabella, who had intimated the previous day that it was she, Jude's lawful wife and sexual mate, who had prior claim upon him. Arabella had detected in Sue's troubled manner, as they stood talking at the door, a perceptible unease which she had rightly intuited to be Sue's uncertainty over the issue of claim. But the self-assurance that yesterday had been Arabella's is Sue's today. She confronts her rival with utmost confidence. Comparing herself favourably with Arabella's frowsiness, playing Lady Bountiful, rebuffing Arabella's open-hearted gesture of proffering a telegram for her to read, Sue stands on her pride and dignity throughout – with just a touch of triumph about her. But it is her chagrin at Arabella's sharp perception of her which is significant (for our purposes) here. 'He is mine', Sue asserts stiffly:

'He wasn't yesterday.'
Sue coloured roseate, and said, 'How do you know?'
'From your manner when you talked to me at the door.' (*JO*, p.278)

For all her morning-bed frowsiness and having to put up with Sue's superior attitude, Arabella is as astute and fair-minded now as always. Disadvantageous circumstances do not urge her to spite or sneers. On the contrary she is candid, warmhearted and not a little forgiving.

As Sue's advocate then, Arabella is exemplary. Her insight

into the unguarded. passionate, sensual Sue struggling to break from the curbing 'ennobled' mould which imprisons her, presents the reader with a deeper understanding of the strong, vital woman conceived by Hardy and tragically misconceived by Jude.

Hardy has come, in *Jude*, to a more dispassionate appraisal of patriarchal circumscriptive attitudes; the gentle Jude bears all the marks of his Wessex predecessors, albeit in smaller measure, in keeping with his exclusion from the middle-class society to which he seeks admission. However mild and forebearing, he cannot help but shape the woman he loves according to a preconceived ideal. In high-ranking her over the sexual act, in denying her a sexual reality, in nullifying her needs and desires, Jude unwittingly enforces her subjugation. A sexless Sue is a disempowered Sue. She may test neither her own active powers, nor, in consequence, his. The power to act at the deepest level of intimate sexual engagement, which she is denied, becomes, in turn, a denial of full participation in sexual union, a denial of caring and sharing, and, ultimately, a denial of sexual equality. And in Sue's world, as elsewhere in Hardy's microcosmic world, the repercussions of this denial are far-reaching and tragic.

6

CONCLUSION

In redefining Hardy's women, my first aim has been to resurrect his original conception of them: his humanly imperfect, unconventional, strong, sexually vital, risk-taking rebels. Each was unorthodox by Victorian standards of femininity; less than conventional, and, in the amalgam, less than feminine. I have also stressed their bitter, frustrating struggle to define *themselves* in a world that would deny them the right to shape their own lives, control their own bodies, explore their own needs and express their own desires.

The critical tendency has been to assess and to shape Hardy's women according to a conventional sexual ethic that emphasises certain traits and qualities believed to be innate in women: passivity, inconstancy, vanity and so forth. So, by way of conclusion, I wish to take a closer look at what I believe to be an ideological conflict here. The danger is that critical exegesis shapes Hardy's more exceptional women to a preconceived pattern, to prescriptive formulae. This, in turn, perpetuates, beyond the life of the novel, the very attitudes Hardy seeks to attack.

I would suggest that, as Hardy presents the case, these so-called innate feminine qualities are not so much gender-determined as determined by preconceptions of gender. According to his conceptual framework, woman continually risks entrapment by male attitudes. For example, Elfride is trapped by the conceptual shape framed principally by Knight (but echoed and reinforced by critics), which construes and, in turn condemns, her generosity of feeling, her need for sexual exploration, as inconstancy. The same distorting mirror is held up to Bathsheba. The self-delighting, adventurous woman as conceived by Hardy, but preconceptually redefined by Oak, barely survives the warping of her true nature in a world in which woman is to be shaped according to man's will.

A major difficulty arises when critics choose to identify with the hero's point of view. For example, one still hears, today, of Bathsheba the irrepressible flirt, never of Oak the blustering browbeater. Yet, there is nothing, either in the novels or in the poetry, to suggest that Hardy himself identified with the Oaks of his world, and a good deal to suggest that he identified, in wish and desire, with the nonconformist rebels – which includes his daring, adventurous, strong women. And in his private correspondence this becomes a self-evident truth.

Victorian accusations of misogynism are perhaps under-standable, since it was a profanity to many that Hardy's great heroines did not personify moral perfection and the 'conscience of man' – the pedestal-role he conscientiously abjures.[1] But for modern critics to be partisan to this view seems inappropriate, to say the least. Particularly since they have access to biographical material not available to the Victorian: Hardy's correspondence and notebooks. From these we learn, if we had not already learned it from his treatment of women in the novels, that Hardy had a love of gifted, imaginative, strong women. We learn, for instance, of his deep, longlasting affection for the intellectually gifted Florence Henniker,[2] and of his high regard for one of the century's strongest women, George Sand.[3] We read too, of his admiration for women rulers: the British Constitution, he says, 'has worked so much better under Queens than Kings the Crown should by rights descend from woman to woman'.[4] The coy flirt, predictably, exasperated him,[5] but, on the other hand, his love of active, free-thinking women noticeably coloured his attitude towards what he called the 'irritated crusty members' of men's clubs who were, in his opinion, 'too selfish' in their reluctance to admit women members to their confines.[6] In attempting, though, to introduce, into his fiction, active, free-thinking women, for whom marriage is not the most desirable goal, Hardy laid himself open, not only to hostile criticism but also to misinterpretation. The culturally valued model was sweetly reasonable and compliant, not free-thinking and rebellious. And, moreover, her highest aim would be, not only to please the men in her life with her attentive, devoted ways, but also to keep herself in constant preparation for a husband.

If he were a woman, Hardy told Florence Henniker in the more liberated climate of 1918, he would think twice about entering matrimony 'in these days of emancipation when everything is open to the sex'.[7] But four or five decades earlier, this view, as expressed in his novels, violated the ethical codes of a culture high-ranking the doll-woman above all others. As late as 1891 Hardy was still wrestling with its hold upon the cultural imagination: 'The doll of English fiction', he protested to H. W. Massingham, 'must be demolished.'[8] But did such demolition denote misogynism? To many a Victorian it did, and against these Hardy reacted with justifiable resentment and the rueful cry that his novels had 'suffered so much from misrepresentation as being attacks on womankind'.[9]

Seeing the necessity of freeing women from the tyranny of the doll/madonna imago in all its incorporeal flawlessness, Hardy sought to restore to woman, or to her fictional counterpart, not only a flesh and blood reality but also a human nature lovable in all its imperfections. He would go so far, in fact, as to demand a fair showing of both malign and benign characteristics – seeing in George Eliot:

A truly magnificent revelation of the nobleness that is in women, [but] the other side is not fairly shown. The mystery of feminine malignity is barely touched upon. Art ought to be impartially representative.[10]

The 'other side' he has in mind has little to do with misogyny. 'Feminine malignity' as a 'mystery' is inexplicable; a matter of hidden origins or deep psychological causes, as we discover in his novels, where man's persistent censure and disparagement drives woman to acts of self-concealment, deceit, secrecy and capriciousness. These are defensive acts resulting from the deep-seated shame, self-distrust and loss of self-esteem produced by that socially approved method of subordinating women: the inculcation of guilt.

Impartial representation then, takes account of the world as it is for Hardy, not excluding 'feminine malignity' and the yet more troubling issues of male domination and sexual inequality. Writing to Gosse he expresses surprise that

such a woman of the people as George Eliot should have carried on the prejudice to some extent in her treatment of Hetty, whom she would not have us regard as possessing equal rights with Donnithorne.[11]

And in declining to write an Introduction to a new publication of Fielding's works, he explains to the publishers that Fielding

as a local novelist has never been clearly regarded to my mind: and his aristocratic, even feudal attitude towards the peasantry (e.g. his view of Molly as a 'slut' to be ridiculed, not as a simple girl, as worthy a creation of Nature as the lovely Sophia) should be exhibited strongly.[12]

And it was surely Hardy's egalitarian principles that turned him against 'the perfect woman in fiction', and to protest, in a letter to Katherine Macquoid, that 'no satire on the sex is intended ... by the imperfections of my heroines'.[13] In more ironic vein, he might have added, 'nor is any satire intended by the imperfections of my heroes'.

Hardy apparently underestimated the conflict his readers might experience in identifying closely with heroines who arouse intensely caring feelings but simultaneously threaten the status-quo – or rather, that all-too-elevated prescription of perfect womanhood so much to be desired and so much to be emulated that few women, if any, might have suspected that in aspiring to the Angel model they were identifying against themselves. None, after all, would achieve perfection, though many would live with a permanent sense of failure, of being in the wrong.

The recurring derogation, by critics, of the unconventional and imperfect Hardy heroine reflects, I think, an unconscious desire to subordinate where subordination is felt to be lacking in his general scheme of things (as I argued in the case of Bathsheba; the same would go for Tess), and where sub-ordination seems to be necessary to public morality and woman's role in the society. It appears that in falling short of angelic perfection, yet, at the same time, beloved of a certain class of men – if not middle-class by birth, middle-class by aspiration – the unconventional Hardy heroine, in her defiance of man's will and expectations, must, in turn, be defied, or, at any rate, undermined and disempowered.

A suitable example is provided by two major critics. To explain the attractiveness of Hardy's women, Havelock Ellis, in the 1880s, and John Bayley, in the 1970s,[14] single them out, reductively, as feminine and weak and 'other', and do so in significantly phallocentric terms: Ellis speaks of their lack of 'virility' and Bayley of their lack of moral 'firmness'. The virile and the firm may of course be imperfect but never weak. They may also, given the phallic connotations, more plausibly be male. Thus by neat sleight-of-hand, by virtue of a lack of virility and firmness which establishes 'otherness' and weakness in the same breath, the Hardy heroine preserves her attractiveness, her femininity, by default. She is, in her moral nonconformity, not firm, and in her sexual attractiveness, not male. And she is now less threatening. The weak, unlike the imperfect, are inherently without power.

Hardy's stress, not upon weakness but upon imperfection, is sufficiently important to his critique to warrant closer attention here. To return to his texts, I would begin by pointing out that he consistently apportions to male and female alike corresponding moral, intellectual and physical attributes. This reduces (without rendering all characters uniform), culturally prescribed gender traits, the 'otherness', that inevitably opens the way for sex-divisive attitudes. By this means, 'feminine' passivity, for instance, becomes as much an attribute of the male as of the female. Compare, say, Stephen Smith's passive withdrawal from the misery of unrequited love with Elfride's hot pursuit of her lover under comparable circumstances. Or, to go to a later work, Giles Winterborne's passive retreat with Fitzpiers' advent to Marty's stoic attempts to build daily upon her longed-for love relationship.

By the same token, no specific gender-connotations attach to the so-called feminine trait of caprice. Henchard's treatment and dismissal of Farfrae, is, although never referred to as such by critics, no less capricious than Bathsheba's treatment of Oak and if Fancy Day is fickle-hearted, so too are Wildeve, Fitzpiers and even Angel Clare who in a feckless moment, invites Izzie to take the place of Tess.

Just as moral traits are equally apportioned to members of both sexes, so too are physical attributes. The invalid woman makes a few brief appearances – significantly brief in the light of the current cult of hypochondria which Hardy might either have disdained as an aspect of woman's negative self-image, or might have eclipsed, quite deliberately, to preserve his voluptuous heroines from any charge of sickness – physical, mental and moral. However, there are examples enough for our purposes. Following a frenzied chess contest with Knight, Elfride lapses into a fever; Bathsheba and Grace, facing matrimonial crises, suffer a temporary breakdown in health; Eustacia, undergoing intense emotional and physical stress, falls into delirium, and Sue, following the death of her babies, suffers a severe nervous breakdown. As to their male counterparts: Owen Graye becomes a permanent invalid; Angel and Clym sicken and become physically wasted; Giles and Jude suffer from congenital disorders, and Boldwood ends up criminally insane. The sickroom, in Hardy, is not reserved, as it was in Victorian society, for woman.

Nor does she have a monopoly on physical beauty. Momentarily ignoring gender attribution, let us consider one of Hardy's characters, a 'full-limbed and somewhat heavy' figure, whose complexion is 'without ruddiness', and whose mouth is 'cut as the point of a spear' – its keenness 'sometimes blunted' as sudden fits of gloom slacken its contours.[15] Alternatively, another character has a 'curly margin of very light shining hair, which accord(s) well with the flush upon (the) cheek' blooming with a 'complexion ... clear ... far removed enough from virgin delicacy' to suggest a fair freshness.[16] The first subject is Eustacia and the second Swithin St Cleeve. If Eustacia's renowned mouth were not such a give-away, the androgynous effect would, no doubt, be more potent still. But it is clear that the 'masculine' or 'feminine' impression (as the case may be) is delightfully ambiguous and most skilfully effected. The insinuation of an image by means of invocation and negation – Eustacia is 'without ruddiness', Swithin's complexion is 'far removed enough from virgin delicacy' – satisfactorily conveys the desired impression of attractiveness or physical beauty which is sensual but not gender-determined. At the same time, in full context, this is achieved without undermining the sexuality of the individual in any way.

That we are invited to appraise the physical attributes, not only of the female, but also of the male, is significant. In relating Bathsheba's pleasure in Troy's body, Hardy's subversive method and intentions can scarcely be mistaken. Appraisal of the erotic body neither is, nor should be, the prerogative of the male.

In keeping with this typological parity, Hardy reserves polymorphic characteristics for his major protagonists. His original Elfride is boyish to Stephen's girlishness; Bathsheba (unmoulded by Oak) conducts herself publicly in a forceful, vigorous manner, and privately with an 'unfeminine' physical zest; and Eustacia's guise of Turkish Knight – 'one would think you were one of the bucks' (*RN*, p.173) – aptly dramatises what Hardy refers to more than once as the 'force' that underlies her 'drowsy latency' (*RN*, p.173). And Sue is, of course, the epicene in whom the gentle 'feminine' Jude sees his own likeness. Tess seems to be exceptional. As a fully realised 'pure woman', a fully actualised self, she is autonomous from the outset, a physical, not to say moral, force in a tale that re-aligns the Edenic myth to have woman gain ascendancy over the fallen Angel. In so far as Hardy identifies closely with her 'feminine' states of being, she is neither inscrutable nor 'other' but twinned to his own consciousness. Similarly, her psychological admixture of assertiveness and compliance, self-willedness and passivity, tenderness and violence, together with her physical attributes of stamina, vigour and hardiness, fit no particular category. They are not so much gender-specific attributes as sexually crosslinked.

It is difficult, in fact, to find any marked trait in Hardy's characters which is not common to both sexes. But all the while convention dictated that woman should equip herself as 'the conscience of man', Hardy continued to incur charges of misogyny. His heroines are not so equipped, he did not intend that they should be, and indeed it would have gone against his most deep-seated principles to promote a single formulated moral code by which all persons at all times should abide, or which an individual, by virtue of sex alone, should personify or exemplify.

On the other hand intersexual imagery is not appropriate to those sexual relationships formed and bound by social codes and prescribed roles. Conventional relationships demand conventional techniques: thus the conventional gender attributes attach to such characters as Knight, Lucetta, Fitzpiers, Alec, and Mrs Charmond. There is nothing bi-sexual, androgynous or polymorphic about any of these men and women.

That the formulated Victorian moral code Hardy's heroines fight against is typically represented by the male in these novels is significant. For all his sympathies with the underprivileged male in his fiction, there is no doubt that for Hardy it is woman's social condition which requires reassessment and revision. His male characters may show individual strengths and weaknesses, but in their capacities as moral 'overseer', censor or watchdog they are uniformly vigilant in maintaining the conventional premise of the status quo. As such, Hardy treats them with an antipathy only thinly concealed by the narrative texture of the novel's structures. Where he, the author, takes pains to deny himself the right of standing in judgement upon his women, so too he refuses to vindicate their male censors – the pedagogical Knight, the spying Oak, the policing Venn. Each, as moral watchdog, partakes of a world of male domination bordering upon absurdity and menace, a world latently vindictive and tyrannical.

An inherent criticism at the heart of Hardy's texts thus levels itself at the puritanical moral bully and his highly questionable motivation. Not one character engaged in such a role effectively benefits the community as a direct result of his moral coercion. Rather the reverse, each enforces so constraining a pressure upon the subject, the censoriously monitored woman, that her nerve eventually fails. Strong in her self-determination, she is at the same time so hard 'up against it' in the man-made world she inhabits that the all-too-often unseen menace of the moral bully eventually drives her into corners so guilt-ridden and fearful that the chances of emerging strengthened prove to be remote. Personal judgement, integrity and the dictates of private conscience eventually give way to an undue concern with appearances, with reputation, with public approval. Woman as an object of public approval/disapproval is thus robbed of her decision-making powers, dignity, pride and self-esteem. Consequently, the trust essential to a healthy, productive community in which the strong, intelligent, resourceful and innovative woman plays an active part is completely undermined. Hardy would not have it otherwise. As I have shown throughout this book, he does not approve of the socially approved method of subduing women, nor the concomitant maladjustment of societal relations.

If, in the context of love relationships, parity between the sexes is Hardy's major platform, which is tacit, not only in his determination to abolish the 'perfect' woman in a world of imperfect men, but also in his polymorphic characterisations and intersexual imagery, this is possibly best exemplified by his anthropomorphised presentation of Egdon, in *The Return of the Native*. 'Perfectly accordant with man's nature' Egdon can weather upheaval, variation, and untoward event. Reciprocity is the by-word, and the Atlantean brow is the pivotal exemplar. Soaring above the heath with its suggestive concavities and convexities, its aggrandised masculine and feminine presences – 'hillocks, pits, ridges and acclivities', 'bossy projections' (*RN*, p.13), 'rounds and hollows' (*RN*, p.4) – and, no less important, its potential for 'fraternization', the Barrow assimilates all opposing and complementary forms and binds them together in perfect unity and reciprocity.

So imaginative a model provides Hardy with an excellent working analogy. Egdon's dual nature (actual and symbolic) manifests perfectly balanced proportions incorporating a design of reciprocation: male and female components set in equipoise, as essential to perfect form as to equitable, interactive relationships.

The Egdon analogy provides the one and only paradigm, in all of Hardy's novels, suggesting alternative possibilities for human sexual relationships. At its most abstract it represents an ideal of harmonious relations; at its most expressionistic a configuration of aspects in which male and female roles, interests, desires, come together in parity. Hope, desire and promise thus shape in his imagination one of the most evocative figurative landscapes in the literary canon: a landscape, a world, a sublime 'upper storey' in which the deepest passions of the human soul find full and free expression.

APPENDIX

The Internal Dating of
Far From the Madding Crowd

The internal dating of *Far From the Madding Crowd* has been set variously at 1840, the 1860s and the early 1870s. John Bayley, for example, argues that 'Bathsheba is a young woman of the 1840s', whereas C.J. Weber's dating based on calendar evidence, sets the action in years 1869–73. Bayley's dating becomes problematical if the youthful Boldwood who features in *The Mayor of Casterbridge* set in the 1840s – a 'silent, reserved young man' (*MC*, p.244) – is to be at the same time the middle-aged suitor of *Far From the Madding Crowd*. Hardy's optional placing of Boldwood suggests an intended temporal gap: approximately thirty years between the two novels to allow for the age discrepancy.

This then favours Weber's dating, which is further supported by information provided by F.R. Pinion who tells us, in *A Hardy Companion*, that Boldwood's farm in *Far From the Madding Crowd* is modelled upon a farm built in 1867 and known to Hardy as Druce Farm. Since Boldwood's house has already been built before the novel's action begins and is actually described by Hardy as 'cobwebbed' [*FFMC*, p.137], suggesting an occupancy of some duration, it seems that Hardy conceived of a late 1860s/early 1870s internal dating.

Further evidence of a contemporary setting is to be found in the *Life*, where Hardy shows every indication of having entered the here and now of his environs into the life of the novel:

While thus in the seclusion of Bockhampton writing *Far From the Madding Crowd*, we find him on September 21, walking to Woodbury Hill Fair, approximately *described in the novel* as 'Green-Hill Fair'. (My italics.)

In reference to the illustrations I have sketched in my notebook during the last summer a few correct outlines of smockfrocks, gaiters, sheep-crooks, rick-staddles, a sheep-washing pool, one of those old-fashioned malt-houses, and some other out-of-the-way things that might have to be shown. (*Life*, pp.96,97)

I have decided to finish it here, which is within a walk of the district in which the incidents are supposed to occur. I find it a great advantage to be actually among the people described at the time of describing them. (*Life*, p.99)

The second extract refers to the serial publication illustrations. Hardy adds that he hopes: 'the rustics, although quaint, may be made to appear intelligent, and not boorish at all' (*Life*, p.97).

Clearly Hardy not only hopes to abolish the generic caricature of Hodge but also wishes to create, down to the last crook and gaiter, a contemporary world. Even Bathsheba's flippant gesture of sending Boldwood a valentine is 'modern' to Hardy, who mentions that regarding 'valentines as things of serious import' is no longer customary (Preface to *FFMC*). Impressionistically too, the novel reads, with its 'modern' concern with marriage laws, as a work of the 1870s – which is a view also held by R.J. White in *Thomas Hardy and History*.

Finally, there is Hardy's 1895–1902 Preface to *Far From the Madding Crowd* which implies a contemporary dating:

The village called Weatherbury, wherein the scenes of the present story are for the most part laid, would hardly be discernible to the explorer, without help, in any existing place nowadays; though at the time, comparatively recent, at which the tale was written, a sufficient reality to meet the descriptions, both of backgrounds and personages, might have been traced easily enough ... the heroine's fine old Jacobean house would have been found in the story to have taken a witch's ride of a mile or more from its actual position.

NOTES

INTRODUCTION

1. 'Gross', in Victorian parlance, denoted, with an aspect of vulgarity, sexual luxuriance. See Elfride's idea (Chapter 1) that things might be made easier between Knight and herself if he were of a 'grosser' nature. Jude also, in speaking of Sue's 'sexlessness', refers to her lack of 'grossness'.

2. Hardy and his contemporaries used the term 'Grundyist' or 'Grundyan' with reference to Mrs Grundy, the symbol of conventional propriety. Although Mrs Grundy never actually appears in the play by T. Morton entitled *Speed the Plough*, (1798), she exists in the background as a constant point of reference on questions of propriety; and she seems to have continued to exist in the background invisibly performing her task as censor for many generations to come.

3. Mrs Oliphant, 'The Anti-Marriage League', *Blackwood's Magazine*, Jan. 1896, clix, pp.135–49. See also the *Saturday Review*, Feb. 1896, lxxxi, pp.153–4. Retaliating against the excess of critical attention being given to sexual issues in *Jude* (dubbed *Jude the Obscene*), the *Saturday* concludes that not only have 'the peculiar matrimonial difficulties of ... Sue ... been treated *ad nauseam* in the interests of purity in our contemporaries', but also that 'so active, so malignant have these sanitary inspectors of fiction become, that a period of terror, analogous to that of the New England Witch Mania is upon us'.

4. For a balanced and highly readable account of Victorian marriage, as it affected women, see Phillip Mallett's 'Woman and Marriage in Victorian Society', *Marriage and Property*, ed. Elizabeth M. Craig (Aberdeen University Press, 1984), pp.159–89.

    Mallett deals essentially with middle-class marriage and middle-class values. Consequently, whereas the locus qualifies the topic it also sets limitations. Thus the harsher, more oppressive aspects of marriage tend to be shaded over by the kindly urbane voices of those educated Victorians elected, by Mallett, to speak.

5. Charles Fourier, 1772–1837, French revolutionary utopian socialist philosopher. He held that a harmonious society could be achieved if organised on a basis of economic units ('phalanx') of 1,620 people sharing a communal dwelling and dividing work to suit their natural inclinations. He also believed in free sexual relationships. Hardy read John Reynell Morell's translation of Fourier's *The Passions of the Human Soul*, 2 vols (London, 1851), and made notes, charts and diagrams on the basis of this work. For fuller information see sections on Hardy and Fourier in *The Literary Notes of Thomas Hardy*, 2 vols, ed. Lennart A. Björk (Gothenberg, 1974), vol. 1.

6. Mona Caird was author of *The Wings of Azreal* (London, 1889), *The Daughters of Danaus* (London, 1894), and *The Morality of Marriage and other Essays on the Status and Destiny of Woman* (London, 1897). Caird shared Hardy's antipathy for Victorian marriage conventions. Levelling her attack at these in particular, she, understandably, experienced difficulties with publishers. In January 1890 she approached Hardy to ask for his help in publishing her article on 'Evolution in Marriage'. Hardy made a recommendation to Percy Bunting, editor of *The Contemporary Review*, but Caird's article was rejected. However, in March of the same year she did publish an article in *The Fortnightly Review*, cclxxix, pp.310–30, entitled *The Morality of Marriage*. This is a fairly judicious piece on marriage so it may well be a sanitised version of the earlier inadmissible product.

Chapter 1
THE HERESY OF PASSION: *A Pair of Blue Eyes*

1. The much-discussed Dr William Acton, one of the more influential Victorian medical theorists, produced his most important work on venereology in midcentury, entitled: *The Function and Disorders of the Reproductive Organs in Childhood, Youth, Adult Age, and Advanced Life Considered in their Physiological, Social, and Moral Relations* (London, 1857). Acton's title, in itself, bears out the point that medical science took upon itself the moral as well as the scientific responsibility for the sexual health of the society.

    Dr Acton held that to ascribe erotic passions to healthy women was to cast a 'vile aspersion' on them. He argued that whereas female sexual activity was much in evidence in lunatic asylums – a characteristic of the abnormal, the diseased, and the insane – healthy women were free from these drives. The 'modest woman' desired no sexual gratification for herself. She submitted to her husband 'only to please him'. 'The best wives, mothers, and managers of households, know little or nothing of sexual indulgence. Love of home, children, and domestic duties, are the only passions they feel.' Acton, *Functions and Disorders*, 3rd edn (London, 1862), pp. 101–2.

Acton's views were shared by many, but W. R. Greg ventured a little further to claim that although sexual desire is non-existent in healthy women, actual intercourse could create such a desire. See Greg's article entitled 'Prostitution', *Westminster Review*, liii (1850).

The opposition was largely discredited, and definitely undermined, by the vagaries of its leading member, Dr George R. Drysdale, whose *The Elements of Social Science: or Physical, Sexual and Natural Religion* was first published in 1854. Drysdale was regarded by the medical profession as unscientific and as something of a charlatan. The following brief outline may help to explain why (I quote from the 3rd edition, 1862).

Drysdale's main thesis, in *Elements*, is that repression of the sexual appetite is, in both sexes, harmful to the health. However, the manner in which this is argued through his book, suggests a conflict between ideology and scientific 'fact'. For example, the advocacy of a freely exercised sexual drive in men is brought up rather short by the observation that nocturnal emissions weaken the nervous system and may affect the mind, turning man 'savage and repulsive', to feel 'hatred and disgust at mankind', and may even 'proceed to insanity or idiocy' (*Elements*, p. 101). Alternatively, in arguing in favour of 'healthy and sufficient' sexual exercise for women, the need for 'female organs to be properly stimulated with a healthy and natural amount of exercise', Drysdale then goes on to discuss a disease called 'chlorosis'. The symptoms of this disease are many: loss of appetite, fatigue, palpitations, breathlessness, digestive disorders, constipation, listlessness, melancholy, and in chronic cases, dropsy and paralytic conditions. But the main problem here is that chlorosis is, according to Drysdale, to be found in married women who are childbearing and suffering miscarriages – women, we must suppose, whose sexual organs have been stimulated with a natural amount of exercise. And now, to fully discredit his argument in favour of stimulation, Drysdale goes on to say that 'masturbation', an 'unfortunate practice', may also cause chlorosis (*Elements*, pp. 163–8).

These examples, none too reassuring to the lay mind, must have been less so to the scientific. And they are, unfortunately, all too typical of Drysdale's epistemology. Credibility is hard to sustain when one reads, first, that women should give vent to natural sexual feelings, and, next, that woman is governed by her emotions: 'feelings have a greater sway over her mind' than over man's, and 'she is so much subject to external influences' that 'immoderate emotions' can cause 'nerves to lose their tone' and the 'power of thought becomes impaired'. Drysdale does not, apparently, detect in his own argument a certain inconsistency between giving vent to sexual feelings (healthy) and giving vent to emotions generally (unhealthy). And in going on, at this point, to recommend that 'self-denial – is often a most valuable quality', he does not attempt to reconcile this with his earlier claim that repression is harmful to the health (*Elements*, pp.174–80).

Elements did run through several editions. It has a very appealing optimistic tone, a utopian air, which must have been refreshing to many a hardened professional. But none, if any, took it seriously.

2. See *The Saturday Review*, lxxxi, Feb. 1896, pp.153–4.
3. Quoted in *Hardy's Personal Writings*, ed. Harold Orel (Kansas, 1966), pp.128–30.
   See also G. W. Sherman's account of Hardy's anecdote concerning his story entitled 'The Distracted Preacher' (1879). This provides an apt illustration of a *de rigueur* convention, and Hardy's reaction to it. Sherman tells us that 'The Distracted Preacher' is an audacious tale of 'rum-smuggling . . . involving a mild-mannered landlady, a Wesleyan minister, and a smuggler, Jim, of which [Hardy] says in a footnote that "the ending of the story, with the marriage of Lizzy and the Minister, was almost *de rigueur* in an English Magazine at the time of writing". But he restored the original version in which Lizzy . . . "stuck with Jim" and after their marriage they emigrated to Wisconsin.' G. W. Sherman, *The Pessimism of Thomas Hardy* (New Jersey and London, 1976), p.60.
4. *The Saturday Review*, xxxvi, Aug. 1873, pp.158–9. Having detected 'a kind of defiance of conventionality' in *A Pair of Blue Eyes*, the reviewer goes on to say that 'we have abstained from any definite analysis of the story, because, where sequence and connection are so delicately worked as they are here, that is hardly fair to either writer or reader'. As this coy face-saver suggests, critical judgement has been suspended, presumably for lack of concrete evidence.

5. James R. Kincaid, for example, argues that *A Pair of Blue Eyes* is a manifestly vaporous and contradictory text. See his essay, entitled 'Coherency in *A Pair of Blue Eyes*', *Critical Approaches to the Fiction of Thomas Hardy*, ed. Dale Kramer (London, 1979).

6. See Gillian Beer, *Darwin's Plots* (London, Boston, Melbourne, Henley, 1983) p.237. Beer writes: 'Hardy wrote in his Journal: "Courage has been idealized: Why not fear? which is a higher consciousness and based on deeper insight." He here inverts the expected value placed on fear, while in his attribution of a "deeper insight" he suggests its power in the natural order.'

7. Stratagem of this kind is more or less pre-empted, in *Desperate Remedies*, by the conventional nature of the heroine. There is, though, an occasional deferential nod, here, to propriety – in the form of a pejorative aside imputing that women are thus, or should be thus – but no dialectical schema, as in *A pair of Blue Eyes*, to subvert the Grundyist wisdom of the proprietary narrator. The first aside occurs where Cytherea, having occasion to call on her rival on behalf of Miss Aldclyffe's 'Ladies Association', seeks information about her own lover. Gaining little ground by oblique promptings, she alters her approach midcourse to adopt a more imperious manner:

> Women are persistently imitative. No sooner did a thought flash through Cytherea's mind that the man was a lover than she became a Miss Aldclyffe in a mild form.
> 'I imagine he's a lover,' she said. (*DR*, p.150)

This generalised reference to role-adoption, indicating something of the deep influence Miss Aldclyffe has had upon Cytherea, is not in itself pejorative, but it does lead away from authorial sympathy towards a disaffecting, superior, worldly-wise stance. And this is not controverted as attention shifts to Miss Hinton, towards whom the aside has surely been flowing:

> Few women, if taxed with having an admirer, are so free from vanity as to deny the impeachment, even if it is utterly untrue. When it does happen to be true, they look pityingly away from the person who is so benighted as to have got no further than suspecting it. (*DR*, p.150)

The magisterial tone here catches at the formal interrogative language of the bench, positioning the speaker in the role of judge. But it is an atypical stance and is no sooner adopted than discarded in favour of affability:

> Women who are bad enough to divide against themselves under a man's partiality are good enough to instantly unite in a common cause against his attack. (*DR*, p.268)

Here language and tone rebuff remonstration. 'Bad', 'good', 'divide' and 'common cause' are devoid of stricture, in contrast to 'taxed', 'deny', 'impeachment'. Dispensing, then, with the magisterial in favour of the affable mode, Hardy's next aside comes as a comment upon the androgyne in his hero, who finds 'echoes of himself . . . sometimes (in) men, sometimes women':

For in spite of a fashion which pervades the whole community at the present day – the habit of exclaiming that woman is not undeveloped man, but diverse, the fact remains that after all, women are Mankind, and that in many of the sentiments of life the difference of sex is but a difference of degree. (*DR*, p.206)

Not of the Separate Spheres school, Hardy here advances his pre-Jungian understanding of the innate bisexuality of human nature. Strictly speaking, this is not a moralistic aside at all: it is neither vapid generalisation – women-are-thus – nor pedagogical preaching – women-should-be-thus. Rather, the tone is quietly contemplative – unusually so for a racy, detective tale. I include it here simply to draw attention to the amiability of the narrative posture, for this most aptly represents the mode of regard reserved for *Desperate Remedies* and its strictly conventional characterisations.

8. In a separate context entirely, Roland Barthes describes this dualistic mode of narration as incorporating a 'proprietary consciousness which retains the mastery of what it states without participating in it'. See his essay, 'To Write: An Intransitive Verb', *The Structuralist Controversy*, ed. R. Macksey and E. Donato (Baltimore, 1972).

Chapter 2
SUBVERTING ORTHODOXY: *Far From the Madding Crowd*

1. Published in *La Revue des Deux Mondes*, 15 Dec. 1875. Quoted in *Thomas Hardy and His Readers*, ed. Laurence Lerner and John Holstrom (London, 1968), pp.41,42.

2. Ibid., pp.30–9. *The Times* piece reads: 'Mr Hardy . . . transforms, with skilful touch, the matter-of-fact prosaic details of everyday life into an idyll or a pastoral poem . . . This idyllic or romantic element is never violent or forced . . . Mr Hardy has his subject well in hand.' The *Saturday Review*, likewise, comments that under Hardy's hand 'Boeotians' become 'Athenians living out their idyllic . . . rustic life'. Andrew Lang takes a similar view. He writes in the *Academy*, vii, Jan. 2, 1875: 'This immobile rural

existence is what the novelist has to paint. . . . There are three
circles of interest in this story – first, the rural surroundings.
. . . Next, there are the minor characters – a sort of chorus of
agricultural labourers. . . . Last, there are the main persons of
the drama – the people in whose passions and adventures the
interest ought to centre. Of these three components of the tale,
the first may be pronounced nearly perfect, and worthy of all
praise.'

3. Hardy's truncation of Thomas Gray's line, in 'Elegy Written in
a Country Churchyard', tends to highlight – by omission – the
significant words, 'ignoble strife'. Gray's first stanza reads:

> Far from the madding crowd's *ignoble strife*
> Their sober wishes never learn'd to stray;
> Along the cool sequester'd vale of life
> They kept the noiseless tenor of their way.
> (My italics)

In common with Gray, Hardy has been lauded a champion of
oppressed humanity. Hardy's theme in *Far From the Madding
Crowd*, however, does not reflect but rather reverses the mood
and theme of Gray's poem, which celebrates the freedom from
social conflict and violence that his countrydweller enjoys. The
episode of Fanny Robin's death encapsulates the atmospheric
turbulence, the dark undertow of brutality and violence in
Hardy's novel. Here, one 'humane' creature, the
Newfoundland dog who comes to Fanny's aid, is stoned from
the door of Parish Relief at the Casterbridge Union following
its journey bearing the dying woman.

4. Lerner and Holmstrom, op cit., pp.30–1.
5. Ibid., p.35.
6. In order of sequence these extracts are taken from: *The
Athenaeum*, 5 Dec. 1874, *The Spectator*, 19 Dec. 1874 (twice), *The
Nation*, 24 Dec. 1874, *The Westminster Review*, Jan. 1875, and
The Saturday Review, 9 Jan. 1875.
    To read in full, see the chapter on *Far From the Madding Crowd*,
in *Thomas Hardy: The Critical Heritage*, ed. R. G. Cox (London,
1970).
7. Mowbray Morris, 'Culture and Anarchy', *Quarterly Review*,
clxxiv, April 1892, pp.319–26.
8. Ibid.
9. For further elaboration see G. W. Sherman, *The Pessimism of
Thomas Hardy* (New Jersey and London, 1976), p.108.
10. The lay-view of Hardy as a Victorian metamorphosed Hodge

still persists today. This scarcely takes into account his cultured childhood, the music, the dance, the Virgil, the French governess and, of course, the close association with Lady Julia Martin. Politicised at an early age (*Life*, p.21), and in adolescence a suitable candidate for higher education in architecture, this son of the property-holding Bockhampton Hardys had neither peasant nor (in the Marxist sense) proletarian origins. To borrow Michael Alexander's apposite phrase, 'This Tolpuddle curmudgeon is not, of course, Thomas Hardy, but the image has stuck.' Michael Alexander, 'Hardy Among the Poets', *Thomas Hardy After Fifty Years*, ed. Lance St John Butler (London and Basingstoke, 1978), p.51.

11. *The Independent*, 25 Feb. 1892. In full: 'It is probable that [Hardy's] method is more dangerous to the moral fibre of young readers than the open French method' (Lerner and Holmstrom, op cit., p.81). Other critics voiced similar sentiments. 'It matters much less' (*The Saturday Review*, 16 Jan. 1892) 'what a story is about than how that story is told, and Mr Hardy ... tells an unpleasant story in a very unpleasant way.' 'The coarse expression which Hardy attributes to Tess' (*Spectator*, 23 Jan. 1892) 'does not admit of a faithful presentation of a "pure woman". We deny altogether that Mr Hardy has made out his case for Tess.' 'The coarseness ... of Mr Hardy's manner' (*Quarterly*, April 1892) comes 'from within rather than from without'. 'The influence of so-called "realism"' (*Review of Reviews*, Feb. 1892) 'as understood in France in the latter part of the nineteenth century, is strong both for good and ill in Mr Hardy's latest work, which in some respects is Zola-esque to a degree likely to alienate not a few well-meaning persons.'

12. Hardy's stance here marks a significant departure from his early caution to establish a proprietary consciousness that faults Elfride at regular intervals. This stance evolved to an undisguised and total authorial commitment in *Tess*, and subsequently brought down more resounding thunders upon his head than upon his heroine's. If she was culpable, then she had been misrepresented. If she threatened to lead the nation's youth astray, this was because her author had distorted the facts. Hardy thus went some way towards pre-empting one conditioned response in his reader: that of instinctively standing in judgement upon woman, automatically laying the blame at her door. This pre-emption no doubt assisted the reception of

Tess, which was intended to disturb rather than shock – the latter response closing more doors than it opens.

13. See, for example, Peter Casagrande's view of Bathsheba whom he regards as a vain, egotistical girl in need of a moral education and whom he accuses of being an 'undeliberate, inadvertent, unconscious agent of evil'. See his essay, somewhat misleadingly entitled 'A New View of Bathsheba Everdene', *Critical Approaches to the Fiction of Thomas Hardy* (New Jersey and London, 1984), pp.50–73, ed. Dale Kramer.

14. Robert C. Schweik, in noticing Hardy's use, here, of the analogical landscape, writes that in rendering Troy's attractiveness to Bathsheba, 'Hardy relied primarily on a more oblique and evocative dramatizing of situations – and with considerably more persuasive art. This more dense and suggestive mode, involving a close interaction of setting, incident, and dialogue ... is developed in such a way which emphasizes the meeting [in the fir plantation] as a sexual encounter.' Robert E. Schweik, 'The Narrative Structure of *From the Madding Crowd*', *Budmouth Essays*, ed. F. B. Pinion (Dorchester, 1976), p.34.

15. 'Voices of Things Growing in a Churchyard', *The Variorum Edition of the Complete Poems of Thomas Hardy*, ed. James Gibson (London, 1979), pp.623–5.

   In Hardy's first edition of *Late Lyrics and Earlier*, in which 'Voices of Things Growing' was first published in 1922, Eve Greensleeves goes by the name of 'Bet' (copy No. 7 of this first edition numbering 25 copies, published by The Chiswick Press, London, 1922, is held by the Beinecke manuscript library at Yale University). Given the character of Hardy's Eve, one might conjecture that he made the change from 'Bet' to 'Eve' with the intention of subverting the Edenic myth and the sexual guilt and shame attached to the original Eve. For, as Tom Paulin so eloquently describes it, in Hardy's poem Eve's world 'of dazzling light fresh breeze and life giving warmth ... become[s] the expression of her free sexuality and her innocent trust. As ever she is eternally virgin and promiscuous.' Tom Paulin, 'Time and Sense Experience: Hardy and T. S. Eliot', *Budmouth Essays*, op. cit., p.198.

16. See Hardy's *The Dorset Farm labourer past and present*, published by the Dorchester and Dorset agricultural workers' union, 1884 (held in the Beinecke Library, Yale University). Farm labourers' wages, according to this source, had, at this time, recently risen to between 10 and 12 shillings a week; at the time

of the publication of *Far From the Madding Crowd*, in the early
1870s, they were closer to 9 shillings a week. However, a
shepherd received a bonus of one shilling for every twin reared;
and an extra 40–60 shillings could be earned during the harvest
season.

17.   Hardy had every reason for dwelling on thoughts of marriage
in the early 1870s, for he was, in life, affianced. But that his
thoughts should turn so deadly seems surprising, unless we take
into account the early influence of Charles Fourier – advocate
of free love and the abolition of institutionalised marriage.
There is nothing to suggest that Hardy did not maintain a
lifelong fidelity to Fourier's ideas: Bathsheba's progressive
notions that she will not become some man's property, that she
would have the wedding but not the man, that she would resist
being coerced into marriage for reputation's sake, anticipate
Sue Bridehead's views by more than two decades.

    Sacrosanct as the Institution of Marriage may have been to
the Victorian of the 1870s, a groundswell of dissent was
gathering force beneath that seemingly unruffled climate of
stability and certitude described by the historian G. M. Young:
'The increasing secularism of English thought might have been
expected to compel a more critical attitude to the family than
in fact we find. Sexual ethic had attracted to itself so great a
body of romantic sentiment: it was closely associated, and even
identified, with virtue in general, with the elevated, the
praiseworthy, the respectable life, that the faintest note of
dissidence might attract a disproportionate volume of suspicion
and censure.' G. M. Young, *Portrait of an Age* (London, 1978),
p.133.

    Mrs Lynn Linton, in the 1860s, was one of the more
suspicious: 'If . . . indignation abounds even in a suppressed
and smouldering state, we should have heard something of it
. . . a general condemnation of marriage has not yet become
common among ladies. Few English novelists, for example,
betray even a latent disposition to preach the doctrines of
George Sand: even the strongest-minded contemplate some
change which shall render man and wife more equal, rather
than any revolt against society.' Mrs Lynn Linton, 'Marriage
and Free Love', *The Saturday Review*, Aug. 24 1867, xxiv, pp.248,
249.

    Linton's attempts to suppress the revolt *ab initio* are
ineffectual. Hardy has picked up the groundswell, and will
shortly be followed by some of those 'few English novelists' who

will also take up the anti-marriage debate – notably Meredith and Gissing.

18. J. Hillis Miller draws attention to the role of the spy as thief. The watcher, he says, 'secretly steals the other's freedom by spying'. J. Hillis Miller, 'History as Repetition in Thomas Hardy's Poetry: The Example of "Wessex Heights" ', *Stratford-Upon-Avon Studies*, 15, ed. Malcolm Bradbury and David Palmer (London, 1972), p.237.

19. The passing of the Married Woman's Property Act, in 1870, was a major turning point in the lives of Victorian women. This act granted a married woman the right to possess her earnings – a right her unmarried sister already possessed. It took approximately fifteen years for Parliament to correct the inequity. The Bill, introduced in 1855, was given a second reading two years later, and then hung fire for another decade before its final resolution in 1870. Such gingerly procedure is insignificant in comparison with the half-century it took Parliament to secure the franchise for women: from John Stuart Mill's 1867 proposed amendment to the Representation of the People Bill, to the 1918 enfranchisement of women over thirty. However, such a protracted passage is a sign of the times. Or as *The Saturday Review* inadvertently reveals, a sign of the times' prejudices. On the Married Woman's Property Act *The Saturday* has this to say: 'The only persons on whose behalf it can seriously be pretended that a change in the law is necessary are the wives of working-men immoderately addicted to beer; and it would be monstrous to alter a state of law which is generally beneficial for the sake of a portion of one class of the community. . . . There is absolutely no evidence of the desirableness of the change as regards the middle and upper classes, and it really is going rather too far to propose to make sweeping innovation for the supposed benefit of the lower class. We are sometimes threatened with the coming of a time when the poor will divide among them the property of the rich. But until that time does come the rich may surely be allowed to enjoy their property in their own way.' 'The Married Woman's Property Act', *The Saturday Review*, April 10 1869, xxvii, pp.482, 483.

As Hardy's Sergeant Troy 'enjoys' his (wife's) property in his 'own way'? Having purchased his discharge from the Army with Bathsheba's hard-earned monies, Troy proceeds to gamble the remainder away at race-meetings – losing more than a hundred pounds in one month (*FFMC*, p.305).

Here, surely, is 'evidence of the desirableness of the change as regards the middle classes'? And Hardy's Troy is by no means unrepresentative, if Millicent Garrett Fawcett's account is indicative. Reporting on her lobbying activities on the proposed Married Woman's Property Bill, Fawcett recalls the indignation of one 'Liberal British farmer' to whom the notion that he should not do as he pleases with his wife's money is utterly preposterous: 'Am I to understand you, Ma'am, that if this Bill passes, and my wife have a matter of a hundred pound left to her, I should have to *ask* her for it?' Millicent Garrett Fawcett, *Women's Suffrage: A Short History of a Great Movement* (London, 1919), p.23.

20. I am indebted to Barbara Murray for directing me to the Old Testament source of Hardy's homiletic address. The Solomonic 'voice' here utters, in paraphrasis, Sol. 8.6: 'Many waters cannot quench love,/neither can floods drown it.' The tone and sentiment in Hardy's piece is strongly reminiscent of his rustic chorus which tends to allude, both sagely and comically, to biblical texts taken, presumably, from public worship ceremonials.

21. Lance St John Butler is surely right to point to the esoterism of this allusion. He writes: 'Hardy's idiosyncrasy overcomes him when he gets to the mouth, whose curve resembles that "So well known in the arts of design as the cyma-recta or ogee". What seems to be wrong here is that his undeniable talent for detail has led him to unearth the most esoteric detail possible in order to convey the *exact* curve of Eustacia's mouth. Alas the detail is too remote and it conveys nothing.' Lance St John Butler, *Thomas Hardy* (Cambridge, 1978), p.44.

But to Hardy (and to the reader furnished with adequate footnotes) the allusion would seem doubly appropriate. In the age of the Gothic revival it may not, of course, have been so esoteric. But more important is the fact that the moulding to which he refers describes an undulating curve and rounded profile and hollow orifice respectively – all too apt an image, as it happens! At a different level the 'cyma-recta or ogee' allusion coheres perfectly with the Palladian imagery in the 'Atlantean' brow sequence where Eustacia features as the necessary finish to the 'architectural' construct of Rainbarrow.

22. The references to Bathsheba's lips in the first half of the novel, before her marriage to Troy, are on pages: 5, 15, 23, 25, 102, 145, 147, 155, 156, 161, 163, 176, 188. In the latter half of the book these references number only three: pp.351, 353, 445.

Chapter 3
ELEMENTAL FORCES: *The Return of the Native*

1. Quoted by Gertrude Himmelfarb in *On Liberty and Liberalism* (New York, 1974), p.173.
2. See *The Literary Notes of Thomas Hardy*, 2 vols, ed. Lennart Björk (Gothenburg, 1974), vol. 1, p.271.
3. See Björk, op. cit., p.272.
4. Florence Nightingale's words in *Cassandra*, 1852. Quoted by Elaine Showalter in *A Literature of Their Own. British Women Novelists from Bronte to Lessing* (London, 1978), p.27.
5. For further elaboration on Hardy's Hellenic view of life, see David de Laura, 'The Ache of Modernism in Hardy's Later Novels', *E.L.H.*, vol. 34, Sept. 1967, pp.388–99.
6. Hardy dates this novel rather vaguely (with hindsight) as 'set down as between 1840 and 1850' (Preface to *RN*, 1895). However, the internal information he provides within the novel is more precise – suggesting the late 1840s/1850. There is, for example, Granfer Cantle's age. Now seventy years of age (p.36) we are also told that he was in his boyhood during the Napoleonic wars, and a dashing young soldier serving with the 'Bang Up Locals' in year four (p.164). If then Granfer Cantle is to be young in year four, as opposed to, say, in his thirties, the setting has to be mid-century. This also coheres with Christian Cantle's recollection of his mother's anecdote on the French Revolution. Christian, now thirty-one (p.27), recalls his mother telling him that as a young maid she received news from the parson that the king's head had been cut off (p.124). Hardy, with his keen sense of history, would, in back-dating this novel, have in mind the 1848 Revolutions which swept Europe towards the end of the decade. And, given his study of Fourier and strong Fourieristic leanings, he might also have been aware that Karl Marx was writing the *Communist Manifesto*, in Paris in mid-century. Clym's study of 'ethical systems popular at the time' (p.203), like Angel Clare's aspirations towards the communistic life, reflect a background of socialist thought. In Britain, the late 1840s saw the rise of Chartism and concomitant fears of social upheaval. Hardy's setting and atmosphere, in *The Return of the Native*, is, according to this internal dating, the setting and atmosphere of incipient social revolution – under whose banner sexual revolution also marches.

7. Michael Millgate, *Thomas Hardy: His Career as a Novelist* (London, Sydney, Toronto, 1971), p.132.

8. Ibid., p.133. Millgate feels that Hardy's Greek allusions go 'stubbornly against the grain of the novel as a whole' (ibid., p.132). This is not what Hardy would have wished. That they go against the grain of the internal world of the novel is an entirely different matter.

9. Reddle, or raddle, is a red ochre compound which, in Hardy's day and region, came from the city of Bristol, in the West of England (which lends force to the idea that Venn is not only an intruder on Egdon but also a representative of the Victorian 'civilised' world).

   The Oxford English Dictionary says that reddle compound was smeared on the fore-bows of the ram, that is, on its breast. This would seem to ensure an effective staining of the ewe's flanks, given the ram's mounting position.

   The practice of reddling continues today. According to Andrew Wheatcroft, in Dumfriesshire, a reddling bag, filled with ochre, is attached under the ram. When the ram has served a ewe the reddle stains announce the fact, showing which ewes will probably be lambing. Under modern conditions, the reddling bag is filled with emulsion paint and changed week by week, with a different colour each time. This is to indicate which batch a ewe belongs to, and hence when it will lamb.

10. With his expert professionalism by now – in the mid- to late-1870s – publicly acknowledged, Hardy evidently feels he can afford to expose the spy/censor, or Grundyan overseer, for the malevolent bully he is.

11. See, for example, Perry Meisel, who claims that Eustacia is both the intruder on Egdon and the agent of disorder. *The Return of the Repressed* (New Haven and London, 1972), p.76.

12. In lighting upon a reddleman for Venn's punitive role Hardy craftily brings together three significant elements: the colour scarlet, the compound used for branding the female, the sexually active woman as outcast. Venn, unlike most Hardy characters, would not seem completely out of place in Nathaniel Hawthorne's world of *The Scarlet Letter* (1850).

   Although I cannot find any evidence of Hardy's having read this particular novel, he was certainly familiar with Hawthorne's work. According to Michael Millgate, Hardy knew the English Men of Letters volume on Hawthorne, and drew upon his reading of Hawthorne's *The Marble Faun*, when writing the poem, 'Rome: Building a New Street in the Ancient

Quarter'. See Michael Millgate (ed.), *Thomas Hardy. A Biography*
(Oxford, Melbourne, 1982), pp.208,282.

13. One of Hardy's most important revisions in the Wessex novels
is his recasting of Eustacia. As John Paterson in *The Making of
'The Return of the Native'* (California, 1960) inadvertently reveals,
Hardy's original 'angry' Eustacia would (if not recast) have
been thoroughly misinterpreted by the sexually prejudiced
reader. Paterson's work demands fuller investigation than can
be given here since critics predisposed to regarding Hardy as
misogynist tend to quote Paterson in support of their views.
(Note: in the following, citations from Hardy's Ur-text are
enclosed in single apostrophes and those from Paterson in
double.)

Working on the assumption that Eustacia, as Hardy
originally conceived her, is wholly evil, Paterson draws the
following conclusions from the Ur-text. Eustacia's 'anger' and
utterances of 'hot words of passion' are "demonic" (Paterson,
p.18). Hardy's ascription 'angrily' denotes "satanic pride and
willfulness" (ibid., pp.18,19). Eustacia's venting 'laughs at
herself . . . sighs between her laughs, and sudden listenings
between her sighs' signifies "diabolism" (ibid., p.19), and her
'angry despair' is "satanic" (ibid., p.21). Readers sharing
Paterson's view of angry women, would not, I suppose, ascribe
evil powers to the angry Christ in the Temple. Paterson
concludes that "If Eustacia belongs to Nature, she formerly
belonged to SuperNature" (ibid., p.22). SuperNature is not,
however, necessarily demonic. Certainly Hardy alludes to
Macbeth in the Ur-novel when he writes (in the 'Queen of
Night' chapter) 'there would have been . . . the same perpetual
dilemmas, the same, sudden changes from fair to foul, from
foul to fair' (ibid., p.20). But this refers to the state of world
government, not to Eustacia.

Hardyan wisdom evidently saw fit to rephrase this passage
for the final version – conceivably with the Patersons of this
world in mind, whose reasoning defies all logic. If, for example –
as Paterson claims – the crooked sixpence Eustacia offers
Johnny Nonesuch is 'a charm against witchcraft' (ibid., p.22),
what then is the 'witch' doing with this charm in the first place?
And why would she pass it on to be (presumably) used against
her? Hardy's logic is preferable to Paterson's: the true witch
on Egdon is Johnny's mother.

Given Hardy's theme of persecution in this novel, it appears
likely that if he conceived of Eustacia as a witch in the first

instance, this was a more enlightened conception than Paterson's. There is nothing to indicate that he was not sufficiently without prejudice to have been aware that, as Nancy van Vuuren puts it: 'The young pretty woman was also subject to accusations of witchcraft, probably because of jealousy and unfulfilled sexual desire. The man who looked upon a young woman with lust would accuse the woman of making him lust by means of witchcraft. If the woman did not respond to the man, this too could be the cause for accusations of witchcraft.' Nancy van Vuuren, *The Subversion of Women* (Philadelphia, 1974), pp.92–6.

14. D. H. Lawrence, *Lawrence on Hardy: 'A Study of Thomas Hardy' and 'Introduction to these Paintings'*, ed. J. V. Davies (London, 1973), pp.29–30.

15. 'An Emancipated Woman', *The Saturday Review*, June 17 1876, vol. XL, p.771.

16. Ibid., p.771.

Chapter 4
Passive Victim? *Tess of the d'Urbervilles*

1.   The term 'rank' rarely connotes luxuriance or abundance in modern parlance. However, it appears that this is Hardy's meaning. See, for example, use of the word in *The Woodlanders*, where he refers to Fitzpiers' midnight readings in 'rank literatures of emotion and passion' (*W*, p.153). See also *Jude*, where Sue gathers 'huge burdock leaves, parsley, and other rank growths' in order to wrap her naked statuettes (*JO*, p.101). It seems unlikely that she would favour foul-smelling shrubs or that the musty, organic smell of parsley could be spoken of as such.

2.   For a corresponding analysis of these sequences see sections on *Tess*, in J. Hillis Miller's *Fiction and Repetition* (Massachusetts, 1982). And for an alternative, fundamentally puritanical, reading of the 'Edenic' scene see Marilyn Stall Fontane's 'The Devil in "Tess"', *The Thomas Hardy Society Review*, 1982, pp.250–4. Fontane sees the 'Garden' as 'dirty'!

3.   This view is expressed by Mary Jacobus in 'The Difference of View', *Women Writing and Writing about Women* (London, 1974), pp.13,14.

4.   Hardy's descriptions of the detailed processes of labour have, Merryn and Raymond Williams write, 'an intensity of feeling

which in most fiction is reserved for interpersonal relationships or landscape and scene'.

Merryn and Raymond Williams, 'Hardy and Social Class', *Thomas Hardy: The Writer and His Background*, ed. Norman Page (London, 1980), p.39.

'Intensity of feeling' is precisely what Hardy feels and projects here as the 'panting ache' induced in Tess by the demonic energy of the machine stuns her to mental insensibility.

5. Jacobus, op. cit., p.14.

See also Richard Swigg who argues, with reference to the 'garden' scene, and which his use of the passive tense insinuates, that Tess is a 'captured, hypnotised creature' undergoing an 'entranced surrender'. Hardy constructs for Tess, Swigg claims, 'hazily lit, somnambulistic scenes, where tragic yieldings are passively conceded to in fog or in the intervals between sleep and waking, in the twilights before complete night and day.'

Richard Swigg, *Lawrence, Hardy, and American Literature* (London and Toronto, 1972), pp.14–16.

It may be useful, in this context, to quote Hardy's contemporary, Havelock Ellis: 'In catalepsy the subject's mental functions are largely or altogether suspended as regards the external world; the muscles are passive and retain any position in which they may be placed. In ecstasy, which cannot be very clearly distinguished from trance, there is not the same absence of muscular control, and the subject's mental functions, instead of being suspended, are actively employed in seeing visions; during the trance the subject's countenance expresses inspired illumination of a more than earthly character . . .' *Man and Woman: A Study of Human Secondary Sexual Characteristics* (New York, 1911), p.302.

6. 'Tess's sexuality has to remain something of an enigma.' Lance St John Butler, *Thomas Hardy* (Cambridge, 1978), p.133.

If this is so, it is not with Hardy's connivance.

7. Jacobus argues that Hardy's omission to explicate openly Tess's sexual experience in the 'Chase' and 'Wedding Night' scenes, effects a silencing of woman's utterance in the event of her attaining a sexual reality. 'Tess's silence makes female desire dumb' (Jacobus, op. cit., p.14).

The problem here is that Tess's physical needs in the 'Chase' episode are not sexual. She is exhausted and longs, not for sexual activity, but for sleep. Hence there *is* no female desire to silence or render dumb.

8. Britta Sandberg Bävner has brought to my attention the following autobiographical detail which clearly twins Tess to Hardy's own consciousness as she waits, exhausted, hungry and dejected for the barn-dancing to finish: 'Tommy perforce stayed on, being afraid to go home without the strapping young woman his companion, who was dancing with the soldiers. There he wearily waited ... till three in the morning, having eaten and drunk nothing since one o'clock on the previous day' (*Life*, p.20).

9. For a contrary reading, see Swigg, who regards Hardy's 'Chase' scene as confused and unfocused, and Tess as sentimentally beautified. 'From confusion such as this, where physicality and blood are distorted by an unfocused vision, Hardy derives his tragic sense.' Swigg, op. cit., pp.16–18.

10. See Rosemary Sumner's comprehensive study of Hardy's anticipation of Freud, Jung, and Adler in *Thomas Hardy: Psychological Novelist* (London and Basingstoke, 1981), p.47.

11. This passage from J. S. Mill is quoted by Richard Evans in his book *The Feminists* (London, 1977) p.20.

12. 'Katabolic' is a term used by geneticists to denote the energy dispensing nature of men, as opposed to 'anabolic', which denotes the energy conserving nature of women. With reference to Tess I deliberately misapply 'katabolic' to revise what appears to be a spurious, sexist, distinction. See Viola Klein: 'The attitude of submissiveness cultivated in women was a far more effective means of their subjection than marriage laws or church precepts. In order to ratify this ostensibly "innate" submissiveness and female passivity, the theory was forwarded by nineteenth-century geneticists, that males were by nature "katabolic" and females "anabolic". Man, it was claimed, consumes energy more readily than woman – she being more conservative of it.' See Viola Klein, *Feminine Character. History of an Ideology* (London, 1971), pp.127–46.

13. This is a phrase borrowed from Sarah M. Gilbert's and Susan Gubar's discussion of analogical, symbolic landscapes and spatial allocations in the nineteenth-century novel. See their book, *The Madwoman in the Attic* (New Haven and London, 1979), pp.108–17.

14. By way of contrast, Swigg views Tess, in this scene, as one of Hardy's 'insignificant specks' requiring inflation. Hardy's defence of his heroine, Swigg writes, 'is ... most readily exercised on behalf of ... Tess when seen as a simple village girl. When Tess baptizes her dead child [Sorrow is dying, incidentally, not

dead] ... without the Church's proper sanction, objections are
waived in deference to this personal illusion of rightness. Thus
the spiritual light upon her face sentimentally condones and
respects the belief, showing her face "as a thing of immaculate
beauty with a touch of dignity which was almost regal" ...
Hardy needs to inflate the value of the seemingly insignificant
specks, who, like Tess, move and labour on vast landscapes, "like
a fly on a billiard Table ... of no more consequence to their
surroundings than that fly".' Swigg, op. cit., p.21.

15. Michael Millgate notes that private baptism was practised by
Hardy's maternal grandmother. See his *Thomas Hardy: A
Biography* (Oxford, 1982), pp.12–13.

   The Baptism scene was omitted from the serial version of *Tess
of the d'Urbervilles*, for reasons of censorship: 'Plans for
publication were begun in the autumn of 1888. About half the
novel was accepted by the newspaper syndicate of Tillotson
and Son, and it was not until the first sixteen chapters were
read at the proof stage ... that objections were raised and the
agreement cancelled at Hardy's request ... The story was later
declined by the editors of *Murray's Magazine*, and *Macmillan's
Magazine*. By this time Hardy knew the "fearful price" he had
to pay "for the privilege of writing in the English language" ...
He decided to excise or alter passages which had proved to be
unacceptable ... (One of) the most important serial omissions
(was) the baptism scene, which was published in *The Fortnightly
Review*, in May 1891, under the bold title of "The Midnight
Baptism: A Study in Christianity".' F. B. Pinion, *A Hardy
Companion* (London, Melbourne, Toronto, 1968), p.46.

16. Nina Auerbach, 'The Rise of the Fallen Woman', *Nineteenth
Century Fiction*, June 1980, vol. 35, No. 1, p.40.

17. Auerbach writes that there was, in the Victorian, a 'pride as
well as pity at the fallen woman's abasement. Admiration
mingled with condemnation, recurs again and again in
Victorian treatments of the fallen woman; her prone form
becomes so pervasive an image that it takes on the status of a
shared cultural mythology. At first glance, the Victorian myth
of the fallen woman seems even more harshly degrading than
its literary archetype in *Paradise Lost*. Milton's Eve gives a
powerful argumentative voice to her longing to reign rather
than to serve, while the Victorian fallen woman is usually
depicted, even in literature, as a mute enigmatic icon, such as
Dante Gabriel Rossetti's Jenny, who sleeps through the poem
that probes her nature. Moreover, Milton's Eve will survive in

the triumphant ascending woman whose heel will bruise the serpent's head, while Victorian conventions ordain that woman's fall ends in death. It seems that an age of doubt has grafted the doom of Milton's Satan onto the aspirations of his Eve, generating a creature whose nature it is to fall. . . . Then, as now, she seems to enlightened minds a pitiable monster, created by the neurosis of a culture that feared female sexuality and aggression and so enshrined a respectably sadistic tale punishing them both.' Auerbach, op. cit., p.30.

Hardy's 'sadistic tale' does, of course, mete out punishment in equal measure: the fallen woman's true love is brought home from his 'Brazil' 'a mere yellow skeleton' condemned to live out his days with a 'spiritualized Tess' whom he may love but may not marry. (See 'The Deceased Wife's Sister Bill', which, after a lengthy passage through Parliament was finally passed in 1907 enabling the widowed partner to wed his sister-in-law. Angel could not, therefore, lawfully wed Tess's sister.) And her seducer suffers death by her own hand, which plunges into his body a *killing blade* – divine retribution surely. Woman's heel will bruise the serpent's head in Hardy as in Milton, despite her end in death.

Chapter 5
PASSION DENIED: *Jude the Obscure*

1. Olive Schreiner, *Women and Labour*, ed. A. Van der Spuy and A. Van der Spuy (Johannesburg, 1975), p.118.
2. G. W. Sherman notes in Hardy, not only a startling comparison in ideas and imagery to Engels but also an affinity with Marxist thought as expressed in the preface to *Capital*. See Sherman's *The Pessimism of Thomas Hardy* (New Jersey and London, 1976). For direct references to Hardy and Marx see pp.262, 291, 410, 420, 422, 425, 434.
3. Frederick Engels, *The Origin of the Family, Private Property and the State* (London, 1972), p.145.
4. This is, as yet, a noticeably under-researched area. Sherman's useful study is by no means comprehensive. See also Lennart Björk, *The Literary Notes of Thomas Hardy* (Gothenburg, 1974), vol. 1, pp.199–203 for brief references to Hardy's study of Fourier. Björk's forthcoming *Psychological Vision in the Novels of Thomas Hardy*, will discuss Fourier's influence on Hardy in more detail.

5. Quoted by Carol Bauer and Lawrence Ritt in *Free and Ennobled* (Oxford, 1979), p.292.

6. Hardy's letter to Millicent Garrett Fawcett, Nov. 7, 1906, held in the Fawcett Library, London. Published in *The Collected Letters of Thomas Hardy*, 4 volumes, ed. Richard L. Purdy and Michael Millgate, vol. 3, pp.238–9.

7. J. S. Mill, *Three Essays* (London, 1975), pp.462–3.

8. See, for example, Lawrence Lerner: 'The New Women of the 1890s – distinguishably different from the organized feminists – were certainly associated with a rejection of marriage, but it is not easy to discover the reality of these bloomered, bicycling, cigar-smoking creatures, the Sue Brideheads and the Herminia Bartons.' Lawrence Lerner, *Love and Marriage. Literature and its Social Context* (London, 1979), p.170. The problems that arise from applying a generalised catchphrase as if to clarify a typology are here well illustrated by Lerner. The New Woman – born phoenix-like from the ashes of the 'Girl of the Period' of the late 1860s, could well be Sue Bridehead's mother, but not Sue. We recall that Sue's mother fled marriage, husband and child, and was thereafter vilified by Sue's father. She exemplifies the 'flighty' type whose 'corrupt' morals so outraged Mrs Lynn-Linton – the Girl of the Period's most ferocious critic.

   Constance Rover argues that the New Woman tended to be Neo-Malthusian. This would also exclude Sue. See Rover, *Love, Morals and the Feminists* (London, 1970), p. 132. Sue is not then Lerner's bloomered, bicycling, cigar-smoking creature, nor is she one of Shaw's sandal-wearing 'village' set, nor is she a Fabian, nor is she of the Annie Besant league – propagandising contraception. Possibly the time has come to dispense with the stereotypical label in Sue's case.

9. Sara Delamont and Lorna Duffin (eds), *The Nineteenth-Century Woman* (London, 1978), pp.12–16.

10. For approval of the decorous approach of the suffragists see R. Fulford's *Votes for Women*, and D. R. Read's *Edwardian England*. For sheer optimism, *The Manchester Guardian* was exemplary – asserting, in 1871, not only that the admission of women to the franchise was merely a question of time, but also that 'time' was likely to be short. Later, in 1886, Millicent Garrett Fawcett was equally optimistic: 'Women's suffrage will come as a necessary corollary of other changes ... it will be a political change ... based on social and educational and economic changes which have already taken place ... a public recognition by the State that the lot of woman in England is no

longer what it was at the beginning of the century.' How, I
wonder, did Fawcett rationalise her optimism when the
prerequisite changes 'which have already taken place' in the
1880s found woman some thirty years later still fighting for
suffrage.

11. *A Dictionary of Modern History. 1789–1945*, ed. A. W. Palmer
     (Harmondsworth, 1962), p.316.
12. J. S. Mill, op. cit., p.520.
13. See, for example, S. M. Elkins, *Slavery: A Problem in American
     Institutional and Intellectual Life* (Chicago and London, 1968),
     and Frank Tannenbaum, *Slave and Citizen: the Negro in the
     Americas* (London, 1946).

To further Mill's analogy, a correspondence can be drawn
between the psychological effects upon women of the rigidly
institutionalised Victorian family and the effects induced in the
North American slave by the institutionalised plantation system.
According to social historians this last is defined as a 'closed'
system, that is one which is subject not to the checks and balances
of alternative institutions but to its own authoritarian,
paternalistic laws in which all lines of authority descend from
the master. Slave and Victorian woman had this much in
common. Under the auspices of their respective institutions,
both were denied legal rights and equality before the law as a
matter of course, and freedom and responsibility as a matter
of practice. The psychological effects of all this are manifold,
but for our purposes can be restricted to the following: an
impaired ability to take and make decisions, to instigate or take
the initiative, an incapacity to exercise judgement and, in the
broader social sphere, an inability to exercise organisational
and co-operational drives. At the same time, development of
self-esteem, sense of self-worth, self-identity and autonomy is
arrested. American slave and Victorian woman were alike
encouraged to adopt 'victim' or 'loser' attitudes and roles as a
means of gaining and retaining social approval without
threatening the power structure of the social formation. Certain
learned behaviour patterns developed in line with this: notably
the submission, compliance, dependency and the child-like
mannerisms we recognise as characteristic of both the Victorian
'doll' and the Black 'Sambo'.

Collaterally, upon liberation, the induction of 'victim' roles
and 'loser' attitudes impeded integration and socialisation
within the 'free' society, for to break the 'second-class-citizen'
mould the 'victim' would have to identify with the 'victor', the

'loser' with the 'champion'. Yet in terms of role-adoption, social attitudes and expectations, and not least self-image, there were no role-models, no opportunity for establishing role-models, no scope for self-advancement, in short, no possibility of making such an identification. When Victorian women embraced the emancipationist's cause, and the freed slave faced liberation in post-bellum America, both were brought up against the same destructive attitudes and low expectations they had experienced in bondage. Moreover, the groundless myths on which the society based its ethic of white male supremacy, which presupposed submissiveness, intellectual inferiority and so forth in the woman and freed-slave who bore such traits, had become more deeply entrenched as science stepped in to assert in all empirical seriousness that such traits were in fact, innate.

The most extreme example given by Elkins of the 'closed' authoritarian system is that of the Nazi Concentration Camp, where it was observed that certain approval-seeking internees not only incited in-group hostilities and aggression, but were also capable of treating their peers with a brutality that exceeded, on occasion, that of their warder.

14. Bauer and Ritt, op. cit., p.266.
15. See Mrs Henry Fawcett's Introduction to Mary Wollstonecraft's *A Vindication of the Rights of Women* (London, 1891). *Vindication* first appeared in London in 1792, but remained out of print for the larger part of the nineteenth century.
16. Mrs Oliphant, 'The Anti-Marriage League', *Blackwood's Magazine*, Jan. 1896, clix, pp.135–49.
17. Lawrence Stone, *The Family, Sex and Marriage. In England 1500–1800* (London, 1977), pp.666–7.
18. Ibid., p.667.
19. Ibid., p.664
20. Engels, op. cit., p.236.
21. I have drawn here upon Ivan Illych's discussion of institutions and the institutionalisation of values. See his *Deschooling Society* (Middlesex, 1971).
22. Edward Shorter, 'Illegitimacy, Sexual Revolution and Social Change in Modern Europe', *The Family in History. Interdisciplinary Essays*, ed. Theodore K. Rabb and Robert I. Rotberg (New York and London, 1971), pp.67–8.
23. Ibid., p.68.
24. S. B. Kitchin, *A History of Divorce* (London, 1912), p.182. See also O. R. McGregor, *Divorce in England* (London, 1957).

McGregor discusses the 1857 Act in detail, including the fact that the provisions for decentralisation (Divorce Courts were London based) did not really take effect until after the First World War. He concludes that one law for the rich and another for the poor (magistrates court separation – post 1878 Act) continued until the Legal Aid and Advice Act of 1949.

25. The last recorded wife sale took place in Sheffield in 1881. See Bauer and Ritt, op. cit., p.166.

26. With James Gibson's discovery of marginalia in Hardy's own copy of *Jude*, any doubts as to the appreciativeness of Hardy's eye may be assuaged. For where Arabella's 'inflated bosom' rises and falls as she sings at matutinal worship in Hardy's vision of her at Kennetbridge (*JO*, p.325), in the margin of his personal edition this has been amended to a phrase of Browning's which reads: 'Breast's superb abundance' – a more luxuriant image from a singularly unimpoverished imagination. Hardy was eighty years old at the time! See Gibson, 'Hardy and His Readers', *Thomas Hardy*, ed. Norman Page (London, 1980), p.207.

Chapter 6
CONCLUSION

1. See Havelock Ellis's 'Concerning *Jude the Obscure*', *Savoy Magazine*, Oct. 1896, vi, pp.35–49. Ellis writes: 'The type of womankind that Mr Hardy chiefly loves to study, from Cytherea Graye to Sue, has always been the same, very human, also very feminine, rarely with any marked element of virility, and so contrasting with the androgynous heroines loved of Mr Meredith.' See also Ellis's 'Thomas Hardy's Novels', *Westminster Review*, April 1883, cxix, n.s., lxiii, pp.334–64. Ellis writes, 'Woman, in Mr Hardy's novels, is far from being the "conscience of man", it is with the men always that the moral strength lies.'
    Ellis shapes a particularly complex dialogue on Hardy's women. They are alternately 'instinctively pure', 'demonic', 'human' yet devoid of 'soul': 'we see at once that they have no souls'. Conceptual confusion is self-evident!

2. See *One Rare Fair Woman* (London and Basingstoke, 1972), xv, ed. Evelyn Hardy and Frank Pinion.

3. See *The Literary Notes of Thomas Hardy*, 2 vols, ed. Lennart Björk (Gothenburg, 1974), vol. 1, pp.271–2.

4. Hardy to Earl Hodgson, July 17, 1900. Published in *The Collected Letters of Thomas Hardy*, 4 vols, ed. Richard L. Purdy and Michael Millgate (London, 1980), vol. 2, p.264.

5. See Hardy to Henniker, June 29, 1893. Purdy and Millgate, ibid., vol. 2, p.18.

6. Hardy to Henniker, July 2, 1893. Purdy and Millgate, ibid., vol. 2, p.20.

7. Hardy and Pinion, op. cit., p.182.

8. Purdy and Millgate, op. cit., vol. 1, p.250.

9. Hardy to Yates, Dec. 12, 1891. Purdy and Millgate, op. cit., vol. 1, p.250.

10. Björk, op. cit., p.158.

11. Hardy to Gosse, Sept. 8, 1898. Purdy and Millgate, op. cit., vol. 2, p.200.

12. Hardy to Archibald Constable and Co., June 24, 1898. Purdy and Millgate, op. cit., vol. 2, p.195.

13. Hardy to Katherine S. Macquoid, Nov. 17, 1874. Purdy and Millgate, op. cit., vol. 1, p.33.

14. Ellis has his modern disciples. John Bayley is one. Regarding his Victorian predecessor as one of Hardy's most sensitive critics he tells us that: 'Havelock Ellis, in his article on Hardy's novels in the *Westminster Review*, in 1883 ... is interested in the more intimate places of the Hardy psychology, though he probes them with delicacy and tact. He points out that all women in his novels must be weak, even when weakness is an aspect of their strength, as with Bathsheba. They are incapable of moral firmness or ascendancy – the natural birthright of George Eliot's women; if they possessed it they would not attract Hardy, or be seen by him and identified with as they are. Naturally Ellis does not speculate on the reasons for this, though as a doctor and psychologist in training he is clearly thinking about it.' John Bayley, *An Essay on Hardy* (Cambridge, 1978), pp.211–12.

Bayley insinuates that there is something untoward in the Hardyan make-up, that his identification with the so-called weak woman calls for pathological explanation. Innuendo of this kind is invariably deprecatory, but it should not inveigle us into overlooking Bayley's prejudicial ability to slant the evidence in order to express, through innuendo, not Ellis's views but his own.

What Ellis touches upon, unknowingly, is the *power* of Hardy's women, which he assiduously diverts, calling it 'demonism'. Likewise, whereas he speaks pejoratively of the 'instinctiveness' of Hardy's women, which he regards as lowering, there is nothing to suggest, in the Wessex novels, that instinctiveness is less than prescient intelligence and the distinguishing mark of what Hardy might call the 'natural aristocrat'. Or again, what Ellis derogates as 'something elemental, something *demonic*' Hardy treats (as with Bathsheba's voluptuous self-delight) as perfectly healthy and natural. By the same token, sexual readiness, sexual responsiveness is read, by Ellis, as a 'yielding to circumstance'. Certainly every major hero in Hardy is inclined to so belittle the woman he loves, or, alternatively, to rarefy her to the point of depersonalisation, that she finally submits to his will. But this is conditioned behaviour, what Sue calls the 'moral enemy, coercion'. So we need to argue, in this instance, from effects to causes. Where there is evidence enough of causal-conditioning by means of disparagement, fault-finding and the induction of shame and guilt, there is none to show innate female passivity. On the other hand, genuinely passive, yielding natures are to be found in Stephen Smith, Swithin St Cleeve and Giles Winterborne.

15. *The Return of the Native*, chapter 7.
16. *Two on a Tower*, chapter 1.

Bibliography

Acton, William, *The Functions and Disorders of the Reproductive Organs in Childhood, Youth, Adult Age, and Advanced Life Considered in their Physiological, Social and Moral Relations* (London, 1857).

Amos, A. K., 'Accident and Fate: the Possibility for Action in *A Pair of Blue Eyes*', *English Literature in Transition*, 1972, vol. vx.

Auerbach, Nina, 'The Rise of the Fallen Woman', *Nineteenth-Century Fiction*, June 1980, vol. 35, no. 1.

Banks, J. A., *Victorian Values. Secularism and the Size of Families* (London and Boston, 1981).

Basch, François, *Relative Creatures: Victorian Women in Society and the Novel*, translated by Anthony Rudoph (London, 1974).

Bauer, Carol and Ritt, Lawrence (eds), *Free and Ennobled: Source Readings in the Development of Victorian Feminism* (Oxford, 1979).

Bayley, John, *An Essay on Hardy* (Cambridge, 1978).

Beatty, C. J. P., 'Two Rare Birds in Hardy's *The Return of the Native*', *Notes and Queries*, March 1961, vol. viii.

Beckmann, R., 'A Character Typology in Hardy's Later Novels', *E.L.H.*, March 1963, vol. xxx.

Beer, Gillian, *Darwin's Plots* (London, Boston, Melbourne, New York, 1983).

Boulmelha, Penny, *Thomas Hardy and Women. Sexual Ideology and Narrative Form* (Sussex, 1982).

Bradbury, Malcolm and Palmer, D. (eds), *Decadence and the 1890s* (London, 1979).

Branca, Patricia, *Women in Europe since 1750* (London, 1978).

Brown, Douglas, *Thomas Hardy* (Connecticut, 1980).

Butler, A. J., 'Mr Hardy as Decadent', *National Review*, May 1896, vol. xxvii.

Butler, Lance St J., *Thomas Hardy* (Cambridge, 1978).

——— (ed.), *Thomas Hardy After Fifty Years* (London and Basingstoke, 1978).

Calder, Jenni, *Women and Marriage in Victorian Fiction* (London, 1976).

Cockshut, A. O. J., *Man and Woman: A Study of Love and the Novel* (London, 1977).

Cox, R. G. (ed.), *Thomas Hardy: The Critical Heritage* (London, 1970).

Crow, Duncan, *The Victorian Woman* (London, 1971).

Davies, J. V. (ed.), *Lawrence on Hardy: 'A Study of Thomas Hardy' and*

'Introduction to these Paintings' (London, 1973).

Deacon, Lois and Coleman, Terry, *Providence and Mr Hardy* (London, 1966).

Delamont, Sara and Duffin, Lorna (eds), *The Nineteenth-Century Woman* (London and New York, 1978).

De Laura, David, '"The Ache of Modernism" in Hardy's Later Novels', *E.L.H.*, Sept. 1976, vol. 34.

Eagleton, Mary and Peirce, David, *Attitudes to Class in the English Novel* (London, 1979).

Ehrenreich, Barbara and English, Deidre, *Complaints and Disorders: The Sexual Politics of Sickness* (New York, 1974).

Elkins, S. M., *Slavery: A Problem in American Institutional and Intellectual Life* (Chicago and London, 1968).

Engels, Frederick, *The Origin of the Family, Private Property and the State* (London, 1972).

Enstice, Andrew, *Thomas Hardy: Landscapes of the Mind* (London, 1979).

Evans, Richard, J., *The Feminists* (London, 1977).

Fawcett, Millicent Garrett, *Women's Suffrage: A Short History of a Great Movement* (London, 1912).

Fernando, Lloyd, *'New Women' in the Late Victorian Novel* (Pennsylvania and London, 1977).

Figes, Eva, *Patriarchal Attitudes* (London, 1970).

Fontane, Marilyn Stall, 'The Devil in *Tess*', *The Thomas Hardy Society Review*, 1982, vol. 1, no. 8.

Fulford, R., *Votes for Women* (London, 1957).

Gay, Peter, *The Bourgeois Experience. Victoria to Freud* (New York and Oxford, 1984).

Gilbert, Sandra and Gubar, Susan, *The Madwoman in the Attic*, (New Haven and London, 1979).

Gittings, Robert, *Young Thomas Hardy* (Harmondsworth, 1978).

—— *The Older Hardy*, (Harmondsworth, 1978).

—— and Manton, Jo, *The Second Mrs Hardy* (London, 1979).

Graham, Kenneth, *English Criticism of the Novel, 1856–1900* (London, 1965).

Gregor, Ian, *The Great Web: The Form of Hardy's Major Fiction* (London, 1974).

Grundy, Joan, *Hardy and the Sister Arts* (London and Basingstoke, 1974).

Guerard, A., *Thomas Hardy* (New York, 1949).

Hardwick, Elizabeth, *Seduction and Betrayal* (London, 1974).

Hardy, Thomas, *The Literary Notes of Thomas Hardy*, edited by Lennart Björk (Gothenburg, 1974).

—— *The Collected Letters of Thomas Hardy*, edited by Richard L. Purdy and Michael Millgate (London, 1980).

—— *The Variorum Edition of the Complete Poems of Thomas Hardy*, edited by James Gibson (London, 1979).

—— *The Poems of Thomas Hardy*, edited by T. M. R. Creighton (London and Basingstoke, 1977).

Hardy, William Masters, *Old Swanage or Purbeck Past and Present* (Kidderminster, 1980).

Harrison, Brian, *Separate Spheres: The Opposition to Women's Suffrage in Britain* (London, 1978).

—— 'Underneath the Victorians', *Victorian Studies* 10, 1966, 7.

Hayek, F. A., *John Stuart Mill and Harriet Taylor* (London, 1951).

Henriques, Fernando, 'Modern Sexuality', *Prostitution and Society*, 1968, vol. III.

Hillis Miller, J., *Distance and Desire* (London, 1970).

—— 'History as Repetition in Thomas Hardy's Poetry: The Example of "Wessex Heights"', *Stratford-upon-Avon Studies* 15, edited by Malcolm Bradbury and David Palmer (London, 1972).

—— *Fiction and Repetition* (Cambridge, Massachusetts, 1982).

Himmelfarb, Gertrude, *On Liberty and Liberalism* (New York, 1974).

Houghton, R. E. C., 'Hardy and Shakespeare', *Notes and Queries*, March 1961, vol. viii.

Howe, Irving, *Thomas Hardy* (London, 1968).

Illych, Ivan, *Deschooling Society* (Harmondsworth, Middlesex, 1971).

Jacobus, Mary (ed.), *Women Writing and Writing about Women* (London, 1979).

Kaplan, S. J., *Feminine Consciousness in the Modern British Novel* (Chicago and London, 1975).

Kitchin, S. K., *A History of Divorce* (London, 1912).

Klein, Viola, *Feminine Character: History of an Ideology* (London, 1946).

Kramer, Dale (ed.), *Critical Approaches to the Fiction of Thomas Hardy* (London, 1979).

Kroeber, Karl, *Styles in Fictional Structure* (New Jersey, 1971).

Laird, J. T., *Shaping of 'Tess of the d'Urbervilles'* (London, 1975).

—— 'New Light on the Evolution of *Tess of the d'Urbervilles*', *The Review of English Studies*, Nov. 1980, vol. xxxi, no. 24.

Lerner, Laurence, *Love and Marriage: Literature and its Social Context* (London, 1979).

—— and Holmstrom, J. (eds), *Thomas Hardy and His Readers* (London, 1968).

Lodge, David, *The Modes of Modern Writing* (London, 1977).

Working with Structuralism: Essays and Reviews on Nineteenth-Century Literature (Boston, London and Henley, 1981).

Lucas, John, *The Literature of Change: Studies in the Nineteenth-Century Provincial Novel* (Sussex, 1977).

Maccoby, Eleanor, *The Development of Sex Difference* (Stanford, 1966).

Macksey, R. and Donato, E. (eds), *The Structuralist Controversy* (Baltimore, 1972).

McGregor, O. R., *Divorce in England* (London, 1957).

Mahowald, M. B., *Philosophy of Woman* (London, 1978).

Mallett, P., 'Women and Marriage in Victorian Society', in *Marriage and Property*, edited by Elizabeth M. Craig (Aberdeen University Press, 1984).

Marcus, Steven, *The Other Victorians: A Study of Sexuality and Pornography in Mid-Nineteenth-Century England* (London, 1967).

Mill, J. S., *Three Essays: 'On Liberty', 'Representative Government', 'The Subjection of Women'*, edited by Richard Wollheim (London, 1975).

Millett, Kate, *Sexual Politics* (London, 1977).

Millgate, Michael, *Thomas Hardy: His Career as a Novelist* (London, Sidney and Toronto, 1971).

—— *Thomas Hardy: A Biography* (Oxford and Melbourne, 1982).

Moore, Katherine, *Victorian Wives* (London, 1974).

Morgan, Elaine, *The Descent of Woman* (London, 1972).

Morrell, Roy, *Thomas Hardy: The Will and the Way* (London, 1965).

Orel, Harold (ed.), *Hardy's Personal Writings* (Kansas, 1966).

Ousby, Ian, 'Love and Hate Relations: Bathsheba, Hardy and the Men in *Far From the Madding Crowd*', *The Cambridge Quarterly*, Nov. 1981, vol. 10.

Page, Norman (ed.), *Thomas Hardy: The Writer and His Background* (London, 1980).

Palmegiano, A. M., *Women and British Periodicals: 1832–1867. A Bibliography* (New York and London, 1976).

Palmer, A. W. (ed.), *A Dictionary of Modern History* (Harmondsworth, 1962).

Paterson, John, *The Making of 'The Return of the Native'* (California, 1960).

Pearsall, Ronald, *The Worm in the Bud: The World of Victorian Sexuality* (Harmondsworth, Middlesex, 1969).

Pinion, Frank, *A Hardy Companion* (London, Melbourne and Toronto, 1968).

Rabb, Theodore and Rotberg, Robert (eds), *The Family in History: Interdisciplinary Essays* (New York and London, 1971).

Read, D. R., *Edwardian England* (London, 1972).

Reade, Charles, *Love Me Little Love Me Long* (London and Glasgow, 1912).

Rose, Phyllis, *Parallel Lives. Five Victorian Marriages* (New York, 1984).

Rover, Constance, *Love, Morals, and the Feminists* (London, 1970).

Salter, C.H., *Good Little Thomas Hardy* (London and Basingstoke, 1981).

Sand, George, *Mauprat* (London, MCMVIII), edited by Edmund Gosse.

Schreiner, Olive, *Story of an African Farm* (London, 1912).

——*Women and Labour* (Johannesburg, 1975).

Segal, Hannah, 'A Psychological Approach to Aesthetics', *International Journal of Psycho-Analysis*, 1952, vol. xxxiii.

Shaw, D.L. and McCombs, Maxwell E., *Mass Media and Society* (London, 1979).

Sherman, G.W., *The Pessimism of Thomas Hardy* (New Jersey and London, 1976).

Showalter, Elaine, *A Literature of Their Own: British Women Novelists from Brontë to Lessing* (London, 1978).

Southerington, F.R., *Hardy's Vision of Man* (London, 1971).

Steig, Michael, 'The Problem of Literary Value in Two Early Hardy Novels', *Texas Studies in Literature and Language* 1970, vol. xii.

Stoller, Robert, *Sex and Gender: On the Development of Masculinity and Femininity* (New York, 1968).

Stone, Lawrence, *The Family, Sex and Marriage. In England 1500–1800* (London, 1977).

Stubbs, Patricia, *Women and Fiction: Feminism and the Novel, 1880–1920* (Sussex, 1979).

Sumner, Rosemary, *Thomas Hardy: Psychological Novelist* (London and Basingstoke, 1981).

Swigg, Richard, *Lawrence, Hardy, and American Literature* (London and Toronto, 1972).

Tannenbaum, Frank, *Slave and Citizen: the Negro in the Americas* (London, 1946).

Thomson, Patricia, *The Victorian Heroine: A Changing Ideal* (London, 1956).

Trudgill, Eric, *Madonnas and Magdalens: The Origin and Development of Victorian Sexual Attitudes* (London, 1976).

Vanderpool, Y. (ed.), *Darwin and Darwinism* (London, 1973).

Van Vuuren, Nancy, *The Subversion of Women* (Philadelphia, 1974).

Vicinus, Martha, *Suffer and be Still* (Indiana, 1972).

——(ed.), *A Widening Sphere* (Indiana, 1971).

Wollstonecraft, Mary, *A Vindication of the Rights of Women* (London, 1891), edited by Mrs Fawcett.

White, R.J., *Thomas Hardy and History* (London and Basingstoke, 1974).

Williams, Raymond, *The English Novel from Dickens to Lawrence* (London, 1970).

Young, G. M., *Portrait of an Age* (London, 1978).

NINETEENTH-CENTURY PERIODICAL PUBLICATIONS ON WOMAN

The following titles are listed chronologically, and periodicals are abbreviated as follows:

Westminster Review WR
Saturday Review SR
Fortnightly Review FR
Spectator S
Blackwood's Magazine B

'Capacities of Woman', WR, vol. xxviii, Oct. 1 1865, pp.352–80.

'Aesthetic Woman', SR, vol. xxv, Feb. 8 1868, pp.165–6.

'The Girl of the Period', SR, vol. xxv, Mar. 14 1868, pp.339–40.

'The Medical and General Education of Women', FR, vol. iv, Nov. 1 1868, pp.554–71.

'The Employment of Women and Children in Agriculture', SR, vol. xxvii, Jan. 16 1868, pp.78–9.

'A Woman's Rights Organs', SR. vol. xvii, Jan. 2 1869, pp.20–1.

'Marriage Settlements', SR, vol. xxvii, Jan. 16 1869, pp.80–1.

'Women's Rights in New York', SR, vol. xxvii, Feb. 6 1869, pp.176–7.

'Charming Women', SR, vol. xxvii, Mar. 6 1869, pp.377–8.

'Instinctive Cruelty', SR, vol. xxvii, Mar. 20 1869, pp.307–8.

'Married Woman's Property', SR, vol. xxvii, Apr. 10 1869, pp.482–3.

'Woman's Oracles', SR, vol. xxvii, April. 17 1869, pp.509–10.

'The Redundancy of Women', SR, vol. xxvii, Apr. 24 1869, pp.545–6.

'Mr J. S. Mill on sex', S, vol. 42, June 12 1869, pp.703–4.

'The Subjection of Women', SR, vol. xxvii, June 19 1869, pp.811–23.

'Flirting', SR, vol. xxvii, June 26 1869, pp.837–8.

'The Physiology of Political Women', S, vol. 43, Feb. 19, 1870, p.232.

'Insanity and Divorce', S. vol. 43, Mar. 5 1870, p.297.

'The Electoral Disabilities of Women', FR, vol. vii, May 1 1870, pp.622–32.

'Condorcet's plea for the Citizen-ship of Women. A Translation', FR, vol. vii, June 1 1870, pp.719–24.

'The Debate of Female Suffrage', S., vol. 45, May 4 1872, pp.554–5.

'The Competition of Women in Physical Work', S, vol. 46, June 14 1873, pp.757–8.

'Women and the Universities', S, vol. 47, May 16 1874, pp.19–20.

'Divorced Women and Property', S, vol. 48, Aug. 21 1875, pp.1060–2.

'Working Women's Clubs', SR, vol. xli, Jan. 15 1876, pp.76–7.

'Women's Disabilities', SR, vol. xli, Apr. 29 1876, pp.539–40.

'Emancipated Woman', SR, vol. xli, June 17 1876, p.771.

'Husbands and Wives', S, vol. 49, Aug. 12 1876, pp.1008–9.

'Man and Woman', FR, vol. xxvi, Nov. 1 1879, pp.672–85.

'Ideals of Feminine Usefulness', FR, vol. xxvii, Apr. 1 1880, pp.656–71.

'Men and Women. A sequel', FR, vol. xxix, June 1 1881, pp.776–93.

'Englishwomen Abroad', SR, vol. lv, Apr. 7 1883, pp.433–4.

'The Marriage Law', SR, vol. lv, June 9 1883, pp.716–17.

'Chinese Ladies', SR, vol. lv, June 23 1883, pp.794–5.

'The Verdict of Christian History on Marriages of Affinity', SR, vol. lv, June 23 1883, pp.793–4.

'Two Books for Girls', SR, vol. lvi, Oct. 6 1883, pp.447–8.

'Marriage and Divorce', FR, vol. xxxvii, May 1 1885, pp.640–53.

'The Women's Protest against Women's Suffrage', S, vol. 62, June 1 1889, p.750.

'The Writings of Mary Wollstonecraft', WR, vol. cxxxiii, Jan.–June 1890, pp.10–23.

'The Marriage Question from a Scientific Standpoint', WR, vol. cxxxiii, Jan.–June 1890, pp.172–80.

'The Morality of Marriage', FR, vol. xlvii, Mar. 1 1890, pp.310–30.

'Women and Politics', S, vol. 64, May 17 1890, pp.686–7.

'The Effect of the New Careers on Women's Happiness', S, vol. 64, June 21 1890, pp.862–3.

'Husband and Wife', SR, vol. lxxii, July 11 1891, pp.48–9.

'Women at Oxford', S, vol. 68, Feb. 13 1892, pp.232–3.

'How Women Propose', S, vol. 86, Apr. 9 1892, pp.492–3.

'The Non-Political Woman', S, vol. 68, Apr. 30 1892, pp.605–6.

'Women's Suffrage', SR, vol. lxxiii, Apr. 30 1892, pp.500–02.

'Why Young Men Do Not Marry', S, vol. 69, Sept. 10 1892, pp.348–9.

'Woman and Her Money', S, vol. 69, Sept. 24 1892, pp.413–14.

'Womanliness and Womanishness', S, vol. 71, Nov. 25 1893, pp.742–3.

'Love and Marriage', WR, vol. clx, July–Dec. 1893, pp.349–51.

'The Impasse of Women', WR, vol. xcli, Jan.–June 1894, pp.566–8.

'The Sexual Problem', WR, vol. cxli, Jan.–June 1894, pp.512–32.

'Dies Dominae. The Fruit of the Tree of Knowledge', SR, vol. lxxix, May 18 1895, pp.646–7.

'Dies Dominae. The Value of Love', SR, vol. lxxix, May 25 1895, pp.687–8.

'A Rejoinder', SR, vol. lxxix, May 25 1895, pp.688–9.

'Dies Dominae. The Practice Marriage', SR, vol. lxxix, June 1 1895, pp.721–2.

'A Rejoinder', SR, vol. lxxix, June 1 1895, p.722.

'Dies Dominae. The Maternal Instinct', SR, vol. lxxix, June 8 1895, pp.752–3.

'A Rejoinder', SR, vol. lxxix, June 8 1895, pp.753–4.

'Dies Dominae. The Sisterhood of Woman', SR, vol. lxxix, June 15 1895, pp.785–6.

'Dies Dominae. The Feminine Potential', SR, vol. lxxix, June 22 1895, pp.824–5.

'The Anti-Marriage League', B, vol. clix, Jan. 1896, pp.136–49.

'The Monstrous Regiment of Women', Fr, vol. lxii, Dec. 1 1897, pp.926–36.

INDEX

Index

Index